AF651150

BUDDHIST EPISTEMOLOGY

BUDDHIST EPISTEMOLOGY

S. R. Bhatt

Anu Mehrotra

Foreword by The Dalai Lama

MOTILAL BANARSIDASS INTERNATIONAL
DELHI

Reprint Edition : Delhi, 2023
First Edition : Delhi, 2017

© MOTILAL BANARSIDASS INTERNATIONAL
All Rights Reserved

ISBN : 978-81-962137-7-0 (Paper)
ISBN : 978-81-962137-8-7 (Cloth)

Also available at

MOTILAL BANARSIDASS INTERNATIONAL

H. O. : 41 U.A. Bungalow Road, (Back Lane) Jawahar Nagar, Delhi - 110 007
4261 (basement) Lane #3, Ansari Road, Darya Ganj, New Delhi - 110 002
203 Royapettah High Road, Mylapore, Chennai - 600 004
12/1A, 2nd Floor, Bankim Chatterjee Street, Kolkata - 700 073
Stockist : Motilal Books, Ashok Rajpath, Near Kali Mandir, Patna - 800 004

No part of this book may be reproduced in any form or by any electronic or mechanical means including information storage and retrieval systems without permission in writing from the publishers, excepts by a reviewer who may quote brief passages in a review.

Printed in India
MOTILAL BANARSIDASS INTERNATIONAL

Contents

Foreword

The Dalai Lama

When Buddha Śākyamuni attained enlightenment beneath the Bodhi tree more than two and a half thousand years ago, his achievement was not only the result of having reached the peak of meditative stabilisation, of having brought great compassion to fruition, but also of clear analytic thought. The lucid simplicity of his subsequent teachings are ample evidence of this. And indeed he encouraged his followers to regard even his own advice in the same rigorously critical light. Thus, the study of logic and the nature of knowledge have been crucial to Buddhist tradition from the outset.

These disciplines continued to develop and flourish in India after the Buddha's passing away, reaching their acme in the works of Vasubandhu, Diṅnāga and Dharmakīrti, which were to become seminal to studies in the great monastic universities, such as Nālandā and Vikramaśilā. And it was this tradition of acute logic and analysis that was transmitted and preserved in Tibet for more than a thousand years, where it was employed not merely to challenge the views of others but to ensure the clarity and authenticity of one's own view.

Therefore, I am delighted that two distinguished contemporary Indian scholars, Dr. S.R. Bhatt and Dr. A. Mehrotra, have written the present book on Buddhist Epistemology, including an English translation of the "Nyāya Praveśa." This valuable work sheds light on abstruse topics and will allow readers to gain a clearer appreciation of the depths of Buddhist knowledge.

Preface

The present work is an analytical exposition of the theory of knowledge as propounded in the Diṅnāga-Dharmakīrti tradition. It expounds the Buddhist theory of knowledge in its totality.

Buddhist thinkers unanimously uphold the view that there are two kinds of objects of knowledge, namely, the unique particular (*svalakṣaṇa*) and the generalized image (*sāmānyalakṣaṇa*). Unique particular is discrete and instantaneous being. It is unique particular in the sense that it is neither identical nor similar to other unique particulars. It is the only objective real (*paramārtha sat*). As distinct from unique particular there are objects that are constructs of our intellect and that are in the form of generalized images. They are subjective in origin but intersubjective in nature.

On the basis of the preceding analysis Buddhist thinkers emphatically maintain that since there are only two kinds of objects of knowldege, there are only two kinds of knowledge (*pramāṇa*) namely, perception (*pratyakṣa*) and inference (*anumāna*). The unique particular is amenable to perception only, whereas generalized image is known through inference only. By implication, unique particular can never be known through inference and generalized image can never be known through perception. Thus, each of the two types of knowledge has its own separate and distinct sphere of operation.

In the following pages is a discussion of Buddhist theory of knowledge, comparing it with other schools wherever necessary.

To make the logical issues more intelligible to readers, a basic text, "Nyāya Praveśa" is given as an appendix of the work. The text of "Nyāya Praveśa" is generally ascribed to Diṅnāga, a pioneer thinker in Buddhist theory of Knowledge. Diṅnāga provided a solid footing to Buddhist epistemology and logic and gave it a distinctive character. He has been regarded as the father of Buddhist epistemology and logic in particular and of the entire medieval Indian epistemology and logic in general. There are several works composed by him in this area, among which "Pramāṇa Samuccaya" and "Nyāya Praveśa" are most important. "Pramāṇa Samuccaya" is not available in its complete form, even though some of its chapters have been restored from Tibetan and other sources. However "Nyāya Praveśa" is available to us in its full form. An attempt has been made here to translate it in English for the benefit of English language readers. The text is presented here in Roman script with a view to have wider readership. Explanatory notes have also been provided to clarify some knotty points.

"Nyāya Praveśa" is a classical work pertaining to the modes of knowing and reasoning in the Buddhist tradition. For centuries it has been studied as a manual of the Buddhist theory of knowledge in India, Tibet, China, and other countries. It provides a foundation to the famous Buddhist art of debate (*vāda-vidhi*). There are several Tibetan and Chinese commentaries and sub-commentaries on "Nyāya Praveśa" apart from the ones in Sanskrit. This accounts for its significance and popularity among classical scholars.

In a cryptic, but succinct, manner "Nyāya Praveśa" presents Diṅnāga's views on the nature of perception and inference and their fallacies. It also elaborately discusses the modes of argumentation and refutation along with their fallacies.

We are grateful to Greenwood Publishing Group and its staff and to Dr. Hoffman who introduced this work to Greenwood. Our thanks are also due to Indian Council of Philosophical Research for providing financial assistance for the preparation of the work.

Introduction

DICHOTOMY OF SUBSTANCE AND NO-SUBSTANCE ONTOLOGIES

The varied and multifaceted Indian philosophical thought is characterized by two broad philosophical tendencies that are antithetical in nature but both of which can be traced in germinal form to the Upaniṣadic thought. One tendency, which can be termed "*ātmavāda*" or "substance ontology," has been dominantly presented in the so-called *āstika* systems, the culmination of which is found in the Advaita Vedānta. The other tendency, which is popularly known as "*anātmavāda*" or "no-substance ontology," finds its advocacy and manifestation in Buddhist thought. The basic contention bifurcating the two tendencies is the view regarding the ontological status of permanence and change, both of which, though opposite in nature, are given to us in veridical experience, and therefore both claim the status of reality. The substance ontology advocates the permanence aspect and tries to explain the phenomenon of change. The no-substance ontology, on the contrary, accepts the reality of change alone and explains the experience of permanence as conceptual superimposition. Thus, the history of Indian philosophical thought could be approached in terms of a dialectic of these two divergent tendencies.

The substance-ontology revolves around the idea of permanence or abidance as the sole criterion of reality. Accordingly, substance, which alone is the substratum of all attributes and modes, has the sole reality or the primary reality, and the attributes and modes have either an apparent existence or a derivative existence. According to Advaita Vedānta substance, which is a unitary, homogeneous, pure consciousness, alone is real, and all attributes and modes are phenomenal in the sense that they are *mithyā* (i.e., neither real nor unreal). The Sāṁkhya system and also the Nyāya-Vaiśeṣika and Mīmāmsā systems, however, assign some reality to change also insofar as matter is regarded as subject to mutation whether in the form of evolution from one mass of matter or in the form of a combination of different elements of matter, thereby producing a different or new complex. But the point to be noted is that even in these schools that display a realistic tendency the primacy of substance and its permanent essence are emphasized. It may be significant to point out that there has also been another tendency in the school of Jainism wherein the exclusiveness of substance ontology and no-substance ontology has been rejected, and equal status is accorded to both permanence and change.

NO-SUBSTANCE ONTOLOGY OF BUDDHISM

Buddhist thought has centered around no-substance ontology. Gautama, the Buddha, who initiated Buddhist thought, was led to philosophizing by an intense longing for the eradication of suffering. He visualized that all suffering is due to '*tanhā*' (longing) and that all longing is due to attachment to the false notion of permanence. He wanted to suggest a way out of the labyrinth of suffering and put forth impermanence or nonsubstantivality as the key to overcoming suffering. The four Noble Truths, therefore, advocate the idea of impermanence and nonsubstantivality as the way to eradicate suffering. The entire reality that is generally understood in terms of matter and consciousness has been understood by the Buddha as a series of changing moments (*kṣaṇa*). The word "moment" is suggestive of the fact that all real or existent is time-embedded. All that exists, exists in time. Therefore, an existence series is identical with time series. The existence series could be physical or psychical or a conglomeration (*saṅghāta*) of the two. Every series in itself is also a conglomeration. Material entity is a physical conglomeration (*bhūta saṅghāta*), whereas mental entity is a psychical conglomeration (*citta saṅghāta*). A living being is a psychophysical conglomeration. Since the psychical conglomeration is of four types, a psychophysical conglomeration is named as *pañcaskandha,* consisting of four psychical and one physical conglomerations. The four psychical conglomerations are *vedanā skandha, saṁskāra skandha, nāma skandha,* and *saṁjñā skandha*. The only physical conglomeration is *rūpa skandha*.

The existence series, whether of a physical conglomeration or psychical conglomeration, consists of distinct units of existence that are discrete but not independent. They are rather interdependent in the sense that every succeeding unit in the series is causally dependent on its preceding unit in that series, and likewise every preceding unit in the series, in order to be real, has to give rise to its succeeding unit. These two ideas are technically known as *pratītya samutpāda* (dependent origination) and *artha kriyā kāritva* (causal efficiency). They constitute the essence of the four Noble Truths propounded by the Buddha.

The concept of existence series (*kṣaṇa santāna*) is pivotal to Buddhist metaphysics. It explains the reality of incessant change in terms of the causal and dependent origin of the succeeding from the preceding unit in the series. The experience of permanence in the series is also explained on the basis of continuity and dependence. The real is always changing, but the change is not random; it is causally regulated. In case of a human being, the series is psychophysical, having a distinct identity of its own. But this poses the problem of memory, recollection, and recognition in every distinct personal identity. Buddhist thought explains these problems also in terms of *kṣaṇa santāna* (existence series). In every psychophysical series that is unique and self-identical the succeeding stems from the preceding, and this conglomeration of fivefold series, which begins with the birth of the conglomeration in a particular form, continues till the death of that conglomeration in that form. From birth to death in this series there is a constant change, and yet there is retention with the possibility of recollection and recognition on the basis of which the past is retained in the present and handed over to the future. In death the total conglomeration does not cease to exist or does not come to an end and gets retained so as to give rise to another conglomeration in some other form in the next birth. In this metamorphosis the psychical series is present only in the form of *saṁskāras* (latent impressions) sustained by *kārmic* forces. The *kārmic* forces determine the nature and form of the next birth. They also determine the *pañcaskandhas* (the fivefold conglomeration), which has to come into existence in the next birth. There is continuity not only within one particular birth but also from one birth to another birth. Thus, in Buddhist thought we find a remarkable explanation of the problems of personal identity, the experience of permanence, and so on expressed in the phenomena of memory, recollection, and recognition.

There are some interesting implications of the no-substance ontology advocated by the Buddha. The idea of impermanence of reality results in the denial of a permanent and immortal soul. However, this does not mean that there is no eschatology or soteriology in Buddhist thought. The Buddhist account of the destiny of the individual self is conditioned by the ideas of *anityatā* (impermanence), *pañcaskandhas* (fivefold conglomeration), and *santāna*(existence series), and accordingly, the destiny of the individual self is characterized as attainment of *nirvāṇa*.

Another implication is in the form of insistence on human autonomy and denial of any suprahuman or divine agency for helping the human being to attain *nirvāṇa*. Buddha spearheaded the *śramaṇa* tradition, which emphasized self-effort and noble conduct (*ārya-aṣṭāṅgika mārga*). In this scheme there is no role assigned to any divine or superhuman agency. Buddha always impressed upon his followers to have a critical attitude and an analytic bent of mind. He was opposed to blind faith, and that is why he rejected all notions about transcendental entities. However, it does not mean that Buddha was antispiritualist. He had an abiding faith in a moral and spiritual order. That is why he was not a materialist like a Cārvāka.

HISTORY OF BUDDHIST THOUGHT

Early Buddhism centers around the teachings of the Buddha, which are contained in the Pāli *Tripiṭakas*. This phase of Buddhist thought is therefore popularly known as Pāli Buddhism. Buddha was not a mere speculative and individualistic thinker. He acquired knowledge and enlightenment not for the eradication of his own suffering but for the eradication of suffering of all living beings. Thus, his thought has a practical and universalistic dimension that is essentially correlated with a theoretical aspect. The teachings of the Buddha were for the benefit of all living beings who have the capacity to acquire knowledge and to practice the noble conduct professed by him. In his thinking he did not concentrate on intricate philosophical issues, this task was subsequently performed by his followers. The history of Buddhist thought evinces two types of following of the Buddha, one philosophical and the other theological. Theologically, his followers form two camps known as Hīnayāna and Mahāyāna, each having many sects and subsects. Philosophically, Buddhist thought in India has four broad divisions, namely, Vaibhāṣika, Sautrāntika, Mādhyamika, and Yogācāra. Nārāyaṇa Bhatta in *Mānameyodaya* cryptically summarizes the basic thrust of each of these four schools as follows:

Mukhyo Mādhyamiko vivartamakhilam śūnyasya mene jagat,
Yogācāra mate tu santi matayaḥ tāsām vivarto' khilaḥ
Artho' sti kṣaṇiko tvasāvanumito kathyeti Sautrāntiko.
Pratyakṣam kṣaṇa bhaṅguram ca sakalam Vaibhāṣiko bhāṣate.

That is, the Mādhyamika is the most important philosophical school, which regards the entire world to be an apparent manifestation of *śūnya*. The next school is Yogācāra, according to which ideas alone are real, and the entire world is an apparent manifestation of ideas. The third school is that of the Sautrāntikas, which maintains that there are objects existing independently of the ideas, but they are momentary, and their existence is known only through inference. The last school is known as Vaibhāṣika, which holds that all objects are momentary and perceivable.

For the sake of easy understanding, these four schools can be put in a particular logical order as Vaibhāṣika, Sautrāntika, Mādhyamika, and Yogācāra. Perhaps this may also be the chronological order. All these four schools claim authenticity and faithfulness to Buddha's thought. Buddha was quite prolific in his ideas, and it may not be difficult to find rudiments of all these four schools in his thoughts. The doctrine of impermanence (*anityatā*), which subsequently was formulated as the doctrine of momentariness (*kṣaṇikavāda*), and the doctrine of dependent origination (*pratītya samutpāda*) are the common planks for all these four schools. All the schools believe in the ideas of rebirth and *nirvāṇa*. Their difference is only in terms of the development of logical structures based on these doctrines and ideas. We shall briefly discuss the major points of difference characterizing each of these schools. The schools of Mādhyamika and Yogācāra (Vijñānavāda) are idealistic in their thrust and are associated with the Mahāyāna tradition. The other two schools have a realistic tendency and are put under Hīnayāna tradition. However, these four schools constitute significant facets of later Buddhist thought.

VAIBHĀṢIKA SCHOOL

The Vaibhāṣika school seems to have acquired this name because it relies upon a commentary on the *Tripiṭaka* known as *Vibhāṣā*. This school upholds a dualism of mental and physical elements. All that is real is momentary, and it is either physical (*bhūta*) or mental (*citta*). The objects of the world are a conglomeration of either physical elements or mental elements or both. No object is permanent or abiding, but since it is in the form of an incessant series, it gives the impression of permanence. These objects are directly known in perceptual cognition. When there is simultaneity of appearance of the cognizing consciousness and the cognized object at a particular time, perceptual cognition of that object takes place. Thus, all three have simultaneous origin at one and the same time. Though the object depends on the cognizing consciousness in order to be known, the dependence is not necessary for mere existence. An object may exist without being known and may thus be independent of the cognizing consciousness. Likewise, a cognizing consciousness may also exist independently of the cognized object. In this way, the Vaibhāṣika school advocates dualism in its metaphysics and realism in its epistemology. The Vaibhāṣika school concentrates more on the analysis of mental phenomena, and we find an elaborate psychological analysis in the literature belonging to this school.

SAUTRĀNTIKA SCHOOL

The Sautrāntika school derives its name from a commentary called *Sūtrānta*. It is also a realistic school, sharing its metaphysics with Vaibhāṣikas. Sautrāntikas believe in the momentary existence of the real and classify them into mental and physical. The mental and the physical are basically independent of each other, though subsequently they may interact. Sautrāntikas regard the object to be existing independently of the noetic process. The object, the cognizer, and the cognition are all distinct. The object may be known or may not be known. If an object is known, it cannot be known in direct perception. In this respect they differ from Vaibhāṣikas. According to Sautrāntikas, the moment of existence of the object and the moment of the cognition of the object cannot be the same because cognition follows and presupposes existence, and every existence precedes its cognition. There cannot be simultaneity of existence and its cognition. The Sautrāntika thinkers examine and refute the Vaibhāṣika position in this respect. In fact, this is the major point of difference between the two schools. The Sautrāntikas argue that the object of knowledge exists independently of the cognizing consciousness, and it ceases to exist in the next moment. So, when it comes into existence at that very moment, it is not cognized, and it cannot be cognized. It does not exist in the next moment to be perceptually cognized, so there is never any perceptual cognition of an object. However, it does not mean that an object can never be cognized. There is another mode of cognizing an object. Before an object ceases to exist, it leaves out its impression. This impression is the exact copy of its original and has semblance (*sārūpya*) with it. The cognizing consciousness perceptually apprehends only this impression, and through this perceptual apprehension of the impression it infers the original object. Thus, Sautrāntikas introduce the concept of object impression and through this advocate the representative theory of perception. For them all cognitions are represented cognitions of the object. An object-qua-object is not directly perceived. Only its impression is perceived, and because of the resemblance of the two and cognitive nonavailability of the object the impression is taken to be the original object.

MĀDHYAMIKA SCHOOL

The third school is Mādhyamika, which is philosophically very significant. Nāgārjuna has been the first known exponent of this school. He argues that Buddha's teachings consist in the *madhyamapratipad* (middle path) to be followed for the realization of *nirvāṇa,* which is cessation of all suffering. According to Nāgārjuna, Buddha advocated *śūnyatā* (essencelessness) of all existence. All existences are *śūnya* (essenceless) in the sense that they do not have self-existence (*svabhāva*). Every existence has a borrowed existence or a dependent existence (*pratītyasamutpanna); svabhāva śūnyatā* (lack of independent existence) characterizes all reals. The same position holds good in respect of all thought and language. Just as all real is self-negating, all thought and all language are also self-negating. Nāgārjuna exposes the hollowness and self-contradictory nature of the important concepts and doctrines prevalent in his time in Buddhist and non-Buddhist philosophies. He successfully employs the weapons of *śūnyatā* and *pratītyasamutpāda* to demolish all systems of metaphysics. He advocates a twofold approach to reality in terms of *samvṛti sat* (empirical real) and *paramārtha sat* (trancendental real). Both are characterized by *śūnyutā* in different ways. Empirical is *svabhāva śūnya* (devoid of intrinsic existence), and transcendental is *prapañca śūnya*. By *prapañca* he means display of thought and language. Nāgārjuna emphasizes the antimetaphysical, practical, and pragmatic nature of Buddha's teachings and lays stress on the attainment of *prajñā* (wisdom) leading to *śīla* (noble conduct) and *samādhi* (state of equipoise). This school is known as Mādhyamika because of its emphasis on *madhyama pratipada*, which is a practical middle path, avoiding all extremes. It is known as Śūnyavāda because of its exposition of essencelessness of all real on account of its dependent character.

YOGĀCĀRA SCHOOL

The pluralistic and realistic philosophy of the Sarvāstivāda culminates in a monistic and idealistic philosophy of Vijñānavāda (Yogācāra) by way of a critique and rejection of Śūnyavāda. The representative theory of perception of the Sautrāntikas implies that all that is cognized is the content of cognition, and the content of cognition has a form of its own, which has sameness of form (*sārupya*) with the form of the object. It resulted in the theory of *sākārajñānavāda*, a theory according to which every cognition has a form of its own apart from the form given to it by its object. From the theory of *sākārajñānavāda* there was a natural transition to the theory that only contents of cognition or *vijñānas* (ideas) are real and that they alone are cognized. The external objects are only hypostatizations. They are presumed to be there, but, in fact, they are only projections of the consciousness. Consciousness alone is real. Thus, in Vijñānavāda we find a repudiation of the theory that the object of cognition exists externally and independently of the cognizing consciousness (*bāhyārthavāda*). The consciousness that alone is primarily real is momentary and is in the form of a continuous flow (*pravāha*). The Vijñānavada advocates three levels of reality, namely, *parikalpita* (imaginary), *pāratāntrika* (dependent or empirical reality), and *pāramārthika* (transcendental reality). Transcendental reality is conceived to be unitary stream of consciousness, technically known as *ālaya vijñāna*. It is a storehouse of consciousness in the sense that it is the foundation of all streams of consciousness that are responsible for the appearance of the world of external objects. It is a repository of the old impressions (*saṁskāras*) and a depository of new impressions. In this way *ālaya vijñāna* is the only ultimate reality. In itself it is pure and cannot be characterized. It can be experienced only in the state of *nirvāṇa*. The other level of reality is empirical, which consists of finite stream of consciousness and objects of consciousness. It is the level of the empirical world that we experience in our ordinary life. It is a reality that is amenable to empirical knowledge and linguistic expression. It is empirical reality (*saṁvṛti sat*), as different from transcendental reality (*pāramārthika sat*).

DEVELOPMENT OF YOGĀCĀRA EPISTEMOLOGY

Maitreya and Asanga

In the Yogācāra tradition prior to Maitreya, Āsaṅga and Vasubandhu initiated systematic philosophical reflections. It seems Maitreya reached Yogācāra position via Śūnyavāda, whereas Asaṅga and Vasubandhu were initially Sautrāntika and Vaibhāṣika, respectively, before coming to Yogācāra. Maitreya was the author of several works such as *Bodhisattvacaryā Nirdeśa, Saptadaśa Bhūmi Śāstra Yogacaryā*, and *Abhisamayālaṅkāra Kārikā*. He discussed in detail the nature of reality and the modes of knowing. In fact he is the forerunner of the art of debate (*vāda-vidhi*) in the Buddhist tradition. Asaṅga followed Maitreya and expounded Yogācāra philosophy. He composed two works entitled *Prakaraṇārya Vācāśāstra* and *Mahāyāna Abhidharma Samyukta Sangiti Śāstra*. By and large he followed Maitreya but differed in respect of the theory of proof (*sādhana*).

Vasubandhu

Vasubandhu carried forward and systematized the Yogācāra philosophy. He was an author of several important works on ontology and epistemology. Some of the works associated with him are *Vāda Vidhi, Vāda Mārga, Vāda Kauśala, Tarka Śāstra*, and *Abhidharma Kośa*.

Diṅnāga

Among the post-Nāgārjuna Buddhist philosophers Diṅnāga has been the most notable thinker who has carried ahead the tradition of Maitreya, Āsaṇga, and Vasubandhu by successfully repudiating the negativistic dialectics of Nāgārjuna and by replacing it with a philosophical positivism that was a synthesis of the Sautrāntika and Vijñānavāda schools. It goes to the credit of Diṅnāga that he reconciled the Sautrāntika ontology with the rubric of Vijñānavāda ontology, formulated an epistemology and logic suited to this new ontology, and propagated a distinct philosophical methodology based on the technique of *apoha* (double negation). He introduces a new mode of philosophizing by interspersing ontological discussion in an epistemological setting, a style that later on fascinated the Navya Nyāya thinker Gaṅgeśa and his followers. Diṅnāga employs the technique of double negation (*apoha*) for clarity and precision in thought and language. He is an abstruse logician. In his logic he advocates a dichotomous classification. This dichotomy is reflected in the advocacy of two types of real, two modes of their cognition, and two shades of meaning. He applies the idea of *svatovyāvartana* (mutual exclusion) in the fields of reality, knowledge, and language. In other words, every real is a class in itself, and everything else constitutes its complementary class. Thus, there is an exclusive ordering in the realm of reality such that there are two and only two types of real, namely, *svalakṣaṇa* (unique particular) and *sāmānyalakṣaṇa* (its generalized image). Whatever is unique particular cannot be its generalized image, and vice versa. The same rigid dichotomy is extended to the field of epistemology. It was innovative of Diṅnāga to point out that every epistemology has to be structured keeping in view the requirement of ontology. Following this ontological commitment in Diṅnāga's epistemology, there are two and only two valid modes of knowing, namely, *pratyakṣa* (perception) and *anumāna* (inference), and only two types of knowledge, perceptual and inferential. The perceptual cognizes the unique particular alone and can never cognize its generalized image. The inferential, on the other hand, cognizes the generalized image alone and cannot cognize the unique particular. So, just as there are rigid dichotomy and strict ordering at the level of reality, there are also a rigid dichotomy and strict ordering at the level of knowledge. Diṅnāga carries forward this dichotomous distinction to the field of language and meaning. Every concept is expressible in language in terms of its meaning. Meaning is conveyed by a word that represents a particular concept.The meaning of a word is the negative of its negative. Thus, there cannot be any overlapping or cross-division in the meanings of any two words. Another great contribution of Diṅnāga is in the form of propagation of the theories of:

1. *Meyādhīnāmānasiddhiḥ* : epistemology is to be constructed to support ontology.
2. *Pramāṇa vyavasthā*: the separation of the two types of mode of knowing (*pramāṇas*)
3. *Hetu cakra* : the theory that provides a schema of formal logic.
4. *Anyāpoha* : the theory of double negation, applied to the fields of ontology, epistemology, and theory of language.

The magnum opus of Diṅnāga is *Pramāṇa Samuccaya* with its

auto-commentary (*Svavṛtti*), *Nyāya Praveśa, Nyāya Mukha, Ālambana Parikṣā,* and *Hetu Cakra Ḍamaru* are some of his major works. Though *Pramāṇa Samuccaya* is lost in its Sanskrit original, it has been partly restored from its two Tibetan versions and Sanskrit fragments.

Dharmakīrti

Dharmakīrti not only mastered the systems of Vasubandhu and Diṅnāga but also excelled in them. Seven works of Dharmakīrti are known and available. Among them *Pramāṇa Vārtika* is most notable. *Pramāṇa Vārtika* is an advancement of the view of Diṅnāga expounded in *Pramāṇa Samuccaya,* and it supersedes the latter. It consists of four chapters. The first deals with the analysis of the *pramāṇas* in general, the second with *pratyakṣa* as *pramāṇa,* the third with inference (*svārthānumāna*), and the fourth with syllogism (*parārthānumāna*). The next work of Dharmakīrti is *Pramāṇa Viniścaya*. It is an abridgment of *Pramāṇa Vārtika*. The third work is *Nyāya Bindu*, which is a further abridgment. The remaining four works are small tracts devoted to specific topics. *Hetu Bindu* is a short classification of logical reasons. *Sambandha Parīkṣā* is an examination of the problem of relations. *Codanā Prakaraṇa* is a treatise on the act of carrying on disputation. *Santānāntara Siddhiḥ* is a treatise on the reality of other minds. It attempts to refute solipsism.

Chapter 1

The Buddhist Theory of Knowledge

Every school of philosophy in India has attempted a theory of knowledge (*pramāṇa śāstra*) on which its metaphysical structure is built. Though the ultimate aim of philosophizing is generally recognized as knowledge of reality (*tattva-jñāna*), it is believed that a theory of knowledge is a necessary prerequisite to a theory of reality. This belief is grounded in the fact that to philosophize is to reflect on the nature of reality given in experience. But since every experience is a cognitive reference to an object, there is always the possibility of going astray in this reference. Though every experience has a built-in transphenomenality or self-transcendence, it is not always guaranteed that it would adequately and faithfully reveal its object. This possibility of error in experience necessitates an inquiry into its veracity. In fact, the entire epistemological pursuit begins with, and centers around, this task. Thinkers belonging to the Buddhist tradition also, therefore, attempt to provide a firm epistemological basis for their theory of reality.

ANALYSIS OF KNOWLEDGE[1]

"All successful human action is necessarily preceded by knowledge."[2] With this prefatory remark Dharmakīrti defines the scope and aim of epistemology and logic in the *Nyāya Bindu*. Human action may be either purposive or instinctive. Human purpose is, again, something either desirable or undesirable. A purposive action based on knowledge consists in attaining the desirable and avoiding the undesirable. Knowledge is efficacious in causing successful action in the sense that it results in the attainment of the desirable aim and avoidance of the undesirable one. A cause may be productive (*kāraka*) or informative (*jñāpaka*). Knowledge is a cause of successful action in the latter sense only. It enables us to reach the real, which alone has practical efficiency.

Different from knowledge is false cognition. Cognition that makes us reach an object different from the one revealed in cognition is false. Objects differ on account of their form and spatiotemporal locations. Thus, cognition representing one form of the object is not to be considered as true when the real object has a different form. Likewise, a cognition is not true if it wrongly represents the place and time of the object.

In the *Pramāṇa Vārtika* Dharmakīrti defines knowledge as a cognition that is not in discordance with its object (*Pramāṇam avisamvādi jñānam*).[3] He further maintains that a cognition that is perfectly in accord with its object will also be characterized by novelty (*Ajñāta artha prakāśo vā*).[4] It is revelatory of an object not yet known because the object is momentary in nature and only that knowledge will accord with the object which arises at that very moment when the object is also in existence. It is the first moment of cognition, the moment of the first awareness. Continuous cognition is not valid or true, according to the Buddhists, because it is not a new cognition but a recognition. Of these two characteristics, the first, nondiscordance, is basic and can be regarded as the differential character of knowledge.

Knowledge thus stands for cognition that is a faithful representation of the real. What it means is that in knowledge the object must be known *as it is* and not *other than what it is*. Since a nondeviating reference is an essential condition of knowledge, the truth of knowledge consists in its accord with the cognized object. Dharmottara puts it as follows: "In common life when we say that truth is being spoken what we mean is that it makes us reach an object. Similarly, that cognition is true which makes us reach an object it points to. In fact, knowledge does not create an object and does not offer it to us, but just makes us reach at it. By making us reach an object nothing else is meant than attending to it."[5] Here Dharmottara points out three distinct, successive stages involved in the process of apprehension of an object, each succeeding one resulting from the preceding. They are cognizing (*adhigati*), attending (*pravartana*), and reaching (*prāpaṇa*). He makes it clear that the first stage alone is knowledge.

Knowledge is of two types. It is intuitive when it springs from inside. It is discursive when it is acquired by directing our attention toward an object with the help of the senses and the cognizing consciousness. Only discursive knowledge is analyzed in epistemology.

THE PROBLEM OF *PRAMĀṆA*

As stated earlier, knowledge is a nondiscordant cognition. This means that not all cognitions are knowledge. Only those cognitions whose nondiscordance is evidenced can claim the status of knowledge. The problem of *pramāṇa* that has given rise to much stimulating debate in the epistemological treatises of Indian origin is basically a problem of evidencing the truth of a cognition. The question of evidencing a cognition arises because all cognitions are unequal in their epistemic status. Some appear to be true and reveal their corresponding objects as they are, whereas others seem to be erroneous and misrepresent their objects. Had all cognitions been true, there would have been no need of evidencing them, and the entire epistemological inquiry would not have arisen. The very possibility of error in a cognition necessitates its subjection to a critical examination with a view to establishing its truth or falsity. If the truth or falsity of a cognition needs to be established, the question arises what sort of criterion is to be resorted to. The problem of *pramāna* has been discussed and raised precisely against this background.

PRAMĀṆAPHALA

Indian thinkers generally adopt a causal approach to knowledge. Knowledge is taken to be an outcome of a particular causal complex in which the most efficient instrumental cause (*karaṇa*) is technically known as *pramāṇa*. In the Buddhist tradition, the word *pramāṇa* refers to both the process of knowing and the knowledge acquired on that basis. Buddhists do not entertain the distinction between the process of knowing (*pramāṇa*) and its outcome (*pramāṇaphala=pramā*). Whether or not *pramāṇa* and *pramāṇaphala* are to be sharply distinguished has been a hotly debated issue between Nyāya and Buddhist thinkers. Nyāya thinkers insist that *pramāṇa* as a process leading to *pramā* should be distinguished from the latter, which is its *phala* (result). For them *pramā* is the *pramāṇaphala,* and *pramāṇa* is the *karaṇa* of *pramā*. Buddhist thinkers, however, maintain that no distinction can be possible between the noetic process and its outcome. The act of cognizing completely coincides with the cognition of an object. In fact, Naiyāyikas have to accept the distinction because for them *pramāṇa* is the evidencing condition for the truth of knowledge, whereas *pramā* is the evidenced knowledge. For Buddhists, knowledge is self-evidencing, and therefore there is no need to distinguish between *pramāṇa* and its *phala*. Thus, the difference between Naiyāyikas and Buddhists is due to the difference in their understanding of the nature and role of *pramāṇa*. Naiyāyikas understand *pramāṇa* as that which is the most efficient causal condition giving rise to, and evidencing, the knowledge (*pramāyāḥ karaṇam iti pramāṇam*), whereas for Buddhists, it means that by which an object is known (*pramīyate artho aneneti*).

Diṅnāga, however, does not refuse to draw this distinction if it is needed from a functional point of view. He writes, "We call the cognition itself *pramāṇa* because it is generally conceived to include the act of cognising although primarily it is a result." Commenting on it, he writes, "Here we do not admit, as the Realists do, that the resulting cognition differs from the means of cognition. The resulting cognition arises bearing in itself the form of the cognised object and is understood to include the act of cognizing. For this reason it is metaphorically called *pramāṇa* although it is ultimately devoid of activity."[6]

Nature of *Pramāṇaphala*

In the Diṅnāga-Dharmakīrti tradition two different views are available about the nature of *pramāṇaphala*. According to one, *pramāṇaphala* consists in the cognition of an object (*viṣayādhigama*). According to the other, it consists in self-cognition (*sva-saṁvitti*). Both these views are complementary and not conflicting and are available in the works of Diṅnāga.[7] They are explicitly restated by Dharmakīrti and Dharmottara.[8] Śāntarakṣita gathers them together and brings out their distinction. He maintains that according to the Sautrāntika tradition, which believes in *bāhyārthavāda* (realism), *sārūpya* (similarity in form) obtaining between a cognition and its object is to be treated as *pramāṇa*, while cognition of an object (*viṣayādhigati*) is to be treated as *pramāṇaphala*. According to *Vijñānavāda*, *sārūpya* is, of course, the *pramāṇa*, but *sva-saṁvedana* or *sva-saṁvitti* (self-cognition) is the *pramāṇaphala*. In the ultimate analysis these views are not different because *viṣayādhigati* and *sva-saṁvedana* are not two different phenomena as they are two facets of the same knowledge.

Sārūpya as *Pramāṇa*

It has been one of the perennial problems of philosophy to put forth a criterion of truth that is cogent and convincing. Since knowledge consists in a cognition's being free from discordance with its object, the criterion of truth has to be formulated in terms of knowledge's being in accordance with its object. Buddhist thinkers therefore put forth *sārūpya* as a *pramāṇa*, in the absence of which no cognition can be taken to be knowledge. The doctrine of *sārūpya* has been formulated keeping in view the self-evidential character of knowledge and also the view that since every knowledge is an awareness of an object, the conditions of its truth are to be determined in terms of its reference to the object.

The Concept of *Sārūpya* in Early Buddhist Philosophy

The doctrine of *sārūpya* advocated by Diṅnāga and Dharmakīrti has its roots in the Sarvāstivāda tradition,[9] though it can further be traced back to the early Buddhist literature in Pāli.[10] In the Sarvāstivāda tradition independent and objective existence of the external object was admitted. Similarity (*sārūpya*) of the form represented in a cognition to that of the object is held to be the *pramāṇa* of the resulting cognition of that object (*viṣayādhigati*). Accordingly, a cognition that is produced along with its object is true with reference to that object. The object, the cognitive sense, and the cognizing consciousness are all simultaneous and momentary. All three exist at the same time (*sahabhu hetu*) and constitute the collocation of causes (*kāraṇa-sāmagri*) that gives rise to the cognition. This Abhidharma account of the genesis of perceptual cognition has been represented by Stcherbatsky in the form demonstrated in Figure 1.1.

Figure 1.1

Sahabhu hetu

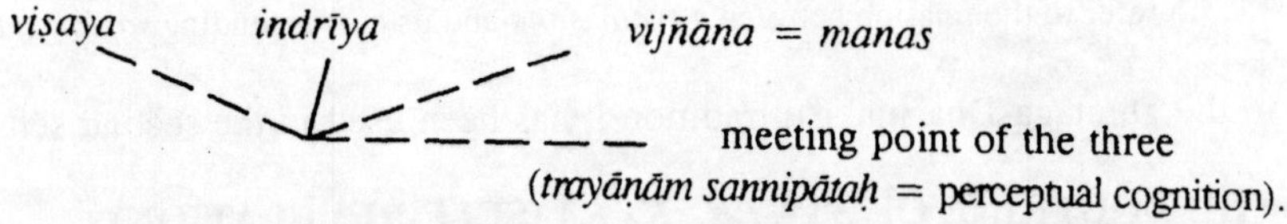

There the perceptual cognition is regarded to be a resultant of three types of causal factors, namely,

1. *samanantara pratyaya* (i.e., perceiving consciousness),
2. *adhipati pratyaya* (i.e., cognitive sense), and
3. *ālambana pratyaya* (i.e., object).[11]

Here a question naturally arises as to why a particular cognition should refer to the object only for its determination and not to the cognitive sense or the cognizing consciousness, which are equally simultaneous with it. This is explained by putting forth the doctrine of *sārūpya*, according to which, though all three causal factors are simultaneously present, the object alone provides a form to the cognition and thus determines it.

The preceding view is put forth by the Vaibhāṣika school but it is not acceptable to Sautrāntikas, who reject the notion of *"sahabhu hetu,"* that is, the simultaneity of object, cognitive sense, and cognizing consciousness. The basic objection raised by them against this position is that in the background of momentariness it poses a serious problem. When the cognition arises, the object is no longer present because, being momentary, it must have by then been destroyed. In such a situation how can it be called the perception of that object alone, and, further, how can that object be the determinant of the truth of the cognition? The Sautrāntikas therefore solve this problem by putting forth the doctrine of *sārūpya*, according to which the object no doubt is momentary but leaves its impression upon consciousness, and through this impression, which has *sārūpya* with the object, the object is cognized.[12]

Though both the Vaibhāṣikas and Sautrāntikas accept the doctrine of *sārūpya*, they use it differently. The former use it to explain why the cognition is determined by the object and not by the cognitive consciousness, though both are the causal factors giving rise to the cognition; while the latter use it to explain how the object that is already destroyed is cognized in perception.

The Doctrine of *Sārūpya* in the Diṅnāga-Dharmakīrti Tradition

In the Diṅnāga-Dharmakīrti tradition the doctrine of *sārūpya* has been primarily put forth as a *pramāṇa* for perceptual cognition, and in this sense it marks a departure from the Sautrāntika use of this concept. In fact, Stcherbatsky[13] has pointed out three different uses of the term *sārūpya*, namely:

1. to refer to the relation between a sensation and a conception,
2. to refer to the relation between *svalakṣaṇa* and its *pratibhāsa*, and
3. to refer to the relation between a *svalakṣaṇa* and its corresponding *sāmānya lakṣaṇa*.

In the Diṅnāga-Dharmakīrti tradition it has been used in the second sense.

THE DOCTRINE OF *SVA-PRAKĀŚA* (SELF-REVELATION)

The doctrine of *sārūpya* has been put forth in the context of the more basic doctrine of *dvairūpya,* which implies that every cognition is necessarily in the form of a twofold appearance, namely, that of the object and that of itself. This doctrine of *dvairūpya* has been an inevitable corollary of the doctrine of *sva-prakāśa* (self-revelation of cognition), which results in the obliteration of the distinction between *pramāṇa* and *pramāṇaphala*, insofar as the same cognition is at once both the evidence and the evidenced.

The doctrine of *sva-prakāśa* has been the basic tenet of the Buddhist epistemology put forth in the context of the theory of momentariness. If a cognition is just a momentary state of existence ceasing to exist the next moment, then either we can have a cognition of that cognition in the very moment of its origin, or we shall have to deny the very possibility of the cognition of that cognition because the next moment that cognition will no longer be there to be cognized by the subsequent cognition. Since the cognition of a cognition is a fact given in our experience, it can be understood only in the context of the doctrine of *sva-prakāśa*. Consistent with the theory of momentariness, Buddhists talk of the cognition of cognition only within the framework of simultaneity and never that of succession. Thus, the only position available would be to advocate the theory of *sva-prakāśa,* which would mean that at the very moment of the cognition's cognizing an object, it also cognizes itself.

Diṅnāga and Dharmakīrti use the expression "*svasaṁvitti*" to express this fact.[14] Thus, when a man has the cognition of something blue, he has at the same time the awareness of the cognition of something blue. This awareness is caused by nothing other than the cognition itself. Thus, the cognition, while cognizing an object, cognizes itself just as a lamp illuminates itself while illuminating an object.

The Doctrine of *Dvairūpya*

The doctrines of *sva-prakāśa* and *svataḥ-prāmāṇya* (self-evidentiality of cognition) go together. Not only is every cognition a cognition cognizing itself but it also evidences itself. Now the question is, How is it that a cognition cognizes itself and thus establishes itself as true? To answer this, as stated earlier, the doctrine of *dvairūpya* has been put forth.[15] Every cognition is produced with a twofold appearance, namely, that of itself (*svābhāsa*) and that of the object (*viṣayābhāsa*). In being *viṣayābhāsa* it establishes its truth because of its being in the form of the object.[16] When a cognition possesses the form of an object, it is a sufficient condition for its being true. Thus, Diṅnāga writes, "The *pramāṇa* is simply the cognition having the form of the object."[17]

Hattori[18] has made an attempt to represent the doctrine of *dvairūpya* using the following symbols:

Viṣayajñāna = C_1
Svābhāsa in $C_1 = S_1$
Arthābhāsa in $C_1 = O_1$
Viṣayajñāna-jñāna = C_2
Svābhāsa in $C_2 = S_2$
Arthābhāsa in $C_2 = O_2$

He writes that, according to Diṅnāga, $C_1 = (S_1 - O_1)$, $C_2 = (S_2 - O_2)$. ("—" indicates relation). Since C_2 takes C_1 for its object, $O_2 = (S_1 - O_1)$. Therefore, $C_2 = \{S_2 - (S_1 - O_1)\}$. Thus, C_2 is distinguishable from C_1.

Now, in case the cognition had only *arthākāra* (= *ābhāsa*), then $C_1 = O_1$, and $C_2 = O_2$. Since C_2 takes C_1 for its object, $O_2 = O_1$. Therefore, $C_2 = C_1$. Thus, *viṣayajñāna-jñāna* would be indistinguishable from *viṣayajñāna*. If, on the other hand, the cognition had only *svākāra (= ābhāsa)*, then $C_1 = S_1$, and $C_2 = S_2$. However, since the cognition, which does not possess the form of an object within itself, remains the same at all times, $S_2 = S_1$. Therefore, $C_2 = C_1$.

In fact, Hattori goes beyond C_2 to postulate C_3 and C_4 and so on ad infinitum. He writes, "In the same manner, the third and the succeeding cognition C_3, C_4 ..... C_n are distinguishable from the preceding ones only when they are acknowledged to possess "*dvi-rūpa.*" The formulas are as follows:

$$C_3 = (S_3 - O_3) = \{S_3 - (S_2 - O_2)\}.$$

$$C_n = (S_n - O_n) = (S_n - (S_{n-1} - O_{n-1})).$$

(S_3 ..... S_n and O_3 .... O_n, respectively, stand for *svābhāsa* and *arthābhāsa* in C_3 ... C_n), C_2, C_3 ... C_n are constituted by adding another *ākāra* to the preceding C_1, C_2 ... C_{n-1}."

This symbolic representation and its explication given by Hattori do not seem to be very appealing, mainly because they are based on the presumption that in the self-cognition of the cognition, which involves two cognitions, namely, C_1 and C_2, C_1 is the preceding, and C_2 is the succeeding one. Hattori proposes to go beyond C_2 to C_3, C_4 ad infinitum. In this venture he seems to be working under the "succession-model." But as we have stated earlier, Diṅnāga's theory of *sva-prakāśa* cannot adequately be understood like that. Diṅnāga is quite explicit in advocating the "simultaneity model" which would preclude any overstepping from C_1 to C_2. If C_1 is granted the dual form of *svākāra* and *arthākāra*, which

Figure 1.2

***Dvairūpya* Model**

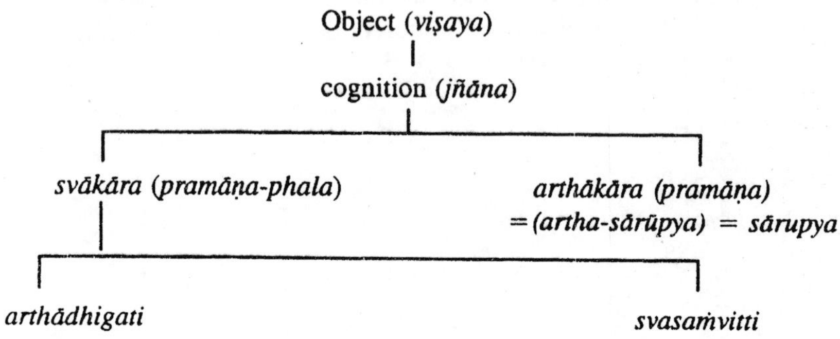

sva-prakāśa theory pronouncedly intends to do, there is no need to bring in C_2, and if C_2 is needless, we also have, ipso facto, not to go beyond C_2 to C_n. Thus, a distinction between C_1 (= *viṣayajñāna*) and C_2 (= *viṣayajñāna-jñāna*) would violate the very spirit of Diṅnāga's theory of *sva-prakāśa*. In fact, within C_1 itself we have *svābhāsa* and *arthābhāsa*, which are inextricably so interspersed that they can be distinguished only for the sake of conceptual clarity but can never be separated. However, this distinction does not in any way imply that *svābāsa* (*viṣayajñāna-jñāna*) and *arthābhāsa* (*viṣayajñāna*) are two different occurrences. In the very act of knowing an object there is an awareness of the knowing because had there been no awareness of the knowing at the initial moment, it could not be possible to have it subsequently, as neither the object nor the cognition of the object would last for the next moment.

Hattori seems to understand the Buddhist theory of *dvairūpya* as implying that at the first moment there is a rise of the first *rūpa*, namely, that of *viṣayākāra*, and then at the succeeding moment there will be the rise of the second *rūpa*, namely, that of *svākāra*, but such an interpretation doesn't do justice to Diṅnāga's position, which explicitly maintains that a cognition has *svākāra* along with *arthākāra* (= *viṣayākāra*).

The Buddhist theory of *dvairūpya* understood in the context of "simultaneity model" is represented in Figure 1.2.

THE CONCEPT OF *VIṢAYĀKĀRA*

The Buddhist theory of *dvairūpya* as represented in Figure 1.2 states clearly that *arthākāritā*, also known as *artha-sārūpya* or just *sārūpya*, is the *pramāṇa* of which *arthādhigati* (apprehension of the object) and *svasaṁvitti* (self-cognition) are the *pramāṇa-phala*. There has been a controversy among Buddhist logicians preceding Diṅnāga as to whether *arthādhigati* is the *pramāṇa-phala* or *svasamvitti*. Of course, this controversy presupposes the distinction between *pramāṇa* and *pramāṇaphala* for pragmatic purposes only. Granting this distinction, Diṅnāga writes that, strictly speaking, *arthādhigati* alone is the *pramāṇaphala,* but *svasamvitti* can also be regarded as *pramāṇaphala.*[19]

Every cognition is a cognition of something and thus inevitably refers to an object. The object gives rise to, and thus determines, the cognition. The object is regarded as the *ālambana pratyaya,* that is, the very ground upon which the cognition is based. In fact, the object not only serves to give rise to the cognition but also differentiates it from other cognitions. Without assigning this task of differentiation to the object, one cognition cannot be differentiated from another cognition. Though from the transcendental point of view every phenomenon is *vijñaptimātra* (pure consciousness), at the empirical level a triple division of *vijñāna* (consciousness) is drawn into *grāhyākāra* (the form that is cognized), *grāhaka* (the cognition), and *svasaṁvitti* (self-cognition).The *grāhyākāra* serves as a differentiating factor between one cognition and another.[20]

Since every cognition is determined by the object, this determination should be understood as the cognition's having the form of the object. Thus, if the object is a pen, the corresponding cognition should have the form of pen. Then only will it be said to be determined by the object "pen" and be a true presentation (*ābhāsa*) of that object. If the cognition is at variance with the object, it will not then be determined by the object, and this will amount to its falsity. In order that a cognition should be true, it has to reflect or represent the object in its real form. This will be possible only when the cognition is arising in the form of the object. The truth of a cognition, therefore, consists in this sameness of form with the object. It is not that knowledge is formless, as is maintained by the *nirākārajñānavādins*. If the cognition were formless while the object had a form, then the cognition itself as distinguished from the object would remain the same whether it cognizes something blue or yellow or anything else. Therefore, the cognition as the apprehension of the object must be admitted to be *sākāra*. To say that cognition is *sākāra* is the same thing as to say that it has the form of the object. The *sākāra* cognition is thus understood to possess the function of assuming the form of the object. For this reason Diṅnāga considers it as *pramāṇa,* although primarily it is a *phala* in its aspect as apprehension of an object.[21]

NIYATA AND *ANIYATA PRATIBHĀSA*

According to Buddhist thinkers since every true cognition (and, for that matter, every cognition) is necessarily caused by an object, and since there are only two types of objects, namely, the *grāhya* (given) and the *adhyavaseya* (construed), there are two types of cognition, the perceptual and the conceptual. Corresponding to these are two types of *pratibhāsa* (mental reflex). The perceptual cognition consists in a *pratibhāsa* that is *niyata*, that is, definite and not vague, because it is caused by an object that is independent of the perceiving consciousness and therefore objectively real. In case of conceptual cognition there is no such objectively existing real object, and hence the *pratibhāsa* here is *aniyata*, that is, indefinite and vague. The apprehended object giving rise to an awareness generates a regulated mental reflex (i.e., a reflex limited to that very object). It is just like a patch of color that, giving rise to visual awareness, generates a definite mental reflex limited to that patch. The conceptual awareness, on the other hand, is not generated by the object. Thus, in the absence of the causal factor to regulate the mental reflex, there is no fixed (definite) mental reflex. However, it should be made clear that from the empirical point of view this *aniyatatva* (indefiniteness of *pratibhāsa*) in no way affects the epistemic status of inferential cognition because the validity (*prāmāṇya*) of a cognition depends not on the vagueness or definiteness of *pratibhāsa* but on its *sārupya* (conformity with the object), and in the inferential cognition it is very much present.

Diṅnāga's Analysis of *Pratibhāsa*

Since the object gives rise to its *pratibhāsa*, the *pratibhāsa* has to be in coordination with its respective object. According to Diṅnāga, every *pratibhāsa* has to be in coordination with its object because it is produced by *that* object only. An object cannot produce any such *pratibhāsa* that cannot accord with it. Logically, therefore, he rules out any possibility of deviation from its object in a *pratibhāsa*.

Dharmakīrti's Analysis of *Pratibhāsa*

Dharmakīrti, however, maintains that sometimes an object may fail to give rise to its genuine *pratibhāsa*. This may be due to several factors like the locus of the object, the circumstances of the presentation of the object, the disturbed state of cognizing consciousness, and so on. If a *pratibhāsa* fails to accord with its corresponding object, it will lack coordination with it, and to that extent it cannot be said to be genuine. Thus, when one has the *pratibhāsa* of a moving tree while traveling in a boat, the *pratibhāsa* cannot be said to be genuine because it is not in accord with its object. Of course, such an analysis of the epistemic situation would not be acceptable to Diṅnāga, who would insist that every *pratibhāsa* has to be in accord with its object because it is produced by that object only.

Irrespective of whether a *pratibhāsa* may or may not deviate from its object, the fact remains that every *pratibhāsa* in a true cognition must be in accord with its object. That is why Buddhist thinkers insist on *avisaṁvādakatva* (nondiscordance) as a necessary condition of a true cognition.

Is There *Arthasārūpya* in Inferential *Pratibhāsa?*

While commenting on the *Nyāya Bindu* of Dharmakīrti, Dharmottara seems to maintain that there can be only one type of real object, namely, the *svalakṣaṇa* (unique particular).[22] There is no real object corresponding to the conceptual cognition insofar as the *sāmānyalakṣaṇa* (generalized image or concept) is not objectively real. This will then mean that in a conceptual cognition there will not be any possibility of *arthasārūpya* (coordination) with the really existing object. But Dharmottara's contention can be sustained only if we overlook the fact that for Buddhist thinkers *sāmānyalakṣaṇa* is also real, although, of course, it is real only from the empirical point of view (*saṁvṛtti sat*).

Justification for Accepting *Sārūpya*

It seems that the only reason for the Buddhist thinkers to advocate the theory of *sākāra jñāna* is to provide for the determination of the cognition by its respective object. Every cognition refers to an object insofar as it is produced by the object. There is no cognition that is not produced by the object and that therefore is not having some form given by the object. Thus, there is no formless cognition, because in the very process of its being produced by the object, it gets, so to say, the form of the object. It may be that the form of a cognition does not accord with the specific object that is given in the epistemic situation and may accord with some other object that is not given but only hypostatized. Such is the case in illusion. Here, there is no *arthasārūpya,* and hence it is not a true cognition. The cognition here has a form but not of the given object. Thus, the doctrine of *sārūpya* serves the purpose of distinguishing between a true cognition and an erroneous one. Buddhist thinkers understand truth in terms of *avisaṁvādakatvam*, that is, nondiscordance with the object of cognition. The necessary as also the sufficient condition for the availability of nondiscordance is *arthasārūpya,* which means the cognition should be determined by that very object and not by any other object. If it is determined by some object other than its own, it will be a case of *vairūpya* (discordance) rather than that of *sārūpya,* because in that case some other object will be the determinant rather than the legitimate one.

Having analyzed the doctrine of *sārūpya,* we may proceed to see the grounds for its acceptance. Though this doctrine is deduced as a corollary of the doctrine of *dvairūpya*, two grounds one positive and the other negative have been put forth to account for its acceptance. The first ground is the fact of recollection, which provides the basis for saying that the cognition has two forms and that it is in accord with its object. As Diṅnāga puts it, "If the cognition has only one form, either that of the object or of itself, then the object which was cognized in the preceding cognition could not appear in the succeeding cognition, because that object of the preceding cognition would not exist when a succeeding cognition arises. But we do have facts of recollection when some time after there occurs to our mind the recollection of our cognition as well as that of the object. We express the fact of the recollection of a past cognition in the form 'I remember that I cognized the object.' The recollection of a past cognition is explainable only by admitting that the cognition is cognized by itself."[23]

The second ground for admitting *sārūpya* as a *pramāṇa* is that if a cognition were not self-cognizing and self-evidencing, this would have resulted in infinite regress, because it would have required another cognition for its cognition and validation, and the second one would have required a third one, and so forth.

The doctrine of *sārūpya* is fully consistent with the idealistic position of Vijñānavāda Buddhism, for which in the ultimate analysis all objects that appear to be objective and external are nothing but projections of the consciousness.

Because of this the Buddhist can talk of the cognition appearing in the form of object. As has been pointed out earlier, the idea of cognition assuming the form of the object should not be mistaken as sameness of form between the object and the cognition. It stands only for the determination of the cognition by the object. However, the term *sārūpya* is slightly misleading insofar as it gives the impression as if cognition has the same or similar form possessed by the object. It is meaningful to talk of the form of an object, but it doesn't make much sense to talk of the form of a cognition unless it is understood in a figurative sense only. All that it should be understood to mean is that every cognition necessarily refers to an object, and every true cognition has to refer to the object as it is. To refer to the object as it is means to be of the form of the object. Understood in this way the contention of the Buddhist seems to be plausible, but to express this with the help of the term "*sārūpya*" is beset with the difficulty referred to before. In fact, the Buddhist logicians should have used another word that would have better expressed the idea of the cognition's being determined by its corresponding object.

THEORY OF *MEYĀDHĪNĀMĀNASIDDHIḤ*

The idea that the truth of a cognition is to be determined in terms of its reference to its object leads Buddhist thinkers to the theory of *Meyādhīna māna siddhi*. According to Diṅnāga, knowledge is no doubt revelatory of its object, and therefore object depends on knowledge for its revelation; the truth of knowledge, however, depends on its exact reference to its object. So far as epistemic dependence is concerned, the object depends upon knowledge, whereas with regard to ontic dependence, knowledge depends on the object. In the context of truth ontic dependence is taken into consideration by Buddhists. However, Naiyāyikas sharply differ from Buddhists and insist that though knowledge is a faithful awareness of its object, the truth of knowledge is not determined and guaranteed by the object but by the most efficient causal condition, which is technically known as *karaṇa*. In fact, this is a natural corollary of the Nyāya distinction between *pramāṇa* and *pramāṇaphala*. Thus, for Naiyāyikas all that is real is knowable, and the truth of knowledge is generated (*utpatti*) and vouchsafed (*jñapti*) by *pramāṇa* only. This is known as the theory of *Mānādhīnāmeyasiddhiḥ*. In other words, for Naiyāyikas epistemology determines ontology, but for Buddhists the reverse is the case.

OBJECTS OF KNOWLEDGE

According to Buddhists, there are only two kinds of objects of knowledge, namely, the real, objective, unique particular (*svalakṣaṇa*) and the generalized concept or image (*sāmānyalakṣaṇa*). This is because the thing to be cognized has the preceding two aspects. The objective real in the form of unique particular has no extension in space and no duration in time. It is devoid of all form, attributes, determinations, and relations. It is just a point instant or a moment in the incessant moments of series of reals. It is unique particular in the sense that it is neither identical with, nor similar to, any other object. It is a distinct existence dissimilar to, and noncomparable with, any other real. It is instantaneous because it never endures for the next moment. It is discrete in the sense that it is an isolated existence not at all related to any other existence. So no relation exists between any two unique particulars, all relations being subjective mental constructions. Such an object alone is objectively real. This is a very distinct and unique view held by Buddhists with regard to the nature of reality. Reality is essentially momentary and dynamic. It is a process in which each moment depends for its existence on a previous moment. Each moment is in itself unique but causally determined by the previous moment. Being momentary, we cannot assign any name to this reality because the act of giving a name implies that (1) the real has to exist for more than one moment in order that a name could be recalled and associated with it and that (2) since the function of naming requires the possibility of identifying a thing whenever its name is uttered, a momentary real cannot be named, and whatever is named is not the reality proper. Therefore, there is one aspect of reality-in-itself, and there is another aspect of reality that is conceptualized and talked about in general terms.

Thus, distinct from the unique particular is another type of object of knowledge, known as *sāmānyalakṣaṇa*, which is a construction of our mind and which is in the form of a generalized image. The generalized image is a form imposed by our mind on the objective reality. A generalized image, also known as concept (*vikalpa*), can be, broadly speaking, of five types, namely, pertaining to substantivality (*dravya*), adjectivality (*guṇa*), relations and spatiotemporal locations (*karma*), class-character (*jāti*), and linguistic determination (*nāma*). A generalized image is a mental construction (*kalpanā*) having no objective existence. Comprehension of objects as having extension in space and duration in time is nothing but generalization, which is only subjective or intersubjective and has no counterpart in the objective world. Similarly, all attributes, relations, and so on are nothing but generalizations.

KINDS OF KNOWLEDGE

On the basis of the preceding ontological analysis Diṅnāga enunciates the theory that since there are only two kinds of objects of knowledge, there are only two kinds of knowledge. Corresponding to the unique particular (*svalakṣaṇa*) we have perceptual knowledge (*pratyakṣa*), and corresponding to the generalized image we have inferential knowledge (*anumāna*). A knowledge is either perceptual or inferential, and there is no knowledge beyond the purview of these two. Thus, the entire Buddhist epistemology is based on the foundations of the theory of twofold knowledge. Perception (*pratyakṣa*) is pure sensation, a direct sense-apprehension of the unique particular. Inference (*anumāna*) is a mental construction in the form of generalized images. Of course, perceptual knowledge is immediately followed by the inferential one; the former is not at all judgmental or determinate. Buddhist thinkers emphatically maintain that the unique particular is knowable in perception only and that the generalized image is known only through inference.

By implication the unique particular can never be known in inference, and likewise the generalized image can never be known in perception. What is known in perception cannot be known in inference, and viceversa. Such a position of radical dichotomy of mutually exclusive modes of knowing is known as *pramāṇavyavasthā*, which means that each of the two modes of knowing has its own separate and distinct sphere of operation.

There is no intermingling in the respective objects of the two. As the unique particular alone is objectively real, while the generalized image is a mental construct, and the one is radically different from the other, there cannot be any cognition that comprehends both at the same time.

Chapter 2

The Buddhist Theory of Perception

In the Buddhist theory of knowledge perception (*pratyakṣa*) is regarded as the foundational *pramāṇa* insofar as inference (*anumāna*) depends on it. Inference presupposes perception, and, therefore, only in this respect does perception acquire primacy over inference. Though all Buddhist thinkers from Diṅnāga onward agree on this point, their understanding of the nature of perception is not the same, and hence they define it in different ways.

DEFINITION OF *PRATYAKṢA*

To give a logically concise and comprehensive definition seems to be a very difficult task. Some thinkers may maintain an extreme position that such a definition can never be given. If the thing is known, they may argue, its definition is useless, and if it is not known, it is still more useless because it is impossible. This, of course, has not been the view of the Buddhist thinkers we are concerned with. Among these thinkers Diṅnāga not only puts forth definitions of philosophical terms in as sharp and clear-cut way as possible but also gives a specific method of defining with the help of double negatives (*atadvyāvṛtti*). Nyāya-Mīmāmsā thinkers attempt to define things in terms of their "essence," that is, their characterizations and relations. Diṅnāga, on the contrary, contends that such definitions are useless because the "essence" doesn't exist. Thus, things-qua-things *(svalakṣaṇas)* are indefinable. However, our conception of a thing (*vikalpa*) is definable. According to him, the characteristic feature of all our conceptual knowledge (and of language) is that it is dialectical. Every conception is a negative corelate of its counterpart and while defining a concept this alone can be stated. So, a definition is only a negative characterization (*vyāvṛtti*). For example, what the color "blue" is we cannot tell, but we may divide all colors into "blue" and "non-blue." The "non-blue" may mean any color other than blue. The definition of "blue" will be "that which is not non-blue," and conversely, the definition of "non-blue" will be "that which is not blue." For Buddhists all knowledge can be dichotomously classified into direct and indirect. The direct is not indirect, and indirect is not direct. The direct cognition is technically known as *pratyakṣa,* and the indirect as *kalpanā* or *parokṣa*. *Pratyakṣa* can therefore be defined in terms of its distinction from *kalpanā* or *parokṣa*. From this it follows that *pratyakṣa* can be understood as the "negative of *kalpanā*."

THREE WAYS OF DEFINING *PRATYAKṢA*

In the later Buddhist epistemology three distinct positions are discernible in an attempt to define *pratyakṣa*. Though there seems to be unanimity among Vasubandhu, Diṅnāga and Dharmakīrti that the definition of *pratyakṣa* should be in terms of "negative of *kalpanā,*" they sharply differ with regard to the phraseology that is to be used to express this point. Vasubandhu does it by using positive phraseology. Thus, he falls on one side, while Diṅnāga and Dharmakīrti on the other. The latter, though they use negative phraseology, differ between themselves not only about the full rendering of the phraseology but also about the epistemic status of *pratyakṣa*. We first state the three positions in detail and then undertake their comparative analysis, particularly of the positions of Diṅnāga and Dharmakīrti.

VASUBANDHU'S DEFINITION OF *PRATYAKṢA*

On the basis of the information available to us Vasubandhu can be regarded as the first systematic epistemological thinker pertaining to the tradition followed by Diṅnāga and Dharmakīrti. In the *Vāda-Vidhi pratyakṣa* is defined as "*tato'rthād vijñānam pratyakṣam,*"[1] that is, "perception is a cognition produced from that object." In this definition Vasubandhu maintains that *pratyakṣa* is a cognition that is determined by its object. Here the word "*tato*" points out the exclusive role of the object (*ālambanapratyaya*) in contradistinction to the role of the cognitive sense (*adhipatipratyaya*) or the cognizing consciousness (*samanantara-pratyaya*).[2] For example, if the object is fire, which is an existing real (*svalakṣaṇa*), and if it is cognized, then cognition of fire is a case of perceptual cognition. Such a cognition has a real object, which is fire, as distinct from the conceptual object, which is the idea of fire. Bare experience of the object without any conceptual element is regarded as perceptual cognition. This differential character of *pratyakṣa,* which consists in being "negative of *kalpanā,*" has been expressed by Vasubandhu with the help of the phrase "*tato'rthād.*" The idea to be expressed by the phrase "*tato'rthād*" is by implication the same as "without any conceptualization." Therefore, Vasubandhu can be interpreted as defining perception as bare experience that is solely and wholly caused by the object without any intermingling of conceptual elements. Though Vasubandhu does not specifically say that a perceptual cognition has no element of conceptualization and verbalization, in fact, he means it when he says that it is exclusively coming from the object.

DIṄNĀGA'S DEFINITION OF *PRATYAKṢA*

Instead of defining *pratyakṣa* in terms of "*tato'rthād vijñānam,*" Diṅnāga defines it in terms of "*kalpanāpoḍham,*" perhaps because the idea of *pratyakṣa* as "negative of *kalpanā*" can be better expressed by the latter phrase rather than by the former. After having stated that there are only two kinds of knowledge,[3] which he conventionally calls *pratyakṣa* and *anumāna*, Diṅnāga turns to *pratyakṣa* and says that this knowledge is *kalpanāpoḍham*[4] (nonconceptual), which is another way of stating that it is "negative of *kalpanā*." Earlier, he argued that there are only two types of cognition and that there is no need to postulate three or more types; otherwise, it may lead to infinite regress.[5] Thus, the object can be cognized either in *pratyakṣa* directly or in *anumāna* indirectly; there is no other way of cognizing it.

Diṅnāga seems to have two objectives in mind when he proceeds to define *pratyakṣa*, namely,

1. to distinguish it from *anumāna* and so on (*anyavyāvṛtyartham*) and
2. to distinguish the Buddhist conception from the views of other schools (*vipratipattinirākaraṇārtham*).

Rejection of Nyāya-Mīmāṁsā Definition

The usual definition of *pratyakṣa* given by Nyāya-Mīmāṁsā and other non-Buddhist traditions in terms of sense-object contact (*indriyārtha-sannikarṣa*) has been rejected by Diṅnāga mainly because it takes no notice of the basic feature of *pratyakṣa,* which is always a new cognition, that is, cognition of something new and not recognition. Such a cognition can be only in the form of sense perception, which is the first moment of every cognition. In the following moments when the attention is aroused and the process of mental construction begins, it is no more that pure sense perception that it was at the first moment. Moreover, that definition contains a concealed confusion between the proper function of sense perception and the function of the mind. Sense perception has its own function, its own object, and its own cause. Its function is to make the object present to the senses (*sākṣātkāritva vyāpāra*), not, of course, forcibly (*na haṭhāt*). Its object is *svalakṣaṇa* (unique particular) since this alone, being real and efficient, can produce a sense impression, and the *svalakṣaṇa* (unique particular) again is its cause. Thus, *pratyakṣa* consists in an awareness (*pratibhāsa*) of the presence of an object, its mere presence and nothing more. To construct an image of an object (*pratibhāsapratīti*) the presence of which has thus been reported is another function, a subsequent operation that follows in the track of the first.

Rejection of Vasubandhu's Definition

Diṅnāga disagrees with Vasubandhu's way of expressing *pratyakṣa* in terms of "*tato'rthād*" mainly because it suffers from ambiguity. Diṅnāga, being an abstruse logician, does not want to leave any lacuna in his definition that he detects in that of Vasubandhu. In saying that a perceptual cognition is that which is exclusively caused by the object, it is not clearly specified whether or not this forbids the involvement of mental construction. Diṅnāga states this point quite explicitly by defining perception as *kalpanāpoḍham*" (non-conceptual).

Comparison of the Definitions of Vasubandhu and Diṅnāga

In fact, there does not seem to be any fundamental difference between Vasubandhu's definition and that of Diṅnāga. The same fact has been positively stated by Vasubandhu and negatively by Diṅnāga. Both agree that what we normally take to be perceptual cognition is, in fact, a complex of perceptual and conceptual, a synthesis of the contribution of the object and of the knowing mind (*citta*). If we represent this complex as "K," the contribution of the object as "S," and the contribution of the knowing mind as "C" and synthesis as "+," then "K" can also be represented as "S + C" (i.e., K = S + C). According to both thinkers, the total "K" is not perceptual; it is a complex of perceptual and conceptual. Out of this complex only "S" is perceptual, not "C." This fact has been stated by Vasubandhu in saying that "S" is perceptual and by Diṅnāga in saying that "K - C" is perceptual. But, in fact, the two expressions, "S" and "K - C" are equivalent. The linguistic expression corresponding to "S" is a little ambiguous, whereas the linguistic expression corresponding to "K - C" does not contain any ambiguity. Perhaps, Vasubandhu's definition could have been improved upon by the addition of the word "*eva,*" which would have meant that a perceptual cognition is that which is determined by the object solely and exclusively. But Diṅnāga thinks it better to put the definition negatively so as to avoid any scope for ambiguity. However, it must be made clear that Diṅnāga does not reject Vasubandhu's definition but only brings out its implication in clearer terms. A perceptual cognition is solely determined by its object; it must be wholly given by the object and not in any way constructed by the mind. Thus, Diṅnāga specifies that it is a cognition that is not at all subjectively determined and conceived of in terms of the *vikalpas* (concepts and words) of the type of *dravya* (substance), *guṇa* (quality), *karma* (action), *jāti* (class), and *nāma* (words). What is perceived by us is unique individual, which is bare existence, devoid of all characterizations. It is just what is immediately given to us in experience. Concepts and words are common (*sāmānyalakṣaṇa)* to several objects, and they are not unique (*svalakṣaṇa*). From this it follows that, according to Diṅnāga, perceptual cognition is the immediately given sensum in complete isolation from all conceptual determinations.

PERCEPTION AS DISTINCT FROM ERRONEOUS COGNITION, INFERENCE, AND SO ON

One of the objectives of Diṅnāga, as stated before, in defining perception has been to distinguish it in clear terms from erroneous cognition, cognition of apparent reality, inference, its result, recollection, and desire, which are not perception because they are not immediate on account of being vitiated by obscurity.[6] Explaining this, Diṅnāga writes in the auto-commentary (*sva-vṛtti*) that erroneous cognition is not perception because it arises due to conceptual construction, for example, the cognition of water in a mirage. Cognition of apparent reality is not a true perception, which is only empirically true. Inference and its resultant cognition and so on are not perception because they superimpose something extraneous upon things because they arise through the conceptualization of what formerly has been perceived.[7]

WHY THE NAME *PRATYAKṢA* AND NOT *PRATIVIṢAYA*?

Perceptual cognition arises when an object gives rise to its reflex (*pratibhāsa*) in the cognizing consciousness through the senses. Here Diṅnāga poses a problem: "For what reason then is it called *pratyakṣa* and not *prativiṣaya*, despite the fact that it is dependent upon both."[8] To this he replies that it is named after the senseorgans, because they are its specific cause. The object is only a common cause because it is common to many cases insofar as it is a cause of similar perceptions in one's own self as well as in other person's. In fact, this problem is earlier posed by Vasubandhu,[9] who gives two reasons, of which Diṅnāga mentions only one. The other reason is that as the cognitive sense is strong or weak, perception becomes clear or dim, and because of this, sense organs should be regarded as the specific cause of perception.

From this account it is quite evident that Diṅnāga is the first systematic exponent of the theory that perception is strictly indeterminate (*nirvikalpaka*) and excludes all conceptual constructions and verbalizations (*vikalpas*). However, for him, every perception has to be nonerroneous (*abhrāntam*) because all errors are consequences of mental construction. At the level of pure sense data there is no question of error because the sense data are wholly given by the object, and there can be no error here. Error arises only when the mental faculty comes to work upon the sense data. That is why he does not include the term "*abhrāntam*" in his definition of perception, as his successor, Dharmakīrti, has done. In the *Nyāyasūtra* of Gautama also, perception has been characterized as *avyabhicāri* (nonerroneous), but for Diṅnāga *vyabhicāra* (error) just cannot be there at the level of sense data.

DEFINITION OF *PRATYAKṢA* BY DHARMAKĪRTI

After having stated that, there being two types of objects, there are two kinds of knowledge, Dharmakīrti, following Diṅnāga, defines *pratyakṣa* as "*kalpanāpoḍham*" (nonconceptual) but, differing from Diṅnāga, adds another term, "*abhrāntam*" (nonerroneous) to it. He defines it in terms of a cognition that is free from conceptual constructions and errors.[10]

Object of *Pratyakṣa*

Perception, according to Dharmakīrti, consists in the apprehension of an object in its own specific character (*svalakṣaṇa*), which has nothing in common with other objects similar or dissimilar and is completely free from association with names and verbal expressions, which are conceptual constructions. The object of perception is thus the real, which is immediately revealed to the consciousness and not such objects that are in the form of concepts and words (*vikalpas*), which are not a part of the given sense data but are conceived in the mind.

The object of perception is different not only from the objects that are in the form of concepts and words but also from a bare figment of imagination. The unique particular (*svalakṣaṇa*) alone is the real object, and, being the real and efficient, it alone can produce a stimulus upon the senses. A figment of imagination, on the other hand, is unreal and, therefore, cannot exercise any such stimulus. Commenting on Dharmakīrti's opening remark in the *Nyāya Bindu* that "all successful human action is preceded by right knowledge," Dharmottara in the context of perception writes that when an object is apprehended by direct experience, it gets converted into an object of purposive action through sense perception. In fact, this characteristic feature of the real object distinguishes it from all objects that are absolutely unreal and that have no practical efficiency (*arthakriyākāritva*).[11]

We may now analyze the two terms, namely, "*kalpanāpoḍham*" and "*abhrāntam,*" that constitute Dharmakīrti's definition. By using the term "*kalpanāpoḍham,*" Dharmakīrti attempts to distinguish a perceptual cognition from all such cognitions that are in the form of conceptual construction. He defines *kalpanā* as "*abhilāpasaṁsargayogyapratibhāsapratīti,*"[12] that is, a determinate cognition that is capable of verbalization. In this definition there are two aspects of *kalpanā* that must be explicitly stated, namely, "*pratibhāsapratīti*" and "*abhilāpasaṁsargayogyatā.*" Every *kalpanā* is a *pratibhāsapratīti*; that is, it is not just bare cognition (*pratibhāsa*) but a determinate cognition (*pratibhāsapratīti*). To be aware of the bare existence of an object is *pratibhāsa* but to recognize that object as "this" object, a particular object, is *pratibhāsapratīti*. The object is capable of giving rise to mental reflex (*pratibhāsa*) only. It cannot produce determination in the form of recognition that "it is such and such", because corresponding to the determination (*pratīti*) there is no object present. The determination cannot be regarded as a part of perceptual cognition. Thus, Dharmakīrti draws a clear-cut distinction between *pratibhāsa* and *pratibhāsa pratīti*. The *pratibhāsa* alone is genuine perception and not *pratibhāsa pratīti,* which follows *pratibhāsa*. The *pratibhāsapratīti* is *kalpanā*, which is *parokṣa jñāna* or *anumāna*.[13] The other apect of *kalpanā* is *abhilāpasansargayogyatā*.

Dharmakīrti points out that a *pratibhāsa* is incapable of verbalization (*anabhilāpya*),[14] whereas only a *pratibhāsapratīti* can be expressed in language. In other words, perception, which is pure sensation, is only to be experienced. It cannot be designated. It is interesting to point out here that Dharmakīrti not only draws a clear distinction between perceiving and designating but also regards designating as absolutely incompatible with perceiving. His argument is that no verbalization can take place in the absence of conceptualization and that there is no conceptualization in perception. In the expression "*abhilāpasaṁsargayogya*" the word "*yogya*" (capable) is quite significant. It clearly states that though it is necessary that there cannot be verbalization without conceptualization, the reverse is not the case. That is, it is not necessary that where there is conceptualization, there must be verbalization. As Dharmottara writes, "We may also have conceptualization, which although not accompanied by corresponding words, is capable of being accompanied, as for example, the conceptualization of a baby which has not been verbalized."[15] Wherever there is verbalization, there has to be conceptualization, but whether the reverse is also the case can be a debatable point. It would, therefore, be in order if we reflect on the relation between conceptualization and verbalization in the context of Dharmakīrti's position.

Following Dharmottara, it can be maintained that by inserting the word "*yogya*" Dharmakīrti wants to point out that it is not necessary that every case of conceptualization should be accompanied by verbalization. Every concept is capable of being verbalized, but, in fact, it may or may not be verbalized. This means only that verbalization is not incompatible with conceptualization in the way in which it is incompatible with perception, but it is not its necessary accompaniment. However, if we keep in view a verse generally ascribed to Diṅnāga in which concept is regarded as having its "*yoni*" (source or place of origin) in words,[16] then Dharmakīrti's position can also be understood as signifying that there are two modes of verbalization, namely, actual and potential. Though all conceptualizations may not be associated with actual verbalization, potential verbalization is necessarily present therein. Such a distinction between "surface language" and "depth language" might have been intended by Dharmakīrti. Accordingly, in every conceptualization there must be necessarily depth language, which means that there can be no thinking without the use of language. The use of language may not be overt but covert.

Besides *kalpanāpoḍham,* the other constituent of Dharmakīrti's definition is "*abhrāntam.*"[17] Perceptual knowledge is that which is free from *kalpanā* and at the same time is *abhrāntam*. While explaining the term "*abhrāntam,*" he mentions different instances of error caused by color blindness, rapid motion, traveling in a boat, mental sickness, and so on. Commenting on it, Dharmottara writes that absence of *kalpanā* and absence of *bhrānti* (error) taken together, not separately, constitute the definition of perception. Dharmottara points out that these four different illustrations represent four different types of illusion. The cause of color blindness is located in the sense organ (*indriyagata*). The cause of rapid motion resulting in the cognition of a fiery circle is located in the object (*viṣayagata*). The cause of illusion of moving trees is located in the external circumstances that condition the perceiver (*bāhyās'rayasthita*). Lastly, the cause of hallucinatory illusions is located in the internal circumstances (*adhyātmagata*) like the mental state of the perceiver. All these causes, whether located in the organ or in the object, whether external or internal, affect the cognitive sense[18] and result in illusory sensation. So, perception should be a sense cognition that is distinct from these illusory sensations.[19] If we undertake a comparative analysis of the definition of *pratyakṣa* given by Diṅnāga and Dharmakīrti, three basic problems come up for our consideration. They are:

1. Is *pratyakṣa* a *pramāṇa* or *samyag jñāna* (knowledge)?
2. What is meant by *kalpanā*? and
3. Is the adjective "*abhrāntam*" necessary?

IS *PRATYAKṢA* A *PRAMĀṆA*?

Both Diṅnāga and Dharmakīrti, before giving a definition of *pratyakṣa,* point out that it is one of the two *pramāṇas*. Of course, in Dharmakīrti we find an explicit and detailed analysis as to what is meant by *prāmāṇya* or *samyakatva* (truth), and no such detailed analysis is available in Diṅnāga as far as our information goes. It is, however, incontrovertible that both of them regard *pratyakṣa* as *pramāṇa*. However, in the context of their insistence on *kalpanāpoḍhatvam* (nonconceptuality of *pratyakṣa*), it can really be asked whether they can justifiably regard *pratyakṣa* as a *pramāṇa*. Śāntarakṣita[20] defines perception exactly on the pattern of Dharmakīrti without using the word *jñānam* or *pramāṇam,* and there Kamalaśīla, his commentator, raises a point as to why the word *jñānam* is not used in this definition. Does it in any way mean that Śāntarakṣita intends to exclude *pratyakṣa* from the sphere of *jñānam?* To this Kamalaśīla responds by saying that the word *jñānam* is not used in the definition because it is implied and therefore not needed. However, it can certainly be inquired as to whether *pratyakṣa,* as it is defined by these Buddhist thinkers, can be a *pramāṇa,* and if it can be, then in what sense? An answer to this question depends on our understanding of *pramāṇa*. If by *pramāṇa* we mean just the presence of *avisaṁvādakatvam* without there being any necessary awareness or confirmation of it (*asaṁdigdhatvam*), *pratyakṣa* can be regarded as *pramāṇa* because it is having *avisaṁvādakatva* with its object insofar as it is exclusively determined by the object (*arthaniyata*) and is of the same form as the form of the object (*arthasārūpya*). But if *pramāṇa* is understood in terms of *avisaṁvādakatvam* and *asaṁdigdhatvam*, that is, a cognition that is true and also indubitable, then, certainly, *pratyakṣa* cannot be regarded as a *pramāṇa* because indubitability or certainty is something that is dependent on confirmation or on the production of some invincible grounds. This would mean that only a *vyavasāyātmaka* (judgmental) or *savikalpaka jñāna* (conceptual) can be a *pramāṇa,* and since *pratyakṣa* by its very definition is nonconceptual, it cannot be put under the rubric of *pramāṇa*. But as we have said, if indubitability is not to be regarded as an essential element of *pramāṇa*, then the *pramāṇatva* of *pratyakṣa* becomes a matter of analytic consequence.

WHAT IS *KALPANĀ*?

The other point that arises for consideration is understanding the word "*kalpanā*" by Diṅnāga and Dharmakīrti. Since Diṅnāga uses the expression "*nāmajātyādiyojanā*" to define *kalpanā*, whereas Dharmakīrti uses the expression "*abhilāpasaṃsargayogyapratibhāsapratīti*" for this purpose, it has to be examined whether both of them are using the word *kalpanā* in the same sense or in two different senses. In other words, what needs to be explained is the meaning of *kalpanā* according to Diṅnāga and Dharmakīrti. When Diṅnāga defines *kalpanā* as "*nāmajātyādiyojanā,*" the question arises whether it is to be understood as *yojanā* (association) of *nāma, jāti*, and so on with things or association of *nāma* with *jāti,* and so on. If it is understood in the former sense, then it goes against Diṅnāga's basic position that the thing (*svalakṣaṇa*) is beyond all associations. Evidently, therefore, it is to be understood only in the latter sense,[21] as has been explicitly stated by Śāntarakṣita.[22] Understood in this sense, there does not seem to be any difference of opinion between Diṅnāga's and Dharmakīrti's understanding of *kalpanā*. Śāntarakṣita defines *kalpanā* as "*abhilāpinipratīti*" on the pattern of Dharmakīrti but takes elaborate pains to point out that it does not go against Diṅnāga's definition given in the *Nyāya Mukha*.[23]

IS THE ADJECTIVE "*ABHRĀNTAM*" NECESSARY?

The necessity of mentioning the characteristic of *abhrāntam* has been controversial right from the time of Diṅnāga. It is first mentioned by Asaṅga, is dropped by Diṅnāga, but is reintroduced by Dharmakīrti. It is again dropped by some of his followers like Vinītadeva but finally reestablished by Dharmottara. However, it must be noted that Diṅnāga is not alone in not using the adjective "*abhrāntam.*" As Śāntarakṣita points out, several Buddhist thinkers regard illusions as purely mental facts having nothing to do with sense perception. These thinkers object to the inclusion of the adjective "*abhrāntam*" in the definition of *pratyakṣa*.[24]

Why Diṅnāga dropped the characteristic "*abhrāntam*" is not known for certain, but Stcherbatsky[25] has pointed out three considerations that seem to be quite plausible. First of all, every illusory cognition has to be judgmental, but no judgmentalization belongs to the sensuous part of the cognition. Every judgment is the construct of the intellect and not the reflex of the senses. Diṅnāga maintains that pure sensation does not contain any judgment, neither the right one nor the wrong one, because it is nonconceptual. It cannot contain any illusion at all, and hence there is no need to add the adjective "*abhrāntam.*" However, this doesn't mean that perceptual cognition is not a *pramāṇa* because for him *pramāṇa* consists only in *arthasārūpya* or *avisaṁvādakatva* and not in *asamdigdhatva*.

Second, Diṅnāga rejects Vasubandhu's definition of *pratyakṣa* because it could be given a realistic interpretation. For the same reason he resolves to drop the characteristic of *abhrāntam* because it could be interpreted as maintaining a position that all conceptual knowledge is erroneous and that perceptual knowledge alone is nonerroneous.

Third, Diṅnāga is aware of the ambiguity of the word "*abhrāntam,*" and to avoid confusion, he must have dropped it. Diṅnāga, of course, doesn't deny that there are illusions, but they must be treated separately. Just as there are inferential fallacies, *hetvābhāsas*, similarly there can be *pratyakṣābhāsas*, but these *pratyakṣābhāsas* are due not to the senses but to the intellect only.

Dharmakīrti disagrees with Diṅnāga on this point and reintroduces the characteristic of *abhrāntam* in the definition. His main argument is that we must distinguish between sense illusion and mental illusion. For example, when we mistake a rope for a snake, the illusion is purely mental and ceases when it is dispelled. But when we see the moving moon in the clouds, this illusion continues even if we are convinced that it is the clouds that are moving.

While explaining Dharmakīrti's contention, Dharmottara points out that the purpose of using the two characteristics is not just to distinguish *pratyakṣa* from *anumāna* but also to clear away wrong cognition.[26] The characteristic of *kalpanāpoḍham* would alone have been quite sufficient for that but if *abhrāntam* were not added, erroneous cognitions, like that of a moving tree, that are not faulty mental constructs but are due to sensual aberrations would not be distinguished from genuine perception. Therefore, Dharmottara insists that the introduction of *abhrāntam* is perfectly in order.

In this context Dharmottara writes that the term "*abhrāntam*" should not be understood in the sense of *avisaṁvādakam* because this would imply that perception alone is *avisaṁvādaka* and not *anumāna* because *anumāna* doesn't represent *svalakṣaṇa*. Had it been Dharmakīrti's intention to maintain that *pratyakṣa* alone is *avisaṁvādaka* and not *anumāna*, the term "*kalpanāpoḍham*" would have been sufficient for that because all *kalpanā* would be *visamvādaka*. But that doesn't seem to be the case. For Dharmakīrti both *pratyakṣa* and *anumāna* are *avisaṁvādaka* in the sense that both are consistent with their respective objects, namely, *svalakṣaṇa* and *sāmānyalakṣaṇa*.

Śāntarakṣita and Kamalaśīla defend Dharmakīrti and argue at length to establish that illusions occur due to sensual aberrations also, and they are not just to be explained as mental distortions. Ultimately, all illusions can be traced to a defect in the sense organ concerned, and if the illusions were not due to this defect and were due to mental aberrations, they would have disappeared when the mental distortion is rectified. Not only this, but the vivid presentation of false objects in illusions cannot be satisfactorily explained unless they are regarded as sensual presentations.[27]

Dharmottara explicitly mentions that there were some thinkers among Buddhists themselves who maintain that even these abnormal experiences are to be regarded as valid knowledge inasmuch as they satisfy the pragmatic tests. He writes, "There are some who maintain that the vision of a moving tree by an observer traveling by ship and similar perceptions are right perceptions because there is in this case an underlying reality which is not a construction. Indeed a man acting upon such a perception reaches something which is a tree; hence it is supposed that experience supports his perception."[28]

Similarly, Śāntarakṣita also writes that because of a successful outcome even in erroneous cognition "some people" maintained that erroneous cognition should also be regarded as valid.[29] While commenting on this, Kamalaśīla explains that "some people," in fact, means some Buddhist thinkers themselves.[30]

Both Dharmottara and Śāntarakṣita point out that what constitutes validity is not pragmatic fitness alone but that plus consistency (*avisaṁvādakam*) with reality. So such presentations, as the light of the jewel for the jewel itself or of yellow conch shell for a really white conch shell or of moving trees for trees that are really stationary are not valid perceptions, though there is actual verification. Mere verification and pragmatic satisfaction cannot, however, be accepted as the test of validity; but consistency of presentation with reality is the criterion. What is presented is the light of the jewel or the yellow conch shell and what is actually attained is not the light of the jewel or yellow conch shell but something different. In the mirage, too, the refracted light of the sun and the determinate experience of water are presented.

Having discussed the divergent views of the Buddhist logicians from Diṅnāga onward, we can while concluding restate our problem. Is not Diṅnāga's definition of perception as *kalpanāpoḍham* complete and sufficient by itself? It seems that addition of the adjective "*abhrāntam*" is not logically necessary. Probably, Dharmakīrti thought that the term "*kalpanāpoḍham*" is competent only to distinguish *pratyakṣa* from *anumāna* but not from *bhrānta jñāna*. But here we can question and perhaps reject Dharmakīrti's contention and uphold Diṅnāga's position on the following grounds.

Indeed, sense perception can be reckoned as a source of knowledge (*pramāṇa*) only under the condition that the knowledge produced by a sensation does not represent the sensory illusion. However, it seems quite superfluous to mention "*abhrāntam*" as characteristic of valid sense perception, because, according to the classification of the system, sense perception is a variety of valid, that is, nonillusive, cognition.

The term "*abhrāntam*" is almost a synonym of "*kalpanāpoḍham,*" since construction represents illusion when compared with pure sensation, the genuine source of knowledge. So it becomes useless to use the synonym in the definition.

A question may arise, How can we have erroneous cognition at the level of perception? Perception being *nirvikalpaka,* we have just the sensations of the object, and no judgment is formed at that stage. Only judgment can be right or wrong. For example, "A" enters a room with a friend of his, and there is a rope lying in the room. Mistaking this rope for a snake, "A" cries, "Snake"

The friend says, "No, it is merely a rope." Thus, the perception of the same object, rope, has resulted in two different mental constructs. The rope must have given the same kind of sensation to both of them, but the first one thought it was a snake, and the second one thought it rightly to be a rope. So, mental construct results in illusion, not bare perception. For distinguishing mental construct from perception Diṅnāga's definition is competent enough, and there is no need to add the adjective "*abhrāntam*" to it.

Dharmakīrti, on one hand, believes in sensual aberrations and, with a view to exclude these from the category of perception, includes the term "*abhrāntam*," but, on the other hand, he strongly advocates the theory of *svataḥ-prāmāṇyavāda*, according to which all cognitions qua cognitions must be true. This fact cannot be overlooked. At the level of sensation there is no error. From this it follows that errors are due to noncognitive factors, that is, factors extraneous to sensation. Hence, the addition of the adjective "*abhrāntam*" seems to be useless.

NATURE OF *PRATYAKṢA*

All the epistemological thinkers in India are unanimous in regarding *pratyakṣa* as a reliable and valid cognition, but there exists a wide difference of opinion with regard to its precise nature. Ordinarily granting a basic distinction between two types of cognition, *nirvikalpaka* (indeterminate) and *savikalpaka* (determinate), it has been debated as to whether *pratyakṣa* is to be regarded as *nirvikalpaka* only or *savikalpaka* only or both *nirvikalpaka* and *savikalpaka*. The Grammarian philosophers and the Jaina thinkers take one extreme view that all cognitions, including perceptual ones, are *savikalpaka* since they are predicative in character and also necessarily embodied in verbal propositions overt or covert. The Buddhist position lies on the other extreme, that *pratyakṣa* is always *nirvikalpaka* and can never be *savikalpaka*. *Anumāna* alone is *savikalpaka*. Before we discuss the Buddhist position in detail, it would be worthwhile if we briefly outline the conflicting non Buddhist positions on this issue.

Advaita Vedāntic View

In the Advaita-Vedānta, particularly in its earlier phase, we seem to have a position akin to the Buddhist one, which is arrived at on a slightly different basis. According to it, the reality being of the nature of pure existence bereft of all characterizations (*śuddha* or *nirviśeṣa sanmātram*), the perceptual cognition that is in the form of presentation of an object must be *nirvikalpaka*. It is a cognition of "this" or "the existent" but not as determined by anything. To determine a thing is to characterize it by this or that quality and is thus to distinguish it from other things having different qualities. All this is the work of *buddhi*. When we have a determinate cognition of an object on the basis of discrimination, the object is determined by certain qualities and relations. Such a cognition, which is ordinarily called *savikalpaka pratyakṣa*, is not valid (*mithyā*) because it is no longer representative of the object, which in the ultimate analysis is one undifferentiated consciousness (*caitanya*). The Neo-Advaita Vedānta, however, accepts a distinction between *nirvikalpaka* and *savikalpaka pratyakṣa* from the *vyāvahārika* or practical standpoint, though from the *pāramārthika* standpoint such a distinction is untenable. According to it, *savikalpaka pratyakṣa* is the knowledge of a thing as qualified by an attribute. The essence of *savikalpaka pratyakṣa* is the determination of its object by way of predication. On the other hand, *nirvikalpaka pratyakṣa* is knowledge of the bare existence of a thing without any predication. Strictly speaking, propositions like "*Tattvamasi*" alone can be regarded as genuine *nirvikalpaka pratyakṣa*. Through "*jahat-ajahat-lakṣaṇā*" such propositions are to be understood as conveying the simple identity between "*tat*" and "*tvam*." Such propositions, technically known as *akhaṇḍārtha vākya*, are nonpredicative in character. For example, when we say "This is that man," we do not predicate "that man" to "this." It is not a case that we relate "this man" with "that man'' but simply assert the identity between the two.[31]

Grammarian's View

Grammarians go to the other extreme, and in this Jainas join them in maintaining that all perceptions are *savikalpaka* because they are necessarily predicative in character and verbalized in form. Not only perception but every cognition, perceptual or nonperceptual, has to be both propositional as well as sentential. In other words, they maintain that the epistemic content and the linguistic form are always inseparable, and all propositions are invariably linguistic in form. There is no pure thinking, but "speech thinking." In the words of Bhartṛhari, a Grammarian philosopher, "There is no thought-content without a language form and always thought-content is inextricably interspersed with language form. If the unfailing form of language had been lost to the thought-content, thought itself would have been lost in oblivion. Thought has a form because it is formed in language."[32]

From this it follows that all cognitions, including perceptual ones, are at once both judgmental and verbal. A corollary of this would be that perception can never be *nirvikalpaka* but should always be *savikalpaka*.

Nyāya-Mīmāmsā-Sāṁkhya-Viśiṣṭādvaita Vedānta Views

In the schools of Nyāya, Mīmāmsā, Sāṁkhya, and Viśiṣṭādvaita Vedānta, the preceding two extreme views are reconciled, and a middle position is put forth. It is held in these schools that any perception, *nirvikalpaka* or *savikalpaka*, is a direct cognition of a real individual that is a unity of universal and particular. The distinction between *nirvikalpaka* and *savikalpaka* is due not to any difference in the contents of perception but to the way in which the same contents of experience may be ordered and arranged.

The Sāmkhya thinkers perhaps initially advocated a distinction between two stages in perceptual cognition, namely, *nirvikalpaka* and *savikalpaka*, and used the term "*ālocana*" (Gestalt view) for *nirvikalpaka pratyakṣa*. The first apprehension of an object is in the form of undifferentiated sensum, and the *manas* is *saṁkalpaka*, that is, differentiates the undifferentiated sensum presented by the senses. While commenting on the *Sāṁkhya Kārikā* Vācaspatimiśra, in his

Sāṁkhya Tattva Kaumudī, introduces a full-fledged distinction between the two kinds of perception.[33]

Kumārila of the Pūrva-Mīmāṁsā school seems to follow the Sāṁkhya line. For him the *nirvikalpaka pratyakṣa* is the first moment of cognition in which there is an undifferentiated apprehension of the object as one individual whole of generic and specific attributes (*sammugdhavastumātra*). Here there is no definite cognition of it as this or that object (*vastu viśeṣa*). *Nirvikalpaka pratyakṣa* thus resembles children's and dumb person's perceptions.[34] It is nonverbal in nature because they lack the capacity to communicate. However, Kumārila's position can also be understood in a different manner, if we take into consideration the following verse and Pārthasārathi's commentary thereon.

Na viśeṣo na sāmānyam tadānim anubhūyate
Tayorādhārabhūtastu vyaktirevāvaśiṣyate.

(In that apprehension neither the particular nor the universal is experienced. What is experienced is only the individual object that underlies the two).[35]

That is, he regards *nirvikalpaka pratyakṣa* as a sort of inchoate cognition in which neither the particular nor the generalized aspect is cognized; nor are they distinguished. Whatever is the interpretation of Kumārila's position, for him it is indeterminate or nonconceptual and therefore nonverbal. The second stage is that of *savikalpaka pratyakṣa*, which is a determinate cognition in which the object is cognized by the mind along with its characterizations.

Like the Sāṁkhya and Mīmāṁsā thinkers, Nyāya-Vaiśeṣika thinkers also accept both stages of perception, and most of them regard them as equally valid. From Vācaspati onward we find a clear-cut distinction between the two stages of *pratyakṣa*. On the distinction between *nirvikalpaka* and *savikalpaka* Jayanta writes, "A universal, a substance, a relation or a quality whatever essence of an object is grasped by *savikalpaka* is equally grasped by *nirvikalpaka*. The remembrance of a meaning-relation of the object with a certain word is the only relation that marks out *savikalpaka* from *nirvikalpaka*. So far as the object is concerned there is not the least difference between the two."[36] From this statement the only thing we can distinctly make out is that for some Naiyāyikas, the distinction between *nirvikalpaka* and *savikalpaka* is only in verbality. The *savikalpaka* is verbalized and predicational, whereas *nirvikalpaka* is nonverbalized and nonpredicational. So in the *nirvikalpaka* we apprehend the object along with all its relations and characterizations, but we do not interrelate them (*vaiśiṣṭyānavagāhi*), and in *savikalpaka* we do so. In the Navya-Nyāya, the distinction between the two is more sharply drawn as compared to Jayanta. However, the consequence of such a sharpness has been some sort of rethinking on the nature of *pratyakṣa* in the Navya-Nyāya. Viśvanātha, in the *Bhāṣā-Pariccheda* and *Siddhānta-Muktāvali*, is unwilling to accept *nirvikalpaka* within the fold of *pratyakṣa* since it is a kind of prejudgmental cognition.[37]

In the Viśiṣṭādvaita Vedānta, even though the distinction between *nirvikalpaka* and *savikalpaka* is accepted, the two are regarded as different quantitatively. Both are predicative and relational in character, but whereas the first one is vague and indefinite, the second one is vivid and definite. The first is the initial awareness (*prathama piṇḍagrahaṇa*) of the object. It is about the total object in which the individual as well as the universal aspects of the object are apprehended in their interrelationship, but there is no complete certainty. In the second or successive apprehensions the judgment becomes decisive and is therefore known as *savikalpaka*. Rāmānuja understands *savikalpaka* not in terms of judgmentalization but in terms of more decisiveness or certainty.

Buddhist View

As against Grammarians, on one hand, and Naiyāyika, Mīmāmsaka, and Sāṁkhya thinkers, on the other, Buddhist thinkers insist on perception being *nirvikalpaka*. A clear-cut distinction between *nirvikalpaka jñāna* and *savikalpaka jñāna* seems to have been introduced for the first time by Diṅnāga. According to him, the difference between *nirvikalpaka* and *savikalpaka* is not just quantitative, a difference in vividness and sequence, but is fundamental and qualitative. The *nirvikalpaka jñāna* is a cognition of an object-qua-object that can be only in the form of pure awareness and that can never be in the form of awareness in terms of thought. The reason is that our thought can never grasp the object-qua-object that is in the form of *svalaksaṇa* because our thought is always restricted to *sāmānya lakṣaṇa*. It is thus clear that the two types of knowledge are quite different not only in their nature but also in the spheres of their operation.

While defining *pratyakṣa,* thinkers from Diṅnāga onward always insist on its being *kalpanāpoḍha*. *Kalpanā* stands for both thought and speech, and, therefore, the phrase *"kalpanāpoḍham"* implies two things: (1) it is nonconceptual, and (2) it is nonverbal.

Buddhists start with a dichotomous distinction between a knowledge that is perceptual and a knowledge that is nonperceptual, that is, conceptual. From this it follows that perceptual cognition cannot be conceptual cognition, and conceptual cognition cannot be perceptual cognition. The nonconceptuality of perception means its freedom from all mental conceptions. In other words, all conceptual contents are mind-given, and mental impositions, whereas perception is given by the object and not at all by the mind. Diṅnāga[38] quotes an *Abhidhamma* treatise in his support where it is stated that one who has ability to perceive, perceives something blue (*Nīlam vijānāti*), but it is not conceived that "this is blue" (*Nīlamiti vijānāti*). The expression "*Nīlam vijānāti*" implies that one has an immediate awareness of the object itself. On the other hand, "*Nīlamiti vijānāti*" implies that one forms a judgment based on perception by associating a name with the object perceived. Thus, the preceding passage expresses the idea that perception is free from conceptual construction. In other words, in respect of an object the perceiver has a sensation of the object but does not possess any conceptual awareness of it.

There are two things we mean when we say that perception is *nirvikalpaka*:

1. (a) In all perceptions we never perceive the universal or the universal qualifying the

individual. Thus, we always perceive an individual, the *svalakṣaṇa*, and nothing more than that because individual is absolutely bereft of all universals. At the level of *svalakṣaṇa* there are no qualifications, and Buddhists are quite vehement in their rejection of *dharma-dharmī bheda* (substance-attribute relationship) because in perception there is no apprehension of qualities and thus there is no determination and so on. For example, "X" is an object, and if "X" is indeterminate then "P" as the knowledge of "X" should also be indeterminate because only then can knowledge be in agreement with its object. If "P" is determinate, then it would mean that it is not given by the object alone because the object has no determination and cannot cause any determination. Consequently, it will be in discrepancy with the object. If the perceived object is indeterminate, its knowledge has also to be indeterminate.

Every *svalakṣaṇa* that alone is the object of perceptual cognition is instantaneous and does not endure for the next moment. Every *svalakṣaṇa*, being momentary, cannot be perceived twice, and therefore every perception is different from another perception. Like *svalakṣaṇa*, every perception is unique *(svatovyāvartaka)*.

(b) There is another sense in which perception is nonconceptual. The conceptual cognition (*savikalpaka jñāna*) is always *vaiśiṣṭyāvagāhi jñāna* (predicative cognition) and *saṁsargāvagāhi jñāna* (relational cognition). In other words, it has to be propositional. Every proposition is a mental construct, and without mental construction there cannot be any formulation of a proposition. Thus, a perceptual cognition is nonpropositional. Though in itself it is nonpropositional, on the basis of it one can formulate a proposition. In this sense it can be regarded as prepropositional. But the moment prepropositional perceptual cognition is transformed into a proposition, that is, conceptualized, it ceases to be perception. To be conceptual is to be nonperceptual.

2. There has been a broad agreement among Indian epistemological thinkers that no determinate knowledge is possible without a language. Buddhists also fall in line with this. Though all determinate knowledge is linguistic, not all knowledge is linguistic. Perceptual knowledge that is indeterminate is nonlinguistic because it does not require the help of language and also because it is beyond the reach of language. The nonverbality of *nirvikalpaka pratyakṣa* is put forth by Nyāya-Mīmāmsā thinkers, perhaps on the first ground rather than on the second, but for Buddhists the second ground is more significant than the first one. *Pratyakṣa* is *anabhilāpya* (inexpressible in language) not only because it does not require the help of language but mainly because it is determined by the object (*svalakṣaṇa*), which is beyond the reach of language.

Buddhists put forth vigorous effort to defend their position vis-a-vis the non-Buddhist ones. We may here present in brief the Buddhist arguments for the rejection of the non-Buddhist positions, which can be broadly represented into three, namely, the Nyāya-Vaiśeṣika, the Jaina, and the Mīmāmsaka.

Refutation of Nyāya Position

In the Nyāya tradition from Vācaspatimiśra onward we have a clear-cut distinction between two stages of perception and hence of two types of perceptual cognition. The Buddhists accept *nirvikalpaka* alone as *pratyakṣa*, and therefore they would deny that there are two stages or types of *pratyakṣa* in the form of *nirvikalpaka* and *savikalpaka*. The main argument put forth by the Buddhists for nonacceptance of *pratyakṣa* as *savikalpaka* is that all determinate perception is capable of being verbalized, and if perception is to be defined in terms of *kalpanāpoḍha* or in terms of *artha-pradatta* (being caused by the object), then it can never be associated with verbal expression. A cognition that is in the form of apprehension of an object (*pratibhāsa*) can never be associated with verbal expression because neither are there words present in the object, nor are the words identical with the object.[39] If it were so, a person ignorant of the meaning of the words would also be capable of communicating through words like the person who knows their meaning. In other words, to cognize is one thing, and to designate is another. The cognizing function is not identical with the designating function, nor is the designating function inseparably associated with the cognizing function. Therefore, a cognition produced by the object should present only the object and not the word, which is wrongly supposed to be denotative of the object. From this it follows that a determinate knowledge that is a mental construction is erroneously held to be a true perception. Determinate knowledge presents an object as associated with a word (*abhilāpa*), although in reality the object is independent of any association with a word. Determinate knowledge is caused by the past mental impression (*vikalpa-vāsanā*), and it grasps an uncertain (*aniyata*) object, not a fixed one. It differs with every individual because it is not a real object and is caused by the past mental impression. The function of mental impression is always concealed in a determinate knowledge, but since that knowledge follows in the wake of perception, it usurps the function of the latter, and because of this determinate knowledge is mistakenly supposed to be perceptual.

The other argument put forth by Buddhists is that the determinate knowledge is always in predicative form in which something is predicated to something (*viśiṣṭavaiśiṣṭyāvagāhi jñāna*). Thus, it is always predicative of a qualifier-qualified relationship. According to Buddhists, first, there is no qualifier-qualified relationship existing between the objects (*svalakṣaṇas*), and second, even if such a relation is objective, one single perceptual cognition cannot apprehend two objects with their interrelation because it is essentially simple in character and cannot be complex.

Refutation of Kumārila's Position

Śāntarakṣita[40] undertakes an elaborate examination of Kumārila's view that there are two stages, namely, *nirvikalpaka* and *savikalpaka,* necessarily involved in perceptual cognition. His main objection is regarding perception as determinate cognition. If in a perceptual knowledge both the qualifier and the qualified, the individual and the universal, are apprehended, then the question is, How can this be possible in a single act of perception? Even granting that universal is perceptually apprehended, when universal is apprehended, individual is not apprehended, and when individual is apprehended, universal is not apprehended. One and the same cognition cannot apprehend both. Then how can a determinate perceptual knowledge be possible? Further, if it is maintained that in the indeterminate cognition itself both the individual and universal are apprehended, then what is left to be apprehended at the determinate level? As a matter of fact, universals and so on do not exist either as different or nondifferent from the individuals. Nor can they be both different and identical.

Refutation of the Jaina Position:

The position that every cognition, let alone a perceptual one, has to be determinate is based on the argument that every object is twofold in character, namely, the individual and the universal, and one cannot know an object without at the same time cognizing both its aspects. If an object is not apprehended along with its differential character, then there will be no difference between one cognition and another cognition, and the cognition of pen will be the same as the cognition of paper. The assertion that a cognition apprehends a qualified thing and yet is not conceptual will be self-contradiction. Thus, the Jaina argument is that to cognize is to cognize a thing with its differential character, which means it has to be a determinate cognition.

To this Śāntarakṣita's[41] reply is that it is one thing to apprehend a qualified thing, and it is an altogether different thing to say that a thing is associated with qualifications. A thing can never be associated with qualifications because by its very nature everything is a unique particular, but every particular thing is different from another thing, and this fact of being "different from" enables us to distinguish one perception from the other perception. Every perception is a negation of all things other than itself, and this accounts for the differentiation from the rest. In fact, all perceptual cognitions are unique and distinct just as their objects are unique and distinct, but the awareness of their distinction is conceptual, and this awareness, which is conceptual, is certainly not perceptual. The perceptual leads to conceptual, but perceptual itself is not conceptual. From the preceding analysis Buddhists conclude that all cognitions concerning *svalakṣaṇas* have to be compatible with the nature of the *svalakṣaṇas*. The *svalakṣaṇas* are devoid of all characterizations, and therefore their perceptual cognition also has to be devoid of all characterizations.

On the basis of the foregoing analysis of the Buddhist and non-Buddhist positions on the nature of *pratyakṣa,* we can restate the Buddhist position consistently and unambiguously put forth by Vasubandhu, Diṅnāga, Dharmakīrti, and so on as follows:

1. *Pratyakṣa* can never be conceptual or determinate (*savikalpaka*) mainly because it is exclusively determined by the object, which is free from all determinations and characterizations.
2. Nor can perceptual cognition be both indeterminate as well as determinate or perceptual as well as conceptual, mainly because perceptual and conceptual are mutually exclusive. A perceptual can never be conceptual, and a conceptual can never be perceptual. This does not mean that a perceptual cognition has nothing to do with a conceptual

one. Though in itself it is nonconceptual, it may give rise to conceptual cognition and thus may become preconceptual. But a cognition remains perceptual only insofar as it is nonconceptual and ceases to be so the moment it gives rise to conceptualization.

TYPES OF *PRATYAKSA*

All Buddhist thinkers of the *Vijñānavāda* tradition from Vasubandhu onward are unanimous in insisting that *pratyakṣa* is *nirvikalpaka* and hence *kalpanāpoḍha*. Thus, the differential character of every perceptual cognition is to be free from all conceptual constructions. In this respect they are all alike, and they are not to be classified under different heads. However, as Diṅnāga[42] points out, they can be classified if such a classification is asked for. Though we have a rough classification of different types of *pratyakṣa* in the *Pramāṇa Samuccaya,* a precise and clear classification is available only in Dharmakirti's works. Perhaps, Diṅnāga is more concerned about giving a precise definition of *pratyakṣa* rather than about the different types of *pratyakṣa*. For him classification of *pratyakṣa* is logically not significant. However, there was a prevalent practice in philosophical circles to discuss types of *pratyakṣa*. Diṅnāga refers to it, but Dharmakīrti feels a need to expound the Buddhist position on the classification of *pratyakṣa* in clear-cut terms.

Diṅnāga's Classification of *Pratyakṣa*

Having stated that all perceptual cognitions are alike so far as they are free from conceptual constructions, Diṅnāga points out that they can be classified into *indriya pratyakṣa* (sense perception), *mānasa pratyakṣa* (mental perception), *svasaṁvedana pratyakṣa* (selfcognition), and *yogi pratyakṣa* (mystic perception).

1. ***Indriya pratyakṣa.*** So far as the *indriya pratyakṣa* is concerned, it is in the form of sensations caused by an external object. Since there are five kinds of cognitive senses, we can talk of five types of *indriya pratyakṣa*.

2. ***Mānasa pratyakṣa.***[43] Besides *indriya pratyakṣa* there is also *mānasa pratyakṣa*, which consists of the awareness of *indriya pratyakṣa*.

3. ***Svasaṁvedana pratyakṣa.*** The third type of *pratyakṣa* is the immediate experience of both *indriya pratyakṣa* and *mānasa pratyakṣa*.

The concept of *svasaṁvedana* has been one of the most significant contributions of Diṅnāga, and its implications in the context of *prāmāṇyavāda* have been worked out while discussing *sārūpya*. The scope of *svasaṁvedana* has been enlarged by Diṅnāga to include the awareness of conceptual constructions also. In his own words, "Even conceptual construction when it is brought to internal awareness is to be regarded as a type of *pratyakṣa* (*kalpanāpi svasaṁvittāviṣtā*)."[44] It is interesting to note here that, according to Diṅnāga, each cognition has a twofold appearance: the appearance of an object (*arthābhāsa*) and that of itself (*svābhāsa*). As such, cognition cognizes itself while cognizing an object. The cognizing of an object through *kalpanā* is *anumāna*, not *pratyakṣa*.

But whether it is *anumāna* or *pratyakṣa*, the essential nature of cognition is the same; that is, it is self-cognized (*sva-prakāśaka*).

4. *Yogi pratyakṣa.* Besides the previous three, the fourth type of *pratyakṣa* accepted by Diṅnāga is *yogi pratyakṣa*. The intuitions apprehended by a *yogi* are also nonconceptual and hence are to be placed under *pratyakṣa*. Here Diṅnāga draws a distinction between a *yogi jñāna* and *āgama jñāna*. The cognition derived from the *āgama* (scripture) is *kalpanā*, but the *yogi jñāna* is not so.[45]

Dharmakīrti's Classification of *Pratyakṣa*

When we come to Dharmakīrti, we find that the problem of types of *pratyakṣa* seems to have been crystallized. Both in the *Nyāya Bindu* and in the *Pramāṇa Vārtika* we have clear statements that *pratyakṣa* is of four types, namely, *indriya pratyakṣa, mānasa pratyakṣa, svasaṁvedana pratyakṣa,* and *yogi pratyakṣa*.

1. *Indriya pratyakṣa.* So far as the *indriya pratyakṣa* is concerned, it is the most primary and at the same time the most pervasive type of *pratyakṣa*. Such a knowledge consists in presentation of an object to consciousness through the medium of senses. The cognitive senses being five in number, it can further be classified under five heads. This fivefold classification is based on the different cognitive senses, which serve as a medium. The cognitive senses are only a medium, not an agent. Their function consists only in creating a sort of link between the subjective consciousness and the objective reality lying outside. This function is over when the object is presented to consciousness and does not continue thereafter. Since in the Buddhist tradition perception has been defined as nonverbal, a question arises as to whether there can be anything like auditory perception. The question is based on an assumption that an auditory perception that cognizes word cannot be free from word association, and if wordassociation is *kalpanā* and not *pratyakṣa,* how can auditory perception be a genuine perception? Moreover, like light and consciousness, a "word" has a dual function of revealing itself and revealing its object. Because of this also an auditory perception must be associated with verbal expression. The answer given by Dharmottara[46] and Śāntarakṣita[47] is that when a word is cognized, it is not the same word that is expressive of some concept. It is cognized only as a sound, which is *svalakṣaṇa* and which does not have the previously referred- to double character. Even if no distinction is drawn between a sound and a word, the object of auditory perception is said to be having the twofold character. In auditory perception we are concerned only with its first character, namely, sound, and only in a conceptual cognition are we concerned with its second character, namely, meaning.[48]

2. *Mānasa pratyakṣa (Mano vijñāna).* The second type of *pratyakṣa* accepted by Dharmakīrti is *mānasa pratyakṣa*. It is a *pratyakṣa* that immediately follows the *indriya pratyakṣa*. It is, in fact, the element of attention when an *indriya pratyakṣa* arises. That is why Dharmakīrti in the *Nyāya Bindu*[49] defines it as "mental sensation which follows sense perception, which is its immediately preceding homogeneous cause." The *mānas pratyakṣa* is generated by the *indriya pratyakṣa,* which acts as its immediately preceding homogeneous cause.[50] If *mānasa pratyakṣa* is to be regarded as different from, and as an effect of, *indriya pratyakṣa,* then a question arises as to what its object is. Does it grasp the same object that is already grasped by the concerned *indriya pratyakṣa*? If it does, then it will not be a valid cognition because it will no longer be "*ajñātārthaprakāśa*" (awareness of an object not hitherto known). On the other hand, if it grasps what is altogether ungrasped by the concerned *indriya pratyakṣa,* then any *mānasa pratyakṣa* can be related to any *indriya pratyakṣa,* or even the blind would perceive color.[51] To this the reply given by Dharmakīrti and Dharmottara is that the objects of the two are different, and yet the two perceptions are interconnected insofar as the *indriya pratyakṣa* along with its object gives rise to the *mānasa pratyakṣa* and its corresponding object at the immediately succeeding moment.[52] This complex phenomenon can be explained with the help of the diagram shown in Figure 2.1.

Figure 2.1

Process of *Mānasa Pratyakṣa*

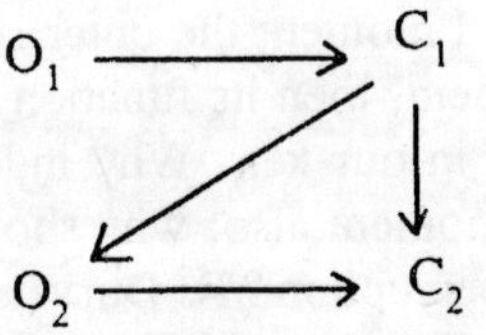

Note: O_1 is *indriya pratyakṣa viṣaya;* C_1 is *indriya pratyakṣa;*
O_2 is *mānasa pratyakṣa viṣaya;* C_2 is *mānasa pratyakṣa;*
C_1 is *samanantara pratyaya* of C_2; O_2 is *ālambana pratyaya* of C_2.

The need for the acceptance of *mānasa pratyakṣa* over and above *indriya pratyakṣa* can be questioned, and justification of its acceptance can be asked for. To this Dharmottara replies that it is a necessary postulate of the system, and no proof need be adduced for its postulation.[53] Stcherbatsky,[54] however, gives some justification, which is not very unconvincing. He opines that after having made a radical distinction between the role of *indriya* and *kalpanā,* Buddhist thinkers are in need of some connecting link between the two insofar as *pratyakṣa* has to lead to *kalpanā*. This connecting link is established by postulating *mānasa pratyakṣa*. There is some basis in Dharmottara for the suggestion given by Stcherbatsky. Dharmottara argues that *mānasa pratyakṣa* has to be postulated as a link between *indriya pratyakṣa* and *kalpanā* because *indriya pratyakṣa,* being momentary, cannot directly give rise to conceptualization unless and until it is first attended to in consciousness, and if *mānasa pratyakṣa* is not accepted, not only will there be a difficulty in accounting for a transition from *indriya pratyakṣa* to *kalpanā,* but there will also be a flaw of *indriya pratyakṣa* being invalid because it will then not have generative efficiency (*arthakriyākāritva*). The *mānasa pratyakṣa,* which is sensory on one side and mental on the other, has the psychological necessity in order to link two heterogeneous types of knowledge, namely, perception and conception.

In fact, the acceptance of *mānasa pratyakṣa* in the Diṅnāga-Dharmakīrti's tradition can be traced back to the Abhidhamma literature, where we have a clear acceptance of *manovijñāna* and *manovijñāna dhātu* in the list of seventy-five categories into which the whole sphere of knowledge and reality is reduced. In the *Nyāya Bindu Tikā Tippaṇi*[55] it is stated that the conception of *manovijñāna* as a type of *pratyakṣa* was a necessary deduction from the import of a scriptural text that declares, "Color is cognised, O monks, by twofold cognition, the sense perception and the mental perception induced by it." Another question may demand our attention concerning the temporal location of *indriya pratyakṣa* and *mānasa pratyakṣa*. It can be asked whether some other *indriya pratyakṣa* can operate even at the time when we are having *mānasa pratyakṣa* in the second moment. Both Dharmakīrti and Dharmottara reply to this view in the negative. They are of the opinion that if the sense organ were to operate even at a time when we are having *mānasa pratyakṣa,* there would be no *indriya pratyakṣa* at all.[56] This point has been further explained and elaborated in the *Tippaṇi* like this: "If we assume that in the second moment the outer sense-organ is engaged just as it is engaged in the first moment, then its function will also be the same, i.e., it will make the object present in our ken. Why indeed should then sense-perception not arise in the second moment also; why should not both the moments receive the same name of sense-perception ?"[57] Durveka's[58] explanation of Dharmottara's statement is as follows: "The first moment of the cognition series is regarded as dependent upon the sense organ because it is invariably concomitant with the presence and absence of the sense organ. If even mental perception were to have invariable concomitance with the presence and absence of the sense organ, this could not be given as a reason to establish a cognition as sense perception, that is, it cannot be called as sense perception on the ground that it depends on the sense organ. So, even the first moment could not be established as sense perception on the ground that it has invariable concomitance with the presence and absence of the sense organ."

It is significant here to point out that the concept of *mānasa pratyakṣa* advocated by Diṅnāga and Dharmakīrti is altogether different from the concept of *mānasa pratyakṣa* advocated by Nyāya-Vaiśeṣika thinkers. In the Nyāya-Vaiśeṣika philosophy *mānasa pratyakṣa* stands for the perception of the qualities of the self, but in the Buddhist tradition it stands for the mental perception caused by the preceding sense perception. Though the object of *mānasa pratyakṣa* in the Buddhist tradition is an internal one, nevertheless, it is caused jointly by the external object and its sense perception. Nyāya-Vaiśeṣika thinkers regard mind as an *antarendriya* (internal sense), but for Buddhists of the Diṅnāga-Dharmakīrti tradition mind is not an *indriya*; mind here stands for the consciousness (*citta*) or, strictly speaking, a specific moment of consciousness.

3. *Svasaṁvedana.* The third type of *pratyakṣa* distinguished by Dharmakīrti is *svasaṁvedana* or *ātmasaṁvedana*. He defines it as "*Sarvam cittacaittānām* *ātmasaṁvedanam*"; that is, all consciousness, cognition (*citta*), and mental states (*caitta*) are self-cognizing. Like Diṅnāga, Dharmakīrti insists that differential character of consciousness as opposed to matter is its self-awareness. Matter is always to be known through consciousness, but consciousness can be known by itself only. This theory is known as *svayaṁprakāśavāda*, the self-luminosity theory of consciousness, which is a distinct contribution of Diṅnāga to epistemology.

The doctrine that every consciousness is also self-consciousness has been a fundamental tenet of the Diṅnāga-Dharmakīrti tradition. Every cognition of the object-external or internal is at the same time a cognition of that cognition. Thus, a cognition can also be understood as an awareness of awareness. To explain the theory of *svayam-prakāsatva* of consciousness, the analogy of a lamp is often put forth. As a lamp illumines the objects in its surrounding and its own self at the same time, not being dependent on any extraneous factor for its own illumination, just so is consciousness self-luminous. Commenting on Dharmakīrti's definition of *svasaṁvedana*, Dharmottara writes, "There is no mental phenomenon whatsoever which would be unconscious of its own existence." Further, he writes that such a self-awareness is not a construction nor an illusion, and hence it is a type of *pratyakṣa*.[59]

Dharmakīrti[60] proves the self-luminosity of consciousness as follows. First, he points out that pleasure, pain, and so on are mental states, but they are of the nature of consciousness and they cannot be cognized by other cognitions. From this it naturally follows that all cognitions and mental states are self-cognized. Dharmottara explains this point with the help of the following example. When a patch of color is apprehended, we at the same time feel something internally in the shape of some emotions. It is not possible to maintain that a patch of color is felt as being itself the pleasure it affords us, because we do not say, "This patch of blue color has itself the form of pleasure." We do not regard blue and pleasure as identical, nor do we feel them as the same. Therefore, we really are experiencing pleasure as something quite different from the object blue, as something that is not equivalent to blue, and this is no doubt knowledge. Therefore, we do experience our own knowledge. Self-consciousness is essentially a case of knowledge; it makes present to us our own-self.

The self-luminosity of consciousness does not in any way mean bifurcation of consciousness into a subject and an object, which would be absurd. Consciousness and selfconsciousness are, therefore, interchangeable terms. In Buddhist writings the word "*citta*" stands for consciousness in general, but the word "*caitta*" stands for feelings and so on, which are classed apart from cognition on the ground that feelings do not contain "intentionality" insofar as they are purely inward in reference. Barring this difference, they are all conscious states, the conscient character being common to cognition and feeling alike.

How one and the same cognition can be both the subject as well as the object has been answered by Dharmakīrti by saying that the cognition directly experiences the form of the external object reflected in it and not the external object itself; so only metaphorically is it said that cognition grasps the external object, which, in fact, simply causes the reflection.[61]

4. *Yogi jñāna.* Besides these preceding three types of perception Dharmakīrti, following Diṅnāga, accepts *yogi jñāna* as the fourth kind of perception.

Dharmakīrti defines *yogi jñāna* as intuition of a mystic that is produced from the subculminational state of deep meditation on transcendental reality. Buddhists, like other mystics, believe in the fact of intuitive realizations, which are available to some gifted persons like saints. In fact, the acceptance of *yogi pratyakṣa* is a necessary prerequisite of the acceptance of the *sarvajñatā* (omniscience) of the Buddha. The Buddhistic way of noble life consists of three broad stages, namely, *prajñā, śīla,* and *samādhi*. The experiences acquired in the state of *samādhi* are perceptual ones because they are vivid, presentational, and direct. Knowledge of the four Noble Truths and so on is an example of such a type of *pratyakṣa*. It is nonerroneous and nonconceptual contemplation on the real.

In order to explain the phrase "*bhūtārthabhāvanā prakarṣaparyantajam,*" Dharmakīrti describes the three stages of contemplation as follows.

First, he states that *yogi pratyakṣa* is generated by deep contemplation, and it is vivid and free from conceptual construction; afterward, he explains each of these qualifying terms in anticipation of the possible objections that might be urged against them. It might be asked how the cognition generated by contemplation can be vivid. Dharmakīrti proves this point by drawing our attention to the fact that the persons possessed of fear, sorrow, and passion vividly see nonexistent things as real because of the repeated thought of those things. Again, someone might ask, "It is conceded that the cognition generated by contemplation is vivid, but how can one accept it to be free from conception?" Dharmakīrti answers that the cognition in question has, indeed, vividness, and just for this reason it ceases to be a conceptual construction. Conceptual constructions are never vivid. Dharmakīrti again observes that all cognitions born of a deep contemplation on either reality or unreality are vivid and nonconceptual; but the cognition born of a contemplation on reality is valid, while the cognition born of a contemplation on unreality is invalid because the former alone is in harmony with successful activity or is efficient to lead to the attainment of the object pointed out by it. This, in short, is how the cognition born of a deep contemplation on reality is vivid, nonconceptual, and efficient to generate the purposive action, and hence it is a case of perception.[62]

Chapter 3

The Buddhist Theory of Inference

INFERENCE (*ANUMĀNA*) AS *PRAMĀṆA*

In different systems of epistemology different numbers of *pramāṇas* are accepted, and with the exception of the Cārvāka system, the acceptance of *anumāna* as a *pramāṇa* has been unanimous. Apart from *pratyakṣa* Buddhists regard *anumāna* as *pramāṇa*. Generally, a distinction is drawn between two kinds of knowledge, namely, *pratyakṣa* (immediate) and *parokṣa* (mediate). *Anumāna*, as opposed to *pratyakṣa,* is a mode that can provide only mediate (*parokṣa*) knowledge.

Anumāna, it is important to note, is at once a mode of knowing and a way of reasoning. Thus, it has an epistemic as well as logical aspect, both of which are inseparably coalesced into one. In fact, the former aspect is the basis for the latter, and that is why *anumāna* is generally known as a mode of knowing.

Development of the Theory of *Anumāna* in the Buddhist Tradition

Among the different systems of logic that developed in India, the Buddhist system is of significance comparable to that of the Nyāya. Though systematic, logical analysis seems to have begun with Vasubandhu, Diṅnāga and Dharmakīrti developed a fullfledged theory of *anumāna* as also that of *pratyakṣa* and *apoha*. The development of logic in the Buddhist system and, for that matter, in the entire Indian thought—has been within the epistemological context and therefore began with the theory of *pratyakṣa*. Some people are of the opinion that the science of logic (*Nyāya śāstra*) developed in India out of a science of dialectics and debate (*Vāda śāstra*), but it seems more probable that it was not so much the dialectics as the art of conducting philosophical debates in public (*Vāda vidhi*) that was the ground for the subsequent rise of the science of logic, a theory of *anumāna*, more specifically, the *parārthānumāna*. Since the technique of *anumāna* was employed as one of the modes of acquiring knowledge and providing proofs or grounds for the truth of that knowledge, the science of logic was also known as the science of reason (*hetu vidyā or pramāṇa śāstra*).

The Buddhist theory of *anumāna* has been developed in the context of the theory of twofold *pramāṇas*, namely, *pratyakṣa* and *anumāna*, which, in turn, is based on the view that there are two types of object of knowledge (*prameyas*). As stated earlier, the Buddhists put forth a process view of reality as opposed to the substantival view of reality advocated by the other schools of thought in India. Such a real being in the form of discrete and momentary existence is given only in our sense-experience, which is pure sensation devoid of all conceptualizations. But for empirical purposes they accept another view of reality (though, of a lower order) in which different thought categories in the form of substance, qualities, motion, class character, etc. and so on are hypostatized and imposed upon the reality. The entire system of logic is interwoven around such mental constructions and their interrelations. However, it also aims at explaining the relation between the dynamic reality and the static construction of thought.

Though the word "*anumāna*" occurs in the Piṭakas, it does not seem to occur in the sense of a science of logic. In the *Anumāna Sūtta*[1] a principle is laid down that one should not do unto others what one doesn't wish others to do unto oneself. This is said to be based on the generalization that what is disliked by oneself is disliked by others as well. This knowledge is said to be inferential. Here one should infer (*svārthānumāna*) as follows: "An evil person who is swayed by evil thoughts is disagreeable and disliked by me; now if I were to be evil and swayed by evil thoughts I, too, will be disagreeable and disliked by others." If we analyze this *anumāna,* it, in fact, consists of two *anumānas*, namely:

1. I dislike an evil person, X is like me (as a person), Therefore, X (probably) dislikes an evil person.
2. X dislikes an evil person (conclusion of (1), I am an evil person, Therefore, X dislikes me.

This apart, we also meet with the expression "*anvaya jñānam,*"[2] meaning inductive knowledge in all the *Nikāyas* as well as in the *Abidhamma*. By this is meant the inferential knowledge of the inductive pattern, which is based on a belief in the uniformity of nature and universality of causal relationships. In the *Sutta Nikāya* we come across several statements expressing causal relations such as "with the arising of birth there is arising of decay and death, and with the cessation of birth there is cessation of decay and death and so on."[3] Knowing such causal relations is called "the knowledge of phenomena" (*dhamma jñānam*). It is further stated, "This constitutes the knowledge of phenomena; by seeing, experiencing, acquiring knowledge before long and delving into these phenomena, he draws an inference (*nayam neti*) with regard to the past and future as follows: All those recluses and *brāhmaṇas* who thoroughly understood the nature of decay and death, its cause, its cessation and path leading to the cessation of decay and death did so in the same way as I do at present; all those recluses and *brāhmaṇas* who in the future will thoroughly understand the nature of decay and death will do so in the same way as I do at present—this constitutes the inductive knowledge."[4]

In the *Abhidhamma* and *Prakaraṇas* we find a more favorable attitude toward the science of debate and logic. Of course, argumentation was always kept subservient to scriptures.[5]

As we remarked earlier, the science of logic was developed in India for the sake of sophistication in debate. Most of the terms and techniques of the science of debate were retained in the science of logic. In *Kathāvatthu* we come across several such terms, like *anuyoga, ādhāraṇa, patijñā, upanaya, niggaha, anuloma, patikamma, and nigamana*.

Yogacaryābhūmiśāstra, a later work dealing with the science of debate, contains a section pertaining to the doctrine of *anumāna* and other *pramāṇas*. Tucci is of the opinion that it is, in fact, there that we find the earliest elaboration of the doctrine of syllogism and *pramāṇas*.[6] Another work by the name *Tarkaśāstra* deals more exhaustively with the theory of *anumāna* and thus forms a link between the science of debate and science of logic. This *Tarkaśāstra* points out unmistakably the existence of *trairūpya* theory before Diṅnāga.[7] Tucci observes: "Whether the work is *Vādavidhi* or a different one, there is no doubt that it contains ideas and doctrines which Diṅnāga found before him and which in many places he refuted in his treatises, and in other places he followed. It is still a *vivāda* text, but it shows an enormous progress upon the first attempts and mere catalogues of the older treatises, as we can see quite well when we compare it with the *vivāda* sections contained in Maitreya and Asaṅga."[8]

ANUMĀNA IN THE WORKS OF PRE-DIṆNĀGA THINKERS

The systematic study of logic and epistemology that began in the Nyāya circle was introduced in the Buddhist tradition by Asaṅga and Vasubandhu, who tried to counter Nāgārjuna's nihilistic dialectics. Nāgārjuna was an absolutist who argued for the futility of all logic for the experience of the Absolute. With the advent of Asaṅga and Vasubandhu the realistic Nyāya logic was introduced in the Buddhist circle with suitable adaptations to their idealistic framework.

Asaṅga was perhaps the first Buddhist writer who talked of the theory of the *parārthānumāna (pañcāvayavi vākya)*. However, we don't find any innovation or significant contribution in the works of Asaṅga. A short summary of the exposition of logic by Asaṅga is found in *Prakaraṇārya Vācāśāstra* and volumes 7 and 16 of *Mahāyānābhidharmasamyuktasangiti śāstra*. Asaṅga was preceded by Maitreya, who composed a treatise on the art of debate by the name *Saptadaśabhūmiśāstrayogacaryā*. In logical views Asaṅga followed Maitreya except in respect of the theory of proof. Proof (*sādhaka*) was understood by Asaṅga in a comprehensive sense of *pramāṇa* and was subdivided as follows: (1) *pratijñā*, (2) *hetu*, (3) *udhāharaṇa*, (4) *upanaya*, (5) *nigamana*, (6) *pratyakṣa*, (7) *anumāna*, and (8) *āgama*. The first five subdivisions constitute *anumāna*. Asaṅga differed from Maitreya in differentiating *anumāna* from *pratyakṣa*, *upamāna*, and *āgama* and in regarding *anumāna* as consisting of the first five divisions only. But in all this he seems to be just imitative of the Nyāya view.

Asaṅga was followed by Vasubandhu, who was a renowned teacher of logic. Vidyabhushana[9] has presented a summary of *Tarka śāstra* authored by Vasubandhu. He points out that Vasubandhu seems to have used two forms of *anumāna*, namely, that of five parts at the time of debate and a syllogism of two parts, namely, *pratijñā* and *hetu*, on an ordinary occasion.[10] Stcherbastsky, however, mentions that mostly he was operating with *pañcāvayavi vākya*, but sometimes he was also making use of the abridged *trayāvayavi*.[11] He further points out that there are only two other significant points on which Vasubandhu differed from the Naiyāyikas: first, the doctrines of *trairūpya* and *avinābhāva* appeared first in the works of Vasubandhu, and second, the classification of *hetus* and *hetvābhāsas* is different from the one accepted in the Nyāya school and agrees in principle with the one introduced by Diṅnāga and developed by Dharmakīrti.

ANUMĀNA IN THE WORKS OF DIṄNĀGA

Diṅnāga gave a new direction and impetus to the study of logic and epistemology in the Buddhist tradition. It goes to his credit that he treated the theory of *pramāṇas* separately from the theory of *prameyas*. In him and perhaps in Vasubandhu prior to him we find an attempt to write independent works on *pramāṇas* without bringing in explicit analysis of *prameyas*. According to him, there are only two *pramāṇas*, namely, *pratyakṣa* and *anumāna*. The other *pramāṇas*, like *śabda*, were reduced to *anumāna*. Diṅnāga's analysis of *anumāna* was so strikingly original that even in the Nyāya circle it was taken cognizance of. Uddyotakara, for example, writes, "*Apare tu bruvate, nāntarīyakārthadarśanam tad vido anumānam.*"[12] Here the expression "*apare*" probably refers to Diṅnāga.

The basic point of difference between Diṅnāga and the Nyāya logicians is that for Diṅnāga *anumāna* may consist of a pure thought process, that is, purely propositional, or it may be sentential.[13] A purely propositional *anumāna* is a thought process that has not been verbally expressed. It is named by him as *svārthānumāna*. When the propositions of an *anumāna* are expressed in language (*prakāśana* or *ākhyāna*), then they are sentential (*śabda*) in nature, and that form of *anumāna* is named *parārthānumāna*. Keith[14] opines that the distinction between the two kinds of *anumāna* was first introduced by Diṅnāga in Indian logic. Probably this two-fold classification of *anumāna* was already prevalent in the Nyāya tradition, but there it was used in a slightly different sense, *svārthānumāna* meaning *anumāna* for one's own sake and *parārthānumāna* meaning for the sake of others. Diṅnāga borrowed the same phraseology to name his twofold classification of *anumāna*. So far as *parārthānumāna* is concerned, it is sentential, according to Diṅnāga, and normally we resort to sentential expression only when we communicate with others. But communication with others is not the necessary condition of using language. Thus, Diṅnāga would not agree with the Naiyāyikas in regarding *parārthānumāna* as inference for the sake of others but would insist that this is one of the motives for undertaking *parārthānumāna*. His basic difference with the Naiyāyikas is with regard to the understanding of *svārthānumāna*. For the

Naiyāyikas *svārthānumāna* is also sentential because for them no conceptual knowledge can be nonverbal. For Diṅnāga, on the other hand, there can be a nonverbalized conceptual cognition, and in *svārthānumāna* we have only such cognitions.

The other point of departure of Diṅnāga is the advocacy of *svabhāvānumāna*, which stands for a sort of analytical entailment. In the Nyāya tradition, because of its predominant realistic attitude there was no such possibility of the acceptance of one concept being subsumed under another concept such that the former could be deduced from the latter. In the Buddhist tradition the entire process of *anumāna* operates at the conceptual level only, and therefore the Buddhist logicians could conceive of one concept being connected with another by the relation of analyticity.

Another innovation of Diṅnāga, which is a corollary of the earlier mentioned point, is that he made explicitly clear the distinction between the objects of perceptual cognition and the objects of inferential cognition. In *anumāna* we are concerned not with the real object (*svalakṣaṇa, grāhya*) but with the conceived object (*sāmānyalakṣaṇa, adhyavaseya*). So a thought process from one conceived object to another conceived object is necessarily connected with it.

Lastly, in Diṅnāga we find a new understanding of the concept of *anumeya*. According to the Nyāya logicians *sādhya* is *anumeya*, but for Diṅnāga it is *paksa* characterized by *sādhya*, which is the *anumeya*. So in the example of the inference of fire on the basis of the perception of smoke Diṅnāga would maintain that the thought process is from smoky hill to fiery hill and not from smoke to fire. The latter Naiyāyikas emphasize the colocushood (*ekādhikaraṇya*) of *hetu* and *sādhya* in *pakṣa*, whereas Diṅnāga talked of *hetu* and *sādhya* being the coproperties of *pakṣa (dharma)*.

Anumāna in the Works of Dharmakīrti

Diṅnāga's formulation of the theory of *anumāna* was further explicated by Dharmakīrti in his *Pramāna Vartika* and *Nyaya Bindu*. In the latter work, the basic concepts and terms involved in the theory of *anumāna* have been clearly analyzed and defined. Dharmakīrti's main contribution lies in his elaboration of the doctrine of *trairūpya*, a detailed account of which is presented later. The doctrine of *trairūpya* regards *hetu* or *liṅga* as the starting point of the process of *anumāna* and grounds its validity on three conditions that a valid *hetu* has to fulfill. In short, they are as follows:

1. There should be a necessary presence of *hetu* in *pakṣa (anumeye sattvam)*. This corresponds to the idea of *pakṣadharmatva* available in the Nyāya position.
2. There should be presence of *hetu* only in such cases that are similar to *pakṣa* (*sapakṣeva sattvam*).
3. Lastly, there should be necessary absence of *hetu* in such cases that are dissimilar to *pakṣa (asapkṣe cāsattvameva niścitam)*.

The second and the third conditions correspond to the two types of *vyāpti*, namely, affirmative (*anvaya*) and negative (*vyatireki*), accepted in the Nyāya tradition. Though these three conditions of *hetu* or *liṅga* have been introduced by Diṅnāga, Dharmakīrti put forth their systematic formulations. In fact, here it is given such a central position that the entire subsequent discussion on *anumāna* pivoted around it.

Further, it goes to the credit of Dharmakīrti to have analyzed *anupalabdhi* into eleven varieties. Such a classification of negative relation is of great significance in the analysis of causal relation. It seems that the later Buddhist theory of *pañcakaraṇi*[15] was formulated as a consequence of the analysis of the negative aspect of causal relation, as it was put forth in the analysis of the different varieties of *anupalabdhi*.

After Dharmakīrti we don't come across any notable thinker in Buddhist logic. Dharmottara, Mokṣākaragupta, Prajñākaragupta, Śāntarakṣita, Kamalaśīla, Ratnakīrti, Jñānaśrī Mitra, and others explained, elaborated, and defended the Buddhist doctrines of logic, but none of them made any new contributions. In the analysis of the theory of *apoha* Ratnakīrti introduced some significant innovations, but he didn't take much interest in the field of knowledge. However, he brought about greater sophistication and cohesion in the Buddhist system. Thus, it appears that Buddhist logic of a serious sort began with Vasubandhu, was developed by Diṅnāga and Dharmakīrti, was defended by Śāntarakṣita and Kamalaśīla, and was later refined by Ratnakīrti and Jñānaśrī Mitra.

ANUMĀNA PRĀMĀṆYA

Svataḥ-Parataḥ Controversy

The problem concerning the *prāmāṇya* of *pramā* can be posed in two different ways. It can be discussed as to whether *anumāna* is a *pramāṇa* or not, or, in other words, whether *anumiti jñāna* has *prāmāṇya* or not. On this point, with the exception of Cārvākas, all other schools of philosophical thought accord *prāmāṇya* to *anumiti jñāna*, but in what way *anumiti jñāna* has *prāmāṇya* there is a difference of opinion. Vedāntins and Bhartṛhari circumscribe the independent operation of *anumāna pramāṇa* by making it subservient to some other *pramāṇa*. The rest of the schools and thinkers grant its independent operation. The Buddhists with whom we are presently concerned accept *anumāna* as an independent *pramāṇa*. However, in Diṅnāga we meet with another position that assigns a status to *anumāna* that is on a par with illusions, hallucinations, and so on. But such a stand is to be understood in its proper metaphysical perspective, which talks of two levels of reality, namely, *pāramārthika* and *sāṁvṛtika*. The validity of inference is denied only from the *pāramārthika* point of view, but at the level of *sāṁvṛtika* it is very much valid, as valid as perceptual cognition.[16]

Whether *anumāna* is an independent *pramāṇa* or not is a question that has a methodological significance, but a question philosophically more significant is the mode of knowing *prāmāṇya* of *anumiti jñāna*. On this issue Indian epistemological thinkers are generally divided into two camps. Some thinkers adhering to *svataḥprāmāṇyavāda* regard the relation between *jñāna* and, for that matter, *anumiti jñāna* and *prāmāṇya* as *svataḥ* (intrinsic). Some others view this relation to be *parataḥ* (extrinsic). Buddhist thinkers, particularly Diṅnāga and Dharmakīrti, advocate the theory of *svataḥprāmāṇya*.

The question about *prāmāṇya* of *pramā* is inseparably bound with the question of the nature of *pramā*. As stated earlier, Buddhists refuse to draw a distinction between *pramāṇa* and *pramāṇaphala,* saying that every cognition-qua-cognition is ab initio valid insofar as it is caused by the object itself. The *sārūpya* of the cognition with its object is a sufficient guarantee for the truth of the cognition, though this *sārūpya* is not something extraneous to that cognition. For Buddhists every cognition has twofold aspects (*dvairūpya*), namely, *svākāratā* and *viṣayākāratā*. *Viṣayākāratā* is the ground for the *prāmāṇya* of a *pramā* since *viṣayākāratā* is the very nature of a cognition. Every cognition has to be inherently true. This consideration led these Buddhist thinkers to advocate the theory of *svataḥprāmāṇya*.

The intrinsic truth of a perceptual cognition is prima facie itself a very plausible position, but the intrinsic truth of inferential cognition may not be that apparent. This is because of the complicated structure of the inferential process. In every inferential process there is a possibility of going astray at every step, giving rise to what is technically known as *hetvābhāsa*. Further, there is a greater need for adducing evidence in an inferential cognition compared to the perceptual one, and this may make the *prāmāṇya* of the inferential cognition contingent upon the adequacy and conclusiveness of the adduced cognition. We may therefore state and examine the grounds on the basis of which Buddhists insist on the *svataḥprāmāṇya* of *anumiti jñāna*. In order to appreciate the sharpness of the Buddhist position it would be very much helpful to refer to Vācaspati,[17] the Naiyāyika, who accepts the *svataḥprāmāṇya* of *anumiti jñāna* even in the context of the Nyāya tradition. His argument of the ab initio apprehension of *prāmāṇya* of *anumiti jñāna* is that among its originating conditions there is certainty about the *vyāpti jñāna*. There is no room left, therefore, for having any subsequent doubt in the validity of inference. It should be pointed out that Udayana is not so very confident, but he, too, hesitatingly concedes that truth is there apprehended ab initio. However, he also makes a desperate attempt to reconcile this with the *parataḥ* theory of the Nyāya tradition by suggesting that there it may be both. Gangeśa is not oblivious of this inconsistency with the Nyāya standpoint and therefore proceeds to explicate what in his view is the true intention of Vācaspati. The general point that he makes is that in all these cases there is no scope for doubt, though truth is apprehended extrinsically. In this he is following Udayana's comment on Vācaspati in his *Pariśuddhi*.[18] The crux of his argument is that it would be too much to claim that since there is no scope for doubt, the truth of an inference is apprehended ab initio. Truth is always to be known subsequently in *anuvyavasāya*.

Diṅnāga and Dharmakīrti seem to be uncompromising in their advocacy of the theory of *svataḥprāmāṇya*. In Pramāṇa Samuccaya Diṅnāga explicitly maintains that the guarantee for the truth of a cognition lies in its being of the form of its object. He writes that, "the means of cognising is simply the cognition having the form of the object."[19] For him every true cognition necessarily refers to an object, and since it is caused by an object, it possesses the form of that object. Diṅnāga is a *sākārajñānavādin* and, therefore, insists on the knowledge being of the form of its object. If every true cognition has to be of the nature of its object, it is a sufficient condition for its truth and therefore leaves no scope for any doubt. The question of doubt will arise only when there is a possibility of the intermingling of such elements that are not caused by the object and that are due to subjective factors. For Diṅnāga, therefore, there is no distinction between knowledge and such factors that evidence its truth insofar as the latter is not something extraneous to knowledge. The question of evidence arises only when falsity is suspected, that is when something that is taken to be a *pramāṇa* (knowledge) is suspected to be a *pramāṇābhāsa* (pseudo knowledge). If, on the basis of any evidence, a particular cognition stands falsified, it does not mean that what was knowledge is now falsified. In fact, knowledge by definition is true, and truth follows from the very definition of knowledge as a matter of analytic necessity. Therefore, it is impossible to falsify knowledge. So when on the basis of some evidence or set of evidences a particular cognition is falsified, all it means is that a pseudoknowledge that was masquerading as a genuine knowledge is now exposed.

In order to appreciate the strength of Diṅnāga's position, it is necessary to first see his metaphysical position. Being an advocate of *Vijñānavāda,* Diṅnāga maintains that in the ultimate analysis the entire empirical reality is nothing but different manifestations of the series of *vijñāna,* and as a consequence of this he maintains that the means of cognition, the cognition that is its result and the object of cognition, are not separate from one another, and though in an epistemological analysis we may analyze these three factors of cognition as *pramāṇa, pramāṇaphala,* and *prameya*, in reality they are not three separate things.[20]

Following Diṅnāga, Dharmakīrti also subscribes to the *svataḥprāmāṇya* theory, though he talks of a true cognition necessarily leading to a successful activity.[21] Knowledge leading to successful activity is only a test and not its criterion. A distinction, therefore, has to be drawn between test of truth and criterion of truth. The truth of a cognition can be tested on the basis of extraneous considerations, like being a means to successful activity. It should not be mistaken as a criterion of truth. The purpose of a test is to verify or ascertain the presence or absence of a particular phenomenon. This can be done on the basis of the possible effect that a particular phenomenon gives rise to; for example, in Dharmakīrti's system successful activity is an outcome of true cognition, and, therefore, the former can be taken as a test of the latter. A criterion, on the other hand, serves a different purpose. Its function is to distinguish a particular phenomenon from its opposite. In the case of knowledge, according to Dharmakīrti, *arthasārūpya* is a criterion of knowledge and is not something extraneous to knowledge. It is rather the very nature or essence of knowledge. Thus, *avisaṁvādakam* is a criterion of knowledge, whereas *sarvapuruṣārtha siddhi hetu* is the test of knowledge.

From this analysis it follows that the criterion of truth of an inferential cognition is intrinsic to it, and this provides a sufficient ground for maintaining that Diṅnāga and Dharmakīrti subscribe to the theory of *svataḥprāmāṇya*.

NATURE OF *ANUMĀNA*

The term *anumāna* literally means "a knowledge that follows'' (*anu+māna*, i.e., *paścānmānamiti anumānam*). This means that the inferential knowledge is necessarily preceded by some other knowledge. In other words, *anumāna* as a *pramāṇa* is a complex knowledge consisting of two elements, one antecedent knowledge and the other consequent knowledge. The antecedent and the consequent have a particular type of relation that is technically known as *gamya-gamaka-bhāva* (entailment). The antecedent leads to, or gives rise to, the consequent and is, therefore, a *gamaka* (that which entails). The consequent results from the antecedent and is, therefore, a *gamya* (that which is entailed).

However, it is not the case that any knowledge will lead to, or entail, any other knowledge. The antecedent knowledge has to be in the form of *liṅga* (necessary mark), of which the consequent knowledge is *liṅgin* (marked). *Liṅga* means that which is a necessary mark of something other than itself (*Līnamartham gamayati saḥ liṅgam*). Likewise, *liṅgin* stands for that which is necessarily marked by a *liṅga*.

Between *liṅga* and *lingin* there is always a *gamya-gamaka-bhāva,*[22] which can roughly be regarded as the relation of entailment such that every case of the presence of *liṅga* is necessarily a case of the presence of *liṅgin*, and, on the contrary, every case of the absence of *liṅgin* is the case of the absence of *liṅga*. The necessary connection between *liṅga* and *liṅgin* on the basis of which *gamya-gamaka-bhāva* is established between the two is technically known in the Buddhist tradition as *avinābhāva* or *vyāpti* (necessary concomitance). The presence of *avinābhāva* provides the basis of the transition from *gamaka* to the *gamya*. *Avinābhāva*, therefore, constitutes the logical ground for the process of *anumāna*. It is significant to note here that unlike the Nyāya tradition in the Buddhist tradition *liṅga* and *liṅgin* are in the form of concepts (*vikalpas*) rather than things or metaphysical reals, a point discussed later.

Nonpresentative Character of *Anumāna*

The inferential knowledge, as we have stated, stands for the knowledge of the *liṅgin* on the basis of the knowledge of the *liṅga*. This implies that the inferential knowledge of the *lingin* is necessarily nonpresentative. By nonpresentative is meant that the object of cognition, which is the *liṅgin*, is not directly given to, or apprehended by, the cognitive senses. The object here is not directly present but is conceived to be so on the ground of the presence of its necessary mark. However, it should not be understood that the conceived object is essentially a nonexistent one. It is an existing object whose presence or absence is indirectly cognized at a particular place on the basis of the presence or absence of its mark. Thus, *anumāna* as a *pramāṇa* offers a mediated knowledge of an object that is not directly given. We know an indirectly given object through a direct one to which it is related.

In saying that *anumāna* is nonpresentative it is to be contrasted with *pratyakṣa,* which is essentially presentative. Presentativeness of perceptual cognition consists in its apprehension of an object that is directly given to the senses (*akṣam akaṣamiti pratyakṣam*). Such an object is named as *grāhya* (sensed) in contrast to the object of inferential cognition named as *adhyavaseya* (conceived). The *grāhya, svalakṣaṇa*, is an objective reality, which is just a point instant, a unique particular, according to Buddhist ontology. The *adhyavaseya, sāmānya lakṣaṇa,* on the contrary, is a mental construction (*kalpanā*), a conceived entity, conceived in terms of either its substantiality or objectivity or relation or generic character. This conceived object is neither purely objective nor purely subjective but intersubjective. It is not objectively real but hypostatized to be so. However, its hypostatized character does not make it illusory or purely imaginary. It is a construction out of sense data and thus has empirical reality.

Judgmental Character of *Anumāna*

According to the Buddhist epistemology as stated earlier, there are only two types of knowledge because there are only two types of objects of knowledge (*mānam dvividham meya dvaividhyāt*). *Pratyakṣa* is knowledge in the form of pure sensation devoid of all conceptualization and judgmentalization (*pratyakṣam kalpanāpoḍham*). In contrast, *anumāna* is necessarily a *kalpanā*, that is, conceptual, and hence judgmental in nature. Thus, in the Buddhist tradition a knowledge can be either nonjudgmental or judgmental. If the former, it is a case of *pratyakṣa,* and if the latter, it is a case of *anumāna*. Of course, every judgmental cognition is ultimately grounded in a nonjudgmental cognition, and that is why *anumāna* is characterized as *pratyakṣa pṛṣṭha bhāvi*.

In the Buddhist tradition *anumāna* is not the only type of judgmental cognition. An illusory cognition (*bhrānta jñāna*) can also be judgmental, but it is not a *pramāṇa,* that is, true cognition. So the only judgmental cognition that is a *pramāṇa* is in the form of *anumāna*.

Relational Character of *Anumāna*

Unlike the perceptual cognition, inferential cognition is relational in nature. The object of the inferential cognition is always a characterized entity (*dharmi*) that is cognized on the basis of the perceptual cognition of one of its *dharmas*. As we pointed out earlier, there are two distinct types of cognition involved in an *anumāna*, namely, the antecedent and the consequent. Both these cognitions are relational in nature. The antecedent cognition is again twofold, technically known as *pakṣadharmatva* and *vyāpti* or *avinābhāva*. The former is in the form of contingent relation, but the latter is a necessary relation. There is an involvement of relation not only in the structure of the premises and the conclusion, so to say, of the *anumāna*, but also in the transition from premises to conclusion. This relation makes possible an extension of our knowledge from premises to conclusion. Thus, *anumāna* operates within a relational framework through and through.

According to Buddhist metaphysics, all relations are mental constructions, as there are no relations in reality. So relations are not apprehended in *pratyakṣa*. That is why perceptual cognition is nonrelational in nature. Thus, only in *anumāna* are relations apprehended. The objects of *anumāna* are relational, and *anumāna* in itself is also a relational cognition.

Verbalizable Character of *Anumāna*

There has always been a difference of opinion regarding the relation between knowledge and language. Bhartṛhari, for example, regards every knowledge to be necessarily embodied in language. Buddhist thinkers, on the other hand, insist that there can be thought even without being associated with language. They talk of two types of knowledge; that which can be verbalized and that which cannot be verbalized. Perceptual knowledge is nonverbalizable. In fact, its nonverbalizability follows from its being nonjudgmental or nonconceptual. Inferential knowledge, on the other hand, is verbalizable. It is controversial whether it is always verbalized or whether it is so only in *parārthānumāna*. However, one thing is certain, that whether actually verbalized or not, it alone is verbalizable. In fact, only when the inferential cognition is verbalized can its fallacious or nonfallacious character be exposed.

Generalized Character of the Object of *Anumāna*

The perceptual cognition has the unique particular as its object. But the object of inferential cognition is a generalized concept that results from the process of mental construction. The constructing activity of intellect is dichotomous. It always begins by conceiving the object in two aspects, the similar and the dissimilar. It operates with the method of agreement with the similar (*anvaya*) and difference with the dissimilar (*vyatireka*). If the aspect of agreement is expressed, then the aspect of disagreement is understood, and viceversa. Thus, according to Dharmakīrti, the object of inference is the exclusion of the opposite (*atadvyāvṛtti*). *Anumāna* does not cognize the positive nature of a thing but only its negative nature, which consists in a thing's exclusion from all types of dissimilar things. What is meant by saying this is only that the object of *anumāna* is a mental concept, a universal and not a real existence. However, this universal is not merely a creation of mental impressions (*vāsanā*). It is generated by real things. According to Dharmakīrti, it is in the nature of real things to generate a mental concept. So, a mental concept is invariably related to those things. Because of this, though an inference cognizes a mental concept, yet it enables us to attain a real thing. Insofar as it does not help attaining a real thing, it is *bhrānta jñāna*.

But so far as it enables us to attain an efficient real thing, it is a *pramāṇa*. Dharmakīrti again proves that an inferential judgment is ultimately grounded in a real thing. The real fire that is the cause of real smoke is the remote object of the inferential judgment "There is fire on the hill." The real fire generates the real smoke, the real smoke generates its own sensation, and this sensation generates the judgment based on conception that there is smoke on the hill. This judgment with the help of memory of the concomitance between smoke-in-general and fire-in-general generates the inferential judgment that "there is fire on the hill." The actual object of inferential judgment, is the fire-in-general, which is necessarily related to real, unique fires.

RELATION BETWEEN *PRATYAKṢA* AND *ANUMĀNA* IN THE CONTEXT OF THE THEORY OF *PRAMĀṆA-VYAVASTHĀ*

Diṅnāga in the beginning of the *Pramāṇa-Samuccaya* draws a radical and essential distinction between pure sensation and a conception. The latter, in his system, includes judgment and inference. This distinction is grounded in a more basic distinction between two types of objects of cognition, namely, *svalakṣaṇa*, the unique particular, and *sāmānyalakṣaṇa* the universal. The former is a particular individual that can never be generalized or conceptualized, and the latter is the universal that is conceptually constructed by the mind through generalizing from many individuals without any regard to the peculiarity or individuality. The former is real, while the latter lacks reality. As one is incompatible with the other, there cannot be anything that possesses both *svalakṣaṇa* and *sāmānyalakṣaṇa* at the same time. Corresponding to this essential distinction between the two kinds of *premeyas* is a radical distinction between the two *pramāṇas*. Diṅnāga was uncompromising in arguing for the distinct spheres of operation of these two *pramāṇas,* and his theory is known as *pramāṇa vyavasthāvāda*.

It is in contrast with the theory of *pramāṇa sampalava* advocated by the thinkers of the Nyāya and Mīmāmsā schools. According to them, the same object can be cognized in many ways by different *pramāṇas*. There are no strict, distinct limits for each of the *pramāṇas*. The basic contention underlying the theory of *pramāṇa vyavasthā* is denied by the Naiyāyikas, who admit neither that there are only two quite distinct types of *pramāṇa* nor that there are only two quite distinct types of *prameya*. According to them, *pramāṇas* are four in number, namely, *pratyakṣa, anumāna, śabda,* and *upamāna,* and the objects can also be of three kinds, the particular, the universal, and the individual thing as possessor of universal.

The main Buddhist argument against the theory of *pramāṇa samplava* is that if *pratyakṣa* and *anumāna* are admitted to have one and the same thing for their object, the cognition produced should also be of the same nature; but that is simply absurd. The sensations of burning as apprehended in *pratyakṣa* and as known through words in *anumāna* are quite different. The Buddhist thinkers maintain that the cooperation or mixture (*samplava ekasmin viṣaye sarveṣām pramāṇānām pravṛttiḥ*) of the different sources of our knowledge in the cognition of one and the same object is impossible, since each one has its own special field of operation.

Thus, Diṅnāga and his followers draw a clear-cut difference between a perceptual knowledge and a conceptual knowledge. Even the perceptual judgment of the form "This is blue" is treated as conceptual and therefore inferential. In the strict sense, therefore, all perceptual judgments are actually inferential.

Diṅnāga insists that an object of knowledge must be either a *svalakṣaṇa* or *sāmānyalakṣaṇa,* for there is no third kind. If it is a *svalakṣaṇa,* it would be an object of perception, and if it is *sāmānyalakṣaṇa,* it would be an object of *anumāna.* Just as *pratyakṣa* cannot cognize a *sāmānyalakṣaṇa,* so also *anumāna* cannot cognize a *svalakṣaṇa*.

Pratyakṣa is capable of cognizing an object only because it is produced through the efficiency (*sāmarthya*) of an object. Such a thing alone can be an object of *pratyakṣa,* which is able to attribute its definite form (*niyata pratibhāsa*) to the cognition. It can be done only by unique particular, which alone is cognized in *pratyakṣa*. On the other hand, the unique particular can never be cognized in *anumāna,* which results from the ascertainment of invariable relation between two entities. Such a relation cannot be established between two unique particulars, and therefore the latter cannot be the object of *anumāna*. Moreover, *pratyakṣa,* which is in the form of stimulus coming from an object, can be produced only by such an object that is present. A universal cannot produce such a result because it can neither cause a stimulus nor call forth its *pratibhāsa,* since it is altogether devoid of any kind of direct causal efficiency. According to Buddhists, *pratyakṣa* can apprehend only such an object that is objectively real. This alone is pure reality in the ultimate sense, the thing-in-itself, because the essence of reality, according to Buddhists, is just the property of being causally efficient.

That a unique particular of this kind should also be cognized by the conceiving faculty of our mind or by *anumāna* is impossible. The sphere of unique particulars is not the sphere of *anumāna*. The latter cognizes relations (*grahita pratibanda hetukam*). In a unique particular no relations can be found. Relations are always conceived between two (or more) universals. The universals are not realities; they are logical constructions produced by our constructing mind, and, therefore, their objective existence in the external world belongs only to the domain of our inferential knowledge, which is either a dialectical superstructure upon reality or an objectivized image. Their source, indeed, is not positive, since they always contain a corelative negation (*anya-vyāvṛtti* or *anyāpoha*).

A universal is, therefore, internal (*abāhyam*) mental construction but related to external reality, since in our behavior we don't notice the differences; that is, we don't think that "a cow" (conceived cow) is not an external object. It is deemed to be external (*bāhyatvena avasīyamānam*) and thus gives reality to inferential knowledge. Being thus indirectly related to external reality, it has efficiency. Thereby it becomes a consistent experience and hence a *pramāṇa*. There is no other *pramāṇa* except these two. Whatsoever has a claim to be a *pramāṇa* is included in these two, or, if it is not included in them, it is not a *pramāṇa*. Since there is neither any other source of valid knowledge nor any other object to be cognized, one has got to admit the theory of *pramāṇa vyavasthā*.

ANALYSIS OF THE NATURE OF INFERENTIAL JUDGMENT

Buddhist thinkers sometimes draw a distinction between a perceptual judgment and an inferential judgment. All cognitions naturally lead to judgments, that is, to interpretation of sensations in concepts. Since a cognition can be distinguished as direct and indirect, the judgment can also be divided into a direct one and an indirect one. The direct one is a synthesis between a sensation and a conception, and the indirect one is a synthesis between a sensation and two concepts. The direct one has two terms; the indirect one has three terms. The direct one is of the form, "This is blue" or "This is smoke," and the indirect one is of the form, "There is fire because there is smoke."

There is a basic difference between a perceptual judgment and an inferential one. The perceptual judgment is a direct cognition in the sense that its object is directly known. "This is smoke" is a perceptual judgment because smoke is directly perceived. The inferential judgment is indirect insofar as its object is not directly perceived. It is a cognition of a nonperceived object through a perceived object that is its mark. The unperceived object has a mark, and this mark, in its turn, is the mark, of a *svalakṣaṇa*. Thus, fire is the unperceived object whose mark is smoke, and this smoke is, in turn, a mark of some *svalakṣaṇa*, the real smoke. The cognition of a *svalakṣaṇa* as possessing the mark of its mark is *anumāna*. In a perceptual judgment we cognize the object "X" through its mark, which is the concept "B." In an inferential judgment we cognize the object through the mark of its mark, that is, through "A," which is a mark of "B." "A" and "B" are related as reason and consequent. When the reason is cognized, the cognition of the consequent necessarily follows. No doubt "A" and "B" have a common substratum "Y" (*pakṣa*); its presence will be necessarily understood without any formal expression. In that case the two interrelated elements "A" and "B" will represent the whole inferential judgment. This judgment will then apparently consist of two concepts only but related as reason and consequent, one being the necessary ground for inferring the other.

Strictly speaking, there cannot be anything like perceptual judgment because the theory of twofold *pramāṇas* is based on a dichotomous distinction between the perceptual, which is nonjudgmental, and the conceptual, which is judgmental. In perceptual cognition there is no involvement of judgment, and hence there cannot be anything like perceptual judgment. However, in a loose sense we can talk of perceptual judgment insofar as every perceptual cognition is capable of leading to a judgment. But then two questions arise, namely:

1. Is this perceptual judgment the same as, or different from, *anumāna*?
2. If it is different from *anumāna*, can it be a *pramāṇa*?

Arcata,[23] commenting upon Dharmakīrti, writes that Buddhist logicians, in fact, don't consider perceptual judgment to be a case of *anumāna* and don't regard it to be a *pramāṇa*. The perceptual judgment is not a *pramāṇa* because it is a cognition of what is already cognized (*grahītagrāhi*). Every perceptual judgment immediately follows in the wake of perception, and, therefore, it apprehends that very object that is apprehended in perception. *Anumāna*, on the other hand, cognizes an object hitherto uncognized (*agrahītagrāhi*).

There is another reason that perceptual judgment as distinct from inferential judgment is not a *pramāṇa*. Though the perceptual judgment has the same object that is already sensed (perceived) in *pratyakṣa*, while determining it, perceptual judgment distorts it, that is, finds it as something general though, in fact, it is something unique. Every judgment consists in superimposition of character(s) on a thing that it doesn't, in fact, possess. The inferential cognition, on the other hand, is conceived only with that object that is a concept. Since every concept is a mental construction, there is no question of its being distorted by mind.

It then becomes a judgment of concomitance or a judgment based on concomitance. Inference or the object cognized in the inference, says Dharmottara, is a complex idea of the substratum together with its inferred property, or, when the invariable concomitance between the reason and the inferred property is considered abstractly, then the inferred fact appears as this property taken in its concomitance with the reason.[24] In the first case, we have just an inferential judgment, and in the second case a judgment of concomitance. The form of the former will be, "There is fire there because there is smoke," and that of the latter, "Wherever there is smoke, there is fire." The term "there" is expressive of the substratum (*pakṣa*) where the two attributes, namely, smoke and fire, are necessarily interrelated such that the latter is deducible from the former. Thus, in every inferential cognition there are three terms involved. However, not every cognition containing three terms of which one is the substratum of the other two will be an inference. Only such a combination of them, where two attributes are necessarily interrelated, the one deducible from the other, represents an inference.

DEFINITION OF *ANUMĀNA*

Before attempting to give a definition of *anumāna*, Diṅnāga, Dharmakīrti, and their followers begin by drawing a distinction between two kinds of *anumāna*, namely, *svārtha*, which is a mere mental process, and *parārtha*, which is a verbalized form of that mental process. Since the first one is nonverbalized, and the second one is necessarily verbalized, the two cannot be comprehended under one single definition, and, therefore, before attempting to a give definition of *anumāna*, it has to be specified whether it is a definition of *svārthānumāna* or that of *parārthānumāna*. This point is clearly stated by Dharmottara in his commentary on the *Nyāya Bindu*. He writes,[25] "*Parārthānumānam śabdātmakam svārthānumānam tu jñānātmakam. Tayoratyantabhedānnaikam lakṣaṇamasti. Tatastayoḥ pratiniyatam lakṣaṇamākhyātum prakaraṇabhedaḥ kathyate.*"

Though two separate definitions for each type are given, we find that the differential property of *anumāna* remains the same in both cases. Different types of definition of *anumāna* are available in the Buddhist tradition. The earliest attempt to define *anumāna* seems to have been made by Vasubandhu, who in the *Vāda Vidhi* defines it as "*Nāntarīyakārtha darśanam tadvido anumānam.*" A similar definition is put forth by Diṅnāga. This definition lays stress upon the inseparable connection that unites the *hetu* with the *sādhya* and defines *anumāna* as a knowledge arrived at on the basis of that inseparable connection by a person who is acquainted with that connection. The term *nāntarīyaka* or *anantarīyaka* means necessary nonexistence of one object in the absence of another object. The Buddhists use another expression, namely, *avinābhāva,* which also means the same. The doctrine of *trairūpyaliṅga* is nothing but an explication of the concept of *nāntarīyaka*. It implies the presence of *hetu* in the *pakṣa*, its presence in the *sapakṣa,* and absence in the *asapakṣa* because in the absence of such a situation there cannot be inseparable connection between *hetu* and *sādhya* leading to inferential knowledge.

Keeping the concept of *trairūpyaliṅga* as the focal point, Diṅnāga[26] puts forth another definition that has been given prominence by Dharmakīrti and that finds greater acceptance in the tradition. In the *Nyāya Bindu*[27] Dharmakīrti expresses it as "*Trirūpāllingād yad anumeye jñānam tad svārthānumānam,*" that is, this definition is based on the actual process that originates inferential cognition. It is a functional definition on a par with a similar functional definition put forth by the Naiyāyikas, namely, "*Vyāptiviśiṣta pakṣadharmatājñānajanyamjñānam anumiti.*" Concerning the Buddhist definition of anumāna, which is on the basis of *trairūpyaliṅga,* Dharmottara[28] remarks that it is put forth keeping in mind the origin of *anumāna*. The inferential cognition arises out of the cognition of the threefold mark. Thus, the cognition of fire (which is not perceived) arises out of the cognition of smoke.

Stcherbatsky[29] refers to another definition given by Buddhists based on the nature of object apprehended in *anumāna*. *Anumāna* is the cognition of an object that is not revealed to the senses. All objects can be divided into present and absent. The present are cognized by perception and the absent by inference.

In Dharmottara[30] we also meet with the etymological definition of *anumāna*. He defines *anumāna* as "*liṅgagrahaṇa sambandhasmaraṇasya paścānmānamanumānam.*" Here *anumāna* is taken to be that cognition that is implied by the perception of the *liṅga* that characterizes the *pakṣa* and the remembering of the necessary concomitance between the *hetu* and the *sādhya*.

Definition of *Parārthānumāna*

The only fundamental difference between *svārthānumāna* and *parārthānumāna* is that the latter consists in linguistic expression of the former.[31] Since the expression aspect is the basic point of distinction in the definition of *parārthānumāna,* this aspect has been highlighted. Thus Diṅnāga defines it as "*Parārthānumānam tu svadṛṣṭārtha prakāśakam*"[32] that is, *parārthānumāna* sets forth an object that has been apprehended by oneself. Dharmakīrti also defines it as "*trirūpaliṅga ākhyānam parārthānumāna.*"[33] *Ākhyānam* is the same as "*prakāśanam,*" and every *ākhyāna* or *prakāśana* is through *vacana*. That is why Dharmottara writes, "*Vacanena hi trirūpam liṅgamākhyāyate.*"[34] Keeping this in mind, he describes *parārthānumāna as śabdātmaka* and *svārthānumāna* as *jñānātmaka*.[35]

To conclude, in the Buddhist tradition we have a variety of definitions of *anumāna* put forth on the basis of different considerations. Here we find some definitions based on etymology and some based on the actual process of *anumāna*. These definitions are substantially different from the ones given in the other schools. Whatever differences are there are due to their divergent ontological positions. All agree that in every inference there are two basic elements, namely, *pakṣadharmatva* and *vyāpti,* which must feature in any functional definition of *anumāna*. Similarly, if any definition is put forth that keep the object in view, then it has to take into account the *parokṣa* (concealed) nature of the object whose necessary mark alone is a perceived object. Likewise, in any definition of the etymological type the implicative nature of the perceptual cognition has to be brought to the fore. However, the basic feature of the Buddhist definition from the functional point of view is the concept of *trairūpyaliṅga,* which is insisted upon as a necessary prerequisite of every valid *anumāna*.

CONSTITUENTS OF *ANUMĀNA*

According to the Buddhist system of logic, like other systems of Indian logic, the process of *anumāna* involves three basic terms and their interrelations. This is quite evident from the analysis of the following definition of *anumāna* given by Dharmakīrti:

Trirupālliṅgād yadanumeye jñānam tad svārthānumānam[36]

These three terms are *pakṣa* (logical subject), *sādhya* (logical predicate), and *hetu* (reason) or *liṅga* (mark), which logically connects *pakṣa* and *sādhya*. An analysis of these constituents of *anumāna* and their interrelations follows.

Pakṣa

Pakṣa stands for the subject under consideration in the inferential reasoning. Every inferential reasoning pertains to some individual or class of individuals[37] about which we want to infer or establish something. It is technically known as *pakṣa*. Etymologically, *pakṣa* (*pacyate iti pakṣaḥ*) means that to which *hetu* and *sādhya* belong as its properties. In this sense it is also referred to as *dharmin*, the underlying substratum, to which *hetu* and *sādhya* are ascribed as *dharmas*. It is also named as *anumeya* because it is an object of inferential inquiry. It is not a mere reference to the bare *pakṣa* but to that *pakṣa* that is a *dharmin* and to which *hetu* and *sādhya* are the *dharmas*. That is why Dharmakīrti defines *pakṣa* or *anumeya* as *jijñāsita viśeṣo dharmī*.[38] Though at the level of objective reality (*paramārtha sat*) Buddhists don't entertain the distinction between *dharma* and *dharmī*, at the conceptual level, which underlies all our worldly behavior, such a distinction is very much necessary because no conceptualization can take place without bringing in distinctions in terms of *dravya, guṇa, karma,* and *jāti*.

With regard to the ontological status of *pakṣa* Buddhists fundamentally differ from Naiyāyikas. For Naiyāyikas, *pakṣa* and so on, stand for the objects that are objectively real. They don't grant any distinction between objectively real and conceptually real. But in the Buddhist system, there being a clear-cut distinction between the objectively real and the conceptually real, *anumāna* is said to pertain to the latter only. Thus, for example, in the *anumāna* "This mountain possesses fire because it possesses smoke," the expression "this mountain" is *pakṣa* insofar as it possesses smoke and fire as its *dharmas*. When we use the expression "this," it should not be understood as referring to some *svalakṣaṇa*. It refers only to the conceptualized experience of some *svalakṣaṇa*. Since *pakṣa* may stand for an individual or a class of individuals, a distinction can be drawn between two types of concept corresponding to a *pakṣa,* namely, a concept having universal denotation and a concept having individual or particular denotation. If the concept of "all men" is the *pakṣa* in an *anumāna* like "All human beings are mortal, and therefore they are living beings," then the term "all men" is the *pakṣa,* which has a universal denotation (*sakaladeśavṛttitva*). But in an *anumāna* like, "This hill possesses fire because it possesses smoke" the expression "the hill" is *pakṣa,* whose denotation is confined to an individual object (*ekadeśavṛttitva*). Thus, a *pakṣa* may have a generalized denotation or a particularized one.

From another point of view, we can draw a distinction between "time-bound" and "time-free" *pakṣa*. A *pakṣa* in *svabhāvānumāna* is time-free in the sense that the *dharmitā* (property possessiveness) of *pakṣa* in respect of *hetu* and *sādhya* is not restricted to any particular time. For example, when we say, "It is a flower because it is a rose," the properties of "roseness" and "flowerness" as they are ascribed to the object stand in a relation that is a matter of analytical entailment. The concept of "flower" is deduced from the concept of "rose" as a matter of analytical entailment, irrespective of any consideration of time. But the relationship of *tadutpatti* (causality) stands on a different footing. It is not a matter of analyticity to arrive at the concept of "fire" from the concept of "smoke." Whatsoever analysis we may give of the concept of smoke, it will not entail the concept of fire. It is because the establishment of this relationship is not a matter of linguistic stipulation but something that is grounded in our experience. It is not that the hill always has smoke and fire as its (*dharmas*) properties so that only at those moments when the hill possesses smoke, can it be inferred that the hill possesses fire. Thus, the relationship of smoke and fire vis-a-vis hill is time-bound, whereas the relationship of the object that is the referent of the word "it" vis-a-vis "rose and flower" is time-free.

The epistemic status of *pakṣa* in the Buddhist analysis is quite different from that of the Nyāya analysis. In the early Nyāya tradition *pakṣa* is understood as *sandigdha sādhyavān*, that is, that in which the presence of *sādhya* is suspected. Thus, *pakṣa* has the status of being doubtful. In the latter Nyāya tradition *pakṣa* may have any of the following three statuses:

1. Having an assured existence of *sādhya* and yet there being an inquisitiveness to prove this.
2. Having no assuredness about the existence of *sādhya* and there being no inquisitiveness to prove this.
3. Having no assuredness but there being some inquisitiveness to prove it.

The difference between the early Nyāya position and the Navya-Nyāya position is that whereas in the former the inferential inquiry begins without doubt, in the latter three different possibilities are accepted in which assuredness and inquisitiveness in their different combinations in terms of their positive and negative relations are viewed.

In Buddhist logic, however, instead of doubt (*sandeha*) being the starting point of inferential inquiry, inquisitiveness (*jijñāsā*) is put forth as the chief motive. This inquisitiveness leads to a desire to prove. It seems that the idea of inquisitiveness of Buddhists enabled the Navya-Nyāya logicians to put forth the idea of will to prove (*siṣādhayiṣā*). In the course of development in the theory of *anumāna* we find a logical transition from *sandeha* to *jijñāsā* and from *jijñāsā* to *siṣādhayiṣā*.

Role of *Pakṣa*

Pakṣa performs a role that is equally significant with the role performed by *hetu* or *liṅga*. It is the perceptual cognition of the object whose conceptualization is *pakṣa*, which provides the starting point of the inferential inquiry. Possession of *hetu* by *pakṣa*, technically known as *pakṣadharmatva*, is thus the necessary condition for an *anumāna* to take place. The significance of the role of *pakṣa* can best be understood when we talk of it as a *dharmī*. If there were no *pakṣa* at the back of which there is a perceptual cognition of some object, the entire process of inference would have been reduced to an abstract intellectual exercise having no relevance to the empirical realities. Therefore, the existence of *pakṣa* having some objective reality at its back provides the ground or basis for the inference of *sādhya*. If the *pakṣa* were such a concept that is barren or empty, having no reality to fall back upon, it would not provide an *āśraya* (basis) to *hetu* and *sādhya*, and it would then be a case of fallacious inference. Not only should the *pakṣa* not be a barren or empty concept, but it should also be such with which the concepts of *hetu* and *sādhya* should not be incompatible. Thus, for example, lake cannot be a *pakṣa* in that case where smoke is the *hetu*, and fire is *sādhya*. Though the Buddhists don't insist on describing the *pakṣa* as being the common substratum (*ekādhikaraṇya* or *samānādhikaraṇya*) of *hetu* and *sādhya*, this idea of being the substratum and having *pakṣa* and *sādhya* as its *dharmas* is not absent in the Buddhist tradition.

Hetu

The other term involved in the process of *anumāna* is *hetu* or *liṅga*. Etymologically, *hetu* means that which takes to an object that is not directly given (*Hinotīti gamayati parokṣārthamiti hetuḥ*). Similarly, *liṅga* means that which leads to the object not directly given (*Parokṣārtho liṅgayate gamyate'neneti liṅgam*). It is also known as *sādhana* because it is a means for the knowledge of *sādhya*" (*sādhyate aneneti sādhanam*).

Hetu is the pivotal element in the process of *anumāna*. It is a necessary mark that leads to the inference of the marked object. In order to do so, a *hetu* has to satisfy three formal characteristics; only then it is known as *sadhetu*, and it acts as a sufficient reason for the inference of its marked object.

Hetu is simultaneously related to both *pakṣa* and *sādhya*. It is a *dharma* of the *pakṣa* and a *liṅga* (mark) or *vyāpya* (pervaded object) of the *sādhya*. In this respect it corresponds to the middle term of Aristotelian logic, the role of which is to connect the minor and the major terms. Here also the *dharmatā* of *sādhya* in respect of *pakṣa* is established on the basis of *hetu's*, being a *dharma* of *pakṣa*.

Diṅnāga, as quoted in the *Nyāya Vārtika Ṭīkā*,[39] defines *hetu* as that property of *pakṣa* that is pervaded by the *sādhya*, which also is a property of the *pakṣa* (*sādhyadharma sāmānyena vyāpto hetuḥ*). In this definition three things are pointed out:

1. *Hetu* is a *pakṣadharma*; that is, *hetu* is a property of *pakṣa* and must be present in *pakṣa*.
2. *Hetu* is the *grāhyadharma*; that is, the *dharmatā* of *hetu* is directly apprehended.
3. *Hetu* is one of the *dharmas* of the *pakṣa* (*pakṣasya aṁśena dharma*) because the *pakṣa* also has *sādhya* as another *dharma*.

On the basis of these three qualities, the three *rūpas* of *hetu* have been formulated, which are discussed subsequently.

Types of *Hetu*

According to Buddhist logicians, there are three types of *hetu*, namely, *svabhāva* (identity), *kārya* (effect), and *anupalabdhi* (noncognition). *Svabhāva* and *kārya* are affirmative, whereas *anupalabdhi* is a negative kind of *hetu*. Now, let us turn to their analysis one by one.

Svabhāva *Hetu* (Reason as Identity)

Svabhāva hetu is defined as the one whose mere existence is sufficient for the establishment of *sādhya*.[40] For example, in the judgment "It is a flower because it is a rose," the *hetu*, namely, rose, is sufficient for proving the *sādhya*, namely, flower. Here the terms "rose" and "flower" have one and the same object for their reference, though they may have different meanings. This sameness of reference is known as *tādātmya* (identity) and is responsible for the existential tie (*svabhāva pratibandha*) between rose and flower. The term "flower" contains the extension of the term "rose," and the term "rose" is a subaltern (*vyāpya*), of which the term "flower" is a superaltern (*vyāpaka*). Both are then said to be existentially identical and become subject and predicate of an analytical judgment.

Kārya Hetu (Reason as Effect)

The second type of *hetu* is *kārya hetu* or *kārya liṅga,* which is in the form of an effect. It necessarily presupposes its cause. Thus, *kārya* as *liṅga* necessarily leads to its *kāraṇa,* which is the *liṅgin.*[41] The relation between seed and sprout, fire and smoke, and so on is a relation of causality. This relation is given to us in our experience. We always find that whenever there is smoke, there is fire, and whenever there is no fire, there is no smoke. The causal relation is a relation of succession in contrast to the relation of identity, which consists in simultaneity or coexistence.

The apprehension of necessary connection between a cause and an effect is based on perceptual experience, but the relation as such is a matter of mental construction. In the Nyāya tradition it is accepted that the process of *anumāna* may proceed from cause to effect and effect to cause, both ways. That is why they draw a distinction between *pūrvavat anumāna* and *śeṣavat anumāna*, the former based on the *kārya hetu* and the latter on the *kārana hetu*. The Buddhists, however, regard the *kārya hetu* alone as *sad-hetu* and not the *kāraṇa hetu* because wherever there is an effect, there must be a cause, but it is not necessary that wherever there is a cause, there must be an effect.

Anupalabdhi Hetu (Reason as Noncognition)

The *svabhāva hetu* and *kārya hetu* are positive, as stated earlier, insofar as they help in proving the existence of a thing. The third kind of *hetu*, known as *anupalabdhi hetu*, is negative in nature. It helps in proving the nonexistence of a thing. *Anupalabdhi* has been defined as the noncognition of such an object that otherwise fulfills the conditions of cognizability; for example, a jar is an object that fulfills the conditions of cognizability. If in a particular place there is noncognition of a jar, this enables us to infer its nonexistence. So, here noncognition of the jar is the *liṅga,* and the nonexistence of the jar is the *liṅgin*.

The noncognition (of a thing) is to be regarded as the *liṅga* for the nonexistence (of that thing) as a *liṅgin*, on the ground that if the thing were present, it would have necessarily been perceived when all other conditions of perceptibility are fulfilled. Since in spite of the conditions of the perceptibility being present, if the thing is not perceived, we can legitimately infer its non existence.[42] For example:

Thesis: On some particular place there is no jar.

Reason: Because it is not perceived, although the conditions of perception are fulfilled.

A "particular place" is a place before the eyes of the cognizer. But not every place is a "particular place" that is present before the cognizer. Now, it can be questioned, How is it possible for a jar to be perceptible in a place where it is absent? It is said to be perceptible, although it is absent, because its perceptibility is imagined. We imagine this object in the following way: "If it were present on this spot, it certainly would have been perceived." In this case the object, although absent, is *ex-hypothesi (samāropya)* visible. It is the object whose absence is cognized, even though all the causes for its perception are present. We can judge that the causes for the perceptibility of the object are all present because we perceive other objects in the same act of cognition but not that particular object. Indeed, when two such objects are before us, we cannot confine our perception to one of them since there is no difference between them as regards possibility of perception (*pratyakṣa yogyatā*). Therefore, if we actually perceive only one of them, we naturally imagine that if the other were present, we should likewise perceive it because the totality of necessary condition is fulfilled. Thus, something fancied as perceptible is imputed. The noncognition of such an object is called negation of hypothetical perceptibility.

Basically, there is only one kind of *anupalabdhi*, known as *svabhāvānupalabdhi*, but in the *Pramāṇa Vārtika*[43] it has been classified under the following four kinds: (1) *Viruddhopalabdhi*, (2) *Viruddhakāryopalabdhi*, (3) *Kāraṇānuplabdhi*, and (4) *Svabhavānupalabdhi*. In the *Nyaya Bindu* seven more kinds are added to them, thus making them eleven in number. These seven are as follows: (1) *Svabhāvaviruddhopalabdhi*, (2) *Kāryānupalabdhi*, (3) *Viruddhavyāptopalabdhi*, (4) *Vyāpakaviruddhopalabdhi*, (5) *Kāraṇaviruddhopalabdhi*, (6) *Kāryaviruddhopalabdhi*, and (7) *Kāraṇaviruddhakāryopalabdhi*.[44] Mokṣākaragupta has added five more to these, making them sixteen in number. They are as follows: (1) *Vyāpakaviruddhakāryopalabdhi*, (2) *Svabhāvaviruddhavyāptopalabdhi*, (3) *Kāryaviruddhavyāptopalabdhi*, (4) *Kāraṇaviruddhavyāptopalabdhi*, and (5) *Vyāpakaviruddhavyāptopalabdhi*.[45]

Sādhya

The third element involved in the inferential process is *sādhya* or *liṅgin*. It is the property (*dharma*) that is to be inferred in a *pakṣa*. It is that property of the *pakṣa* that is cognized through *anumāna* on the basis of the perceptual cognition of the other property, earlier referred to as *liṅga*. Though *sādhya* may be expressed as a substratum, for example, fire, and it is so in the Nyāya analysis, in the Buddhist analysis with respect to *pakṣa*, it is a property, say, the "fieriness" of a given place. In *anumāna* it is the *sādhya*, the property belonging to *pakṣa*, which is inferred. The *sādhya* does not have a status independent of *pakṣa*. So in the Buddhist tradition it is not the *sādhya* that is the *anumeya*, nor is the *pakṣa* by itself *anumeya*, but the *anumeya* is that *sādhya* that is a *dharma* of *pakṣa*.

Anumeya (Object of Inferential Inquiry)

In the Nyāya tradition *sādhya* is given an independent status, and that accounts for its being the object of inferential inquiry. So in the logical process, it is more significant than *pakṣa*. Only in epistemic terms it has a status lower than the status of *pakṣa* insofar as its exisntece is either doubted or is intended to be established. But in the Buddhist tradition the importance of *sādhya* is, so to say, passed on to *pakṣa*. Even then, the role of *sādhya* cannot be minimized because it is the cognition of *sādhya* being the property of *pakṣa*, which is the concluding part of inferential inquiry. So if it is asked what is cognized in *anumāna*, the answer will not be that the *liṅga* is cognized because with its cognition the inferential process starts. Nor can it be said that *pakṣa* is the object of cognition because the *pakṣa* is to be cognized either with the *liṅga* or with the *liṅgin* and never without them, and its cognition with *liṅga* is the starting point. So, the real object of inferential inquiry is the *sādhya* as it is possessed by the *pakṣa*, which is technically known as *anumeya*.

A proposition that is unproved and is desired to be proved makes inference possible. But what exactly is to be inferred or proved? To make the point clear, let us suppose that the proposition "The hill has fire on it" is to be proved; but the hill is already known through perception, and hence the question naturally arises as to what exactly is here sought to be inferred. It is not quite impossible to find persons who would declare the hill as such to be the *anumeya*. But common people naturally think that, the hill being already perceived, what remains to be inferred or proved is just the fire. This is the second alternative. We get two other alternatives as we put major emphasis on either the subject (S, hill) or predicate (P, fire), and again we get a third one if we put equal emphasis on both subject and predicate, that is, hill qualified by fire or, in other words, fiery hill. Those who put major emphasis on the predicate (fire) feel that the *anumeya* is predicate qualified by subject, that is, fire qualified by hill or hilly fire. Those who put equal emphasis on both subject and predicate feel that the *anumeya* is subject plus predicate. Thus, we get various answers to the question as to what exactly we infer or what precisely is the *anumeya*.

Pakṣadharmatā

Pakṣadharmatā constitutes one of the two necessary grounds for the process of *anumāna*, the other being *vyāpti*, which we discuss subsequently. *Pakṣadharmatā* stands for the relation between *pakṣa* and *hetu*. It consists in the judgmentalization of the perceptual cognition of *hetu* located in *pakṣa*. It is a relational cognition in which *hetu* is cognized as being a property (*dharma*) of *pakṣa*. *Pakṣa* is said to possess two different properties, which are *hetu* and *sādhya*. The fact of *pakṣa* being the *sādhyadharmī*, that is, possessing the *sādhya* as its property, is inferred on the ground of the *pakṣa* being *hetudharmī*, that is, possessing the *hetu* as its property. Since *hetudharmatā* of *pakṣa* is directly cognized (i.e., not inferred), and it stimulates the process of *anumāna*, it has been taken to ba more significant property than that of the *sādhya*. Without the cognition of *pakṣa* possessing *hetu* as its property, the process of *anumāna* cannot start or be valid. This relation of *hetu* and *sādhya*, therefore, is given special consideration. To take the classical example of the *anumāna* of fire on a hill on the basis of the perceptual cognition of smoke there, the cognition of smoky hill is characterized as *pakṣadharmatā*. Without the cognition of smoky hill, it is not possible to infer the fiery hill. Mere knowledge of the *vyāpti* between smoke and fire cannot generate the knowledge of the fire on the hill unless the smoke is also cognized on the hill. The relation between hill, which is *pakṣa,* and smoke, which is *hetu,* is possible only when the two are cognized to be so related. The *sādhya,* which is known in *vyāpti,* is a universal, but the *sādhya,* known through the *pakṣadharmatā* of *hetu,* is a particular one. In other words, the *vyāpti* relation is always between two universals, and therefore at the back of the two relata, there are no individuals to fall back upon, but that is not the case with *pakṣadharmatā*. Here, both types of *dharmatā* of *pakṣa,* whether that of *hetu* or *sādhya,* are established as having an immediate reference to some individual facts. Thus, for example, the *vyāpti sambandha* between smoke and fire is between two universals, but the *pakṣadharmatā sambandha* is grounded in the conceptual cognition of *hetu* and *pakṣa,* which also have some underlying *svalakṣ aṇas* (*svalakṣaṇa pṛṣṭha bhāvi*). The relation of *pakṣadharmatā* is conditional and contingent. In this respect it differs from the *vyāpti* relation, which is necessary and unconditional. The conditionality and contingency of the *pakṣadharmatā* are because of the fact that the *pakṣa* does not necessarily possess *hetu* as its *dharma,* as it depends on the presence of certain conditions. Similarly, the *hetu* also is not exclusively present in *pakṣa*. It can be present in any other thing where conditions conducive to its presence are available; for example, it is not necessary that the hill should always be smoky or that the smoke must be present only on the hill.

The relation of *pakṣadharmatā* is the relation between a substantive and an adjective-*dharmī-dharma sambandha. Pakṣa* is always a substantive, and *hetu* an adjective. The order of the relata can never be reversed, and if it is reversed, then it will be an altogether different thought process. The idea of smoky hill necessarily implies that smoke is the *dharma* and hill is the *dharmī*. If the position of the relata is reversed, then it will be a case of "smoke on the hill," and in this case hill becomes the *dharma,* and smoke becomes the *dharmī*. The concept of "smoky hill" is altogether different from the concept of the "smoke on the hill."

The *hetu* that is a *dharma* of *pakṣa* is not any object that may be taken to characterize that *pakṣa*. It should be rather such an object that is essentially in the form of a *liṅga* being necessarily concomitant with another object that is its *liṅgin*. The implying power of *hetu* is by virtue of its being a necessary associate of *sādhya,* and, therefore, only such a *hetu* is a *dharma* of *pakṣa*. Thus, in the case of smoke it is in enabling us to infer fire that it is a *hetu,* not as smoke-qua-smoke.

Vyāpti or Avinābhāva

The concept of *vyāpti* is central to every theory of *anumāna*. *Vyāpti* stands for a relation of necessary concomitance, positive or negative, between two classes of facts such that one inevitably leads to the other. The entire process of *anumāna,* as has been said, is based on such a relation between the *liṅga* (one that leads) and the *liṅgin* (one that is led), which can be understood in terms of necessary dependence (*avinābhāva niyama*). The significance of *vyāpti* is indicated by the facts that there can be no *anumāna* in its absence and that every definition of *anumāna* directly or indirectly has to bring it in.

Though we do not have any information about the analysis of *vyāpti* by pre-Diṅnāga thinkers, Diṅnāga referred to it in his statement expressing the *pakṣadharmatā* and *vyāpti* as the two grounds of *anumāna*. In the *Pramāṇa Samuccaya*[46] he writes, "*Grāhya dharmastadanśena vyāpto hetuḥ.*" In Dharmakīrti we find its detailed analysis. Etymologicaly, the word "*avinābhāva*" means "*a + vinā + bhāva,*" that is "in the absence of *sādhya* necessary absence of *hetu.*" Here, the term "*vinā*" stands for absence of *sādhya*, the term "*bhāva,*" stands for presence of *hetu,* and the term "*a*" stands for the negation (of the presence of *hetu*). Thus, it implies absence of *hetu* in the absence of *sādhya*. Apparently, it seems to have a negative meaning, but it has a positive implication also. *Avinābhāva* is a relation between two such things where one thing cannot be present without the other. Dharmakīrti also uses the expression "*svabhāva pratibandha,*" which means "existential tie." "Existential tie" means the existence of one thing tied to the other, which means a dependent existence. This may be in the form of a causal relation or an analytical relation. For example, the dependence of effect is known to us. Similarly, an analytically deduced fact by its very essence depends on the fact from which it is deduced. Thus, there is a *svabhāva pratibandha* (existential tie) between cause and effect and between the deduced object and that from which there is deduction. The example of the former type is the relation between smoke and fire, and of the latter, between rose and flower. We can deduce one fact from another only if the two facts are simultaneous, and we can have causal connection only between two such facts that are in immediate succession.

It may be asked, Why is it that we can infer one fact from another only if there is existential dependence? The answer given by Buddhist logicians is that this is so because if a fact is not dependent on the other, it cannot be invariably and necessarily concomitant with the latter.[47] There will be no invariability.[48] Thus, the possibility of deducing one fact from another depends on an invariable and necessary connection that precludes the existence of one without the existence of other. Therefore, if two facts are existentially connected, we can assert that one of them cannot exist independently of the other, and therefore from the presence of the one follows the presence of the other.

The *svabhāva pratibandha* (existential tie) is always that of the *liṅga* with *liṅgin*. Explaining this, Dharmottara writes that *liṅga* is always dependent on the *liṅgin,* whereas the *liṅgin* is independent of *liṅga*. That is why *liṅga* is said to be "tied-to," and the *liṅgin* is said to be "not-tied." That which is tied is the *gamaka,* and the one to which it is tied is said to be its *gamya*. That which is not existentially tied to anything particular will not have the relation of invariable concomitance with the thing, but that *liṅga* that is not untied has the relation of invariable concomitance with its *liṅgin* (which itself is not tied) because the former does not deviate in its occurrence with the latter. This invariable concomitance is known as *avinābhāva*. On the basis of this invariability the *gamya-gamaka-bhāva* is established. In the absence of invariable concomitance there can be no *gamya-gamka-bhāva* because the *liṅga* by itself cannot reveal the *liṅgin,* unlike a lamp, which can illuminate its objects. The determination of *liṅgin* is on the basis of invariable concomitance. Thus, on the basis of *svabhāva pratibandha* there is *avinābhāva,* and from *avinābhāva* follows *gamya-gamaka-bhāva*. This is meant when it is said that on the basis of *svabhāva pratibandha* alone one object leads to another.[49]

Hetu is known as *vyāpya,* and *sādhya* is known as *vyāpaka*. According to Dharmakīrti, *vyāpti* being the *dharma* of both *vyāpaka* and *vyāpya,* it can be expressed in two ways: the presence of *vyāpaka* is necessary for the presence of *vyāpya,* and *vyāpya* can exist only when *vyāpaka* exists. These two conditions are, respectively, known as *anvaya* and *vyatireka*.[50] Arcaṭa has explained this as follows: An object that has *vyāpya* as its property will also necessarily have *vyāpaka* as its property. This is technically known as *vyāpakadharmatā*. Here the *vyāpyatā* of the *vyāpya* is known through the *vyāpaka*. Similarly, when an object has *vyāpya* necessarily by virtue of its possessing *vyāpaka,* then it is known as *vyāpyadharmatā*. By violating this regulation there cannot be the establishment of *liṅgā-liṅgi-saṃbandha*.[51] Thus, in short, the *avinābhāva* stands for the regulation that the *liṅga* can be present only in the presence of *liṅgin* and that the absence of *liṅgin* necessarily implies the absence of *liṅga*.

According to Buddhist logicians, there are only two types of *vyāpti*, namely, *tādātmya* and *tadutpatti*. It can, therefore, be asked why there are only two types. The answer is that the necessary connection of one with another means that the existence of the former is necessarily dependent on the existence of the latter. Now one thing's existence could necessarily depend on the existence of the other only under two conditions: (1) if the latter causes the former or (2) if the latter is a part of the former. No other condition makes the existence of one thing necessarily dependent on the existence of another. Hence, Dharmakīrti asserts that the relation of causality and that of essential identity are the only two necessary relations.[52]

Vyāpti or *avinābhāva* is a relation of necessary concomitance that is universal and invariable, but the problem is how we apprehend the *vyāpti* relation between any two given phenomena. For this different schools of logic in India have given different answers. According to Buddhists, the relation of *vyāpti* is not directly apprehended in perception, as all relations are conceptual construction. According to Dharmakīrti, the relation of *vyāpti* is based on our knowledge of either causality (*tadutpatti*) or identity (*tādātmya*), as an effect cannot be conceived to be independent of a cause, and hence effect is a proof of the cause, and as regards the two things whose nature is fundamentally identical, there can be no separation between the two,[53] as that would be tantamount to forfeiture of their own essential character, which is inconceivable.

It can be objected that Buddhists have reduced all *vyāpti* relations to causal or identity relations. But it can be pointed out that certain relations of uniformity cannot be reduced to relations of causality or identity. Thus, for instance, the impending rainfall is inferred from the movement of ants, but the concomitance in such a case cannot be traced to causality or identity.

Buddhists may reply that mere concomitance in presence and absence cannot constitute sufficient evidence of its inevitability unless the contrary possibility is debarred by the method of *tarka*. The method of *tarka* can be employed only if the relation is understood to be one of causality or identity because no other relation can be conceived to be invariable and uniform. It should be observed that there must be a causal relation, though indirect, between two sets of connected phenomena. They must be coeffects of the same set of causes and conditions; otherwise, the invariability of the relation cannot be explained. Such a relation of invariability is to be constructed or established on the basis of observation. However, it must be noted that the mere observation of positive and negative instances does not give rise to the knowledge of *vyāpti,* which has to be constructed by the conceiving mind. Of course, the mind has the capacity of doing so, and observation only provides a stimulus for that.

In granting the constructing capacity of mind to give us the knowledge of *vyāpti*, Dharmakīrti assumes two things: every event has a cause, and the same cause always uniformly produces the same effect. In other words, there is general regularity or uniformity in the universe. Whatever is a cause of particular type of a thing remains forever a cause of that type of a thing. To think otherwise, namely, that one type of cause does not always produce only one type of effect, is to go against the logic based on experience. "Y" cannot be treated as an effect of "X," even in a single case, if *all* "Y" is not an effect of *some* "X." It is so because we call "X" the cause of "Y" only if "X" invariably produces "Y." Moreover, to say that at times "Y" is produced by "X" and at times it is produced by something other than "X," that is "non-X," would mean that "Y" possesses two contradictory natures. Again, this would suggest that the nature of a thing does not depend on its cause, and to grant this suggestion would mean that the thing comes into existence without any cause. This, in turn, would make it eternal and consequently devoid of efficiency, which is the criterion of reality. So, one type of effect can never be regarded as being produced at times by this type of cause and at times by that type of cause. When we feel that there are instances of one type of effect at times being produced by this type of cause and at times by that type of cause, our feeling is not justified. We commit a fallacy of nonobservation. The two effects produced by two different types of causes are not merely of one type. We are deceived by their outward similarity. A close examination may reveal that they, in fact, belong to two different types.[54]

Thus, according to Buddhist logicians, what we directly perceive is nothing but *svalakṣaṇa*. Perception is a series of sensations without any connection or order in them. Only the *buddhi* constructs a system or order out of them, through the instrumentality of the two necessary relations of *tādātmya* and *tadutpatti*. Perceptual cognitions are discrete in nature, and the *vikalpa buddhi* superimposes order and uniformity on them. The necessity underlying the relation of *tādātmya* and *tadutpatti* is superimposed upon the perceptual cognition that provides an occasion for the functioning of the *vikalpa buddhi*.

Sapakṣa

Another significant concept that figures in the analysis of inferential process is *sapakṣa*. *Sapakṣa* means that which is similar to *pakṣa*. Dharmakīrti defines it as:

> *Sādhyadharmasāmānyena samāno'rthaḥ sapakṣaḥ.*[55]

It is similar to *pakṣa* by virtue of the common possession of the *śādhya*, which is the inferred property and, therefore, metaphorically called its copartner. In other words, all those objects that possess the property to be inferred are to be known as *sapakṣa* in as much as they are similar to *pakṣa* in that respect. The word "*sa*" is a substitute for *samāna*.[56] It should, however, be borne in mind that this similarity is not absolute because the possession of *sādhya* in *sapakṣa* is a matter of certainty, whereas the possession of a similar property by the *pakṣa* needs to be proved. That is why some of the thinkers belonging to the early Nyāya school define *pakṣa* as *saṃdigdhasādhyavān pakṣaḥ* (i.e., *pakṣa* is that object where the presence of *sādhya* is suspected) and *sapakṣa* as *niścitasādhyavāna sapakṣaḥ* (i.e., that object where the presence of *sādhya* has been well known). However, the two are similar by virtue of the fact that they possess *sādhya* as their property. This property in Buddhist thought is always a *sāmānyalakṣaṇa* because no *svalakṣaṇa* can ever be a property.[57] Thus, in the example of fire being inferred on a hill on the basis of smoke, fire is the property that is inferred in relation to the hill. Therefore, hill becomes a *pakṣa*, and all those instances, like kitchen, where fire is known to be a property, constitute *sapakṣa*, because they are similar to *pakṣa* in commonly possessing the property of fire.

The *pakṣa* and *sapakṣa*, even though similar in their possession of the common property, which is *sādhya*, are dissimilar in several other respects. *Pakṣa* refers to an object that is presently given, whereas *sapakṣa* refers to such object(s) that have been known in the past. Therefore, a *sapakṣa* is always to be remembered and not presently perceived. Second, in the case of *pakṣa* it is always numerically one, but *sapakṣa* may be more than one. However, Buddhists do not insist on numerical multiplicity of *sapakṣas*. In the *Hetu Cakra Ḍamaru* Diṅnāga maintains that there should be "at least one" instance of *sapakṣa* where *hetu* is present along with *sādhya*.

Asapakṣa or Vipakṣa

That which is not similar to *pakṣa* is known as *asapakṣa* or *vipakṣa*. That is why Dharmakīrti defines it as :

Na sapakṣo'sapakṣaḥ[58]

In fact, it is dissimilar to both *pakṣa* and *sapakṣa*. Though the basic contention here is to point out its dissimilarity with *sapakṣa*, its dissimilarity from *pakṣa* also becomes evident. *Asapakṣa* is dissimilar from *sapakṣa* in that it is never a possessor of the property commonly possessed by *pakṣa* and *sapakṣa*.

Asapakṣa can be of the following three types:

1. Different from *sapakṣa (anya);*
2. Contrary to *sapakṣa (viruddha);*
3. Absence of *sapakṣa (abhāva)*.[59]

Of the three, *abhāva* is the most fundamental, and *anya* and *viruddha* cannot be conceived so long as there is no *abhāva*. The conceptions of *anyatva* and *viruddhatva* include the conception of *abhāva* because through the analysis of these two conceptions the third one is revealed. When the *anya* and *viruddha* are realized, they are realized as possessing the form of *abhāva* of the *sapakṣa*. Thus, *abhāva* is conceived as something representing the *sapakṣābhāva* directly, and *anya* and *viruddha* are conceived indirectly.[60]

Role of *Sapakṣa* and *Asapakṣa*

Sapakṣa and *asapakṣa* are basically relational concepts. *Sapakṣa* stands for the positive relation consisting of the presence of *sādhya* in *pakṣa,* and *asapakṣa* stands for the negative relation indicating the absolute absence of the former in the latter. These two become elements of the process of *anumāna* when they are taken as aspects of *trairūpya liṅga*. Here they are concerned with the regulations of the presence and absence of *liṅga* in *sapakṣa* and *asapakṣa,* respectively. The *liṅga* must be present apart from *pakṣa* at least in one *sapakṣa,* and it must be absolutely absent in every case of *asapakṣa*. Thus, we get the two *rūpas* of the *liṅga* as *sapakṣe sattvam* and *asapakṣe asattvam*. The concepts of *sapakṣa* and *asapakṣa* are only bilateral as they involve the relation between *pakṣa* and *sādhya,* whereas the concepts of *sapakṣe sattvam* and *asapakṣe asattvam* are trilateral as they involve *hetu* also, along with *pakṣa* and *sādhya*. In *sapakṣa* and *asapakṣa* the sole consideration is the presence and absence of the *sādhya,* whereas in *sapakṣe sattvam* and *asapakṣe asattvam* prominenace is given to the presence and absence of *hetu*. In *sapakṣe sattvam* and *asapakṣe asattvam* the presence or absence of *hetu* is governed by the rule of concomitance. Therefore, we have only these two types of regulation.

Hetu and Its *Rūpas*: *Trairūpya* and *Pañcarūpya*

The Buddhist theory of *anumāna*, as we saw earlier, is rooted in the concept of *gamya-gamaka-bhāva*. *Anumāna* is that thought process in which the cognition of the *liṅga* acts as a *gamaka* and leads to the inferential cognition of the *liṅgin*, which thus is the *gamya*. No doubt this *gamya-gamaka* relationship cannot be established between any two cognitions; there has to be the necessary connection in the form of *avinābhāva*. This implies that only a particular cognition can be a *liṅga* for another specific cognition, which will be its *liṅgin*. The process of *anumāna* begins with the cognition of the *liṅga* Therefore, the *liṅga* provides the starting point of the inferential process. It is the logical ground upon which the subsequent cognition of *liṅgin* depends. In the Buddhist tradition *liṅga* and *liṅgin* stand for construed facts (*adhyavasita*) rather than real facts (*grahita*). The two construed facts are so conceived that one is taken to be a *liṅga* of the other. But, as we said, any two such facts cannot be arbitrarily taken to be the *liṅga* and *liṅgin*. Therefore, it has to be seen that a particular fact is really a *liṅga* of another fact, which is its *liṅgin*.

The establishment of the relation between *liṅga* and *liṅgin* and the cognition of the *liṅga* constitute the basis of inferential process, and therefore they can be taken to be premises. The transition from *liṅga* to *liṅgin* is the conclusion. If the premises are not wellgrounded, the conclusion entailed by them also cannot be logically valid. The *liṅga* constitutes the pivotal element in the premises. Whenever anything is taken to be a *liṅga* in respect of another thing taken as a *liṅgin*, there are always two possibilities conceivable. A *liṅga* may be a genuine *liṅga* if it really stands for its *liṅgin*. But that *liṅga* will be termed fallacious that does not lead to something conceived as its *liṅgin*. In such a situation the *liṅgin* doesn't have that *liṅga* as its proper *liṅga*. In fact that *liṅga* is not at all a *liṅga* in respect of that *liṅgin*. That *liṅga* may be a *linga* as some other *liṅgin* than the one in question. Thus, in the case of the present *liṅgin*, that *liṅga* is not a *liṅga* but a *liṅgābhāsa*. When a *liṅga* is employed as a ground for inferring the *liṅgin*, the *liṅga* is known as *hetu*. So, if *hetu* is not genuine, then it is known as *hetvābhāsa*. Thus, a distinction has to be drawn between *hetu* and *hetvābhāsa* or, to use a different set of phraseology, between *sadhetu* (valid reason) and *asadhetu* (fallacious reason). In other words, there has to be some distinctive marks of *sadhetu* to differentiate it from *asadhetu*. Since the process of *anumāna* is grounded in *hetu*, if the *hetu* is *sadhetu*, the *anumāna* will be valid, and if it is *asadhetu*, then the *anumāna* will be invalid. In order to have a logically valid and sound *anumāna* we must take care to see that *hetu* is *sat* and not *asat*. Different systems of logic in India have put forth a different number of characteristics a *sadhetu* has to possess. Buddhists have advocated the theory of *trairūpya*, whereas Jainas have reduced the three *rūpas* to one (*ekarūpya*), and Naiyāyikas have added two more *rūpas* to these three, making them five (*pañcarūpya*).

THE THEORY OF *TRAIRŪPYA*

According to Diṅnāga and Dharmakīrti, *anumāna* stands for the cognition of the *liṅgin* on the ground of the cognition of *liṅga*. The *liṅga* has to be characterized by three *rūpas* in order to be a logically valid *liṅga*. The Buddhist system of logic insists that there are three and only three essential characteristics of a valid *liṅga*. This is so because there is only a threefold requirement of the *liṅga* being related to (1) *pakṣa*, (2) *sapakṣa,* and (3) *asapakṣa*. Every *liṅga* must possess all the three characteristics simultaneously, only then it is a *trirūpaliṅga* or *trilakṣaṇa hetu* and can be made use of in the process of inference. The doctrine that a *liṅga* must possess three essential characteristics is known as *trairūpyavāda* or the theory of *trairūpyaliṅga*.

(a) Diṅnāga's Formulation

The first systematic formulation of the theory of *trairūpya* is said to be by Diṅnāga, though a reference to it is also found in the works of Vasubandhu.[61] Uddyotakara in his *Vārtika* cites Diṅnāga's formulation of *trairūpya* as follows: "*anumeye'tha tattulye sadbhāve nāstitāsati*," that is, existence in the *anumeya (pakṣa),* in what is like the *pakṣa (sapakṣa*), and nonexistence in what is not like the *pakṣa (asapakṣa)*.[62] We can render in English Diṅnāga's version as follows:

1. Its presence in the subject of inference.
2. Its presence in similar instances.
3. Its absence in dissimilar instances.[63]

The first condition lays down the requirement of *pakṣadharmatā*. It regulates the relation between *liṅga* and *anumeya*. The term *anumeya* has been ambiguous and is used differently in the Buddhist and the Nyāya traditions. In the Nyāya tradition it stands for *sādhya,* which is the object of inferential cognition. But for Diṅnāga and his followers it always stands for the *pakṣa,* which is a *dharmī* and of which *sādhya* is a *dharma*. Though Diṅnāga doesn't seem to be very explicit on this, by *anumeya* he meant *anumeyadharmin*, that is, *pakṣa* and not *anumeyadharma* because the other expression "*tattulya*" clearly means "like that," that is, like the *pakṣa* (*sapakṣa*). The second condition regulates the relation between *liṅga* and *sapakṣa*. It states the necessity of the presence of *liṅga* in a *sapakṣa,* but from its wording it is not clear whether the presence is essential or not, nor is it clear whether the presence is in all *sapakṣas* or in at least one only. However, it should be understood as expressing the necessity of the presence of *liṅga* at least in one *sapakṣa*. This is so because the second condition refers to the positive concomitance between *hetu* and *sādhya*, the reference to one instance of which is logically sufficient to fulfill the requirements of an *udāharaṇa*. The third condition regulates the relation of *liṅga* with *asapakṣa* and states its absence in the same. Like the first two conditions this also is ambiguous and may be understood as requiring the necessary absence of *hetu* in *asapakṣa* or as requiring the necessary absence of *hetu* alone in *asapakṣa*. The intention of Diṅnāga seems to be that *hetu* should be absent in all *asapakṣas*. This is because of the requirements of inverted concomitance. Not only must there be a statement giving out the conditions for the presence of *hetu*, but there should also be a statement of the conditions that necessitate the absence of *hetu*. The conditions that necessitate the absence should be more than the conditions that guarantee the presence of *hetu*, because when we talk of presence, it is always in respect of one individual, whereas when we talk of absence, it is necessarily in respect of the entire class. Thus, the statement of *sapakṣa* is particular in nature and that of *asapakṣa* is universal. The element of necessity or unexceptionality is available only in the latter. From this it is quite evident that the logical status of the two statements is not the same, and hence the *asapakṣa* cannot be regarded as just the negative corollary of the first.

(b) Uddyotakara's Objection

It seems that Uddyotakara was not fully aware of the precise sense in which Diṅnāga talked of the three *rūpas* of *hetu*. Because of the apparent ambiguity he pointed out alternative interpretations of each of the three *rūpas* and tried to expose their untenability on some logical grounds. Uddyotakara's examination of Diṅnāga's formulation is as follows.

In the statement of the first *rūpa*, the expression "*anumeye sadbhāva*" was not free from ambiguity, and as a consequence of that, Uddyotakara examined its two possible interpretations, namely,

1. The *hetu* is present in the *pakṣa* only, and
2. The *hetu* alone is present in the *pakṣa*.

To point out the difference in the two interpretations the following symbolic formulation may be helpful:

(i) *b* is present in *a* only = every *b* is *a* = no *non-a* is *b*.
(ii) only *b* is present in *a* = every *a* is *b* = no *non-b* is *a*.

From the preceding it is quite evident that these two interpretations don't mean the same thing, and therefore the formulation of Diṅnāga was replete with ambiguity. The formulation of the second *rūpa* given by Diṅnāga was also ambiguous in the same way, which led Uddyotakara to give two different interpretations, namely,

(i) The *hetu* is present in similar instances only.
(ii) The *hetu* is present in "all similar instances."

In the same way Diṅnāga's formulation of the third *rūpa* was subjected to two different interpretations by Uddyotakara as follows:

(i) *Only the hetu* is absent in the "*dissimilar instances.*"
(ii) The *hetu* is absent in the *dissimilar instances* only.

Though Diṅnāga has given his unambiguous version in the *Hetu Cakra Damaru,* where the presence or the absence of *hetu* in relation to *sādhya* is well regulated, perhaps he did not do so in the *Pramāṇa Samuccaya*, from which Uddyotakara has quoted him.

(c) Dharmakīrti's Reformulation

Diṅnāga's account of *trairūpya* was given a more rigorous form by Dharmakīrti. He did so by associating the word "*eva*" with each of the three marks and by qualifying the entire expression by the word "*niścitameva.*" The other modification he introduced was the use of the terms "*sapakṣa*" and "*asapakṣa*" to remove all sorts of ambiguities.

We find that it was only to give Diṅnāga's formulation more precision that Dharmakīrti put the emphasizing particle "*eva*" with the entire expression. With this addition the first condition, for example, gives the emphatic meaning of "impossibility of absence" to the assertion.

(d) Dharmottara's Modifications

The ambiguity of nonquantification that vitiated Diṅnāga's formulation was sought to be removed by Dharmakīrti by adding the restrictive word "*eva,*" but unexpectedly, his modification caused further ambiguity. That is why commentators from Dharmottara onward had to struggle hard to interpret it in a satisfactory way. Dharmottara had to face a dilemma on this account while commenting upon the second and third *rūpas*. The second *rūpa* apparently meant "only in the *sapakṣa hetu* must be present," but by implication it meant the *hetu* must be absent in all *asapakṣas*. But then the second *rūpa* will be another way of saying the same thing as the third *rūpa*. This renders the third *rūpa* superfluous, but this was not the intention either of Dinnāga or of Dharmakīrti.

In order to remove this ambiguity Dharmottara suggested another modification, that the expression "*niścitam*" should be added to all the three *rūpas* to render them free from ambiguity.[64]

Thus, his statement, "*liṅgasyānumeye eva sattvam sapakṣe eva sattvam asapakṣe cāsattvameva niścitam*" can be interpreted as follows:

1. *Liṅgasyānumeye (eva) sattvam niścitam.*
2. *Sapakṣe (eva) sattvam niścitam.*
3. *Asapakṣe cāsattvam (eva) niścitam.*

In English it can be rendered as follows:

1. Existence only (never nonexistence) in the *pakṣa*.
2. Existence only in those things that are similar to *pakṣa* (never in things that are not similar to *pakṣa*).

3. Only nonexistence (never existence) in things that are not similar to *pakṣa*.

(e) Stcherbatsky's Interpretation

Stcherbatsky has expressed Dharmakīrti's version in three different ways as follows:

(i) The presence of the reason in the subject, its presence "just," that is, never absence.
(ii) Its presence in similar instances, "just" in similars, that is, never in dissimilars, but not in the totality of the similars.
(iii) Its absence from dissimilar instances, its absence "just," that is, never presence, absence from the totality of the dissimilar instances.

It seems that the expression of the second condition just given has been defective in two ways. First, the implication, namely, "never in dissimilars" is not intended by Dharmakīrti, nor does it follow from the expression *sapakṣe eva sattvam (niścitam)*" as implying "necessary presence of the *hetu* in at least one similar instance." Second, the expression "but not in the totality of the similars" is also faulty insofar as it implies that there should not be presence of *hetu* in the totality of similars. Its proper wording should have been "but not necessarily in the totality of similars." Because of these defects the second and the third conditions have been seen to be mutually implying each other.[65]

The second mode of the expression of *trairūpya* is as follows:

(i) The necessary presence of the reason in subject's totality.
(ii) Its necessary presence in similars only, although not in their totality.
(iii) Its necessary absence from dissimilars in their totality.

This way of expressing *trairūpya* is free from the defects referred to earlier because it draws a clear distinction between "presence only in *sapakṣas*" and "necessary presence in at least one *sapakṣa.*" Only when the second *rūpa* is understood in the former sense does it overlap with the third *rūpa*, but not when taken in the latter sense.

The third way of expressing *trairūpya* is nothing but an abbreviation of the second. It is as follows:

1. In subject wholly.
2. In similar only.
3. In dissimilar never.

(f) Chi's Exposition

Chi has given the Chinese version of *trairūpya*, which seems to be free from ambiguity as follows:

(i) The "*pervasive presence*" of the *hetu* in the subject.
(ii) The "*necessary presence*" of the *hetu* in some similar instances.

(iii) The *"pervasive absence"* of the *hetu* from dissimilar instances.

In the preceding rendering the use of the word "pervasive" in the first and the third *rūpas* and of the word "necessary" in the second rūpa refer to the distributive quantification of *hetu*. Similarly the phrase "necessary presence" means "assured presence" or "not failing to be present." Chi has defined the notion of "pervasive presence" as follows:

"Pervasive presence of *b* in *a*."
= "*b* is present in every *a*."
= "every *a* is *b*."

The notion of "pervasive absence" is defined by him as follows:

"Pervasive absence of *b* from *a*."
= "*b* is absent from every *a*."
= "no *a* is *b*."

The notion of "necessary presence" is defined by him as follows:

"Necessary presence of *b* in *a*."
= "*b* is present in atleast one *a*, almost every *a*"
= "at least one *a*, at most every *a* is *b*."

In accordance with this understanding he interprets *trairūpya* as follows:

I *rūpa*:
"The property of *g* is present in every thing which possesses the property *f*."
= "Everything which possesses the property *f* possesses the property *g*."
= "For every *x*, *x is an* f *implies x is g*."

II *rūpa*:
"There is at least one occasion in which the property *g* is present in a thing which possesses the property *h* apart from the thing which possesses the property *f* which remains to be proved."
= "Apart from the thing which possesses the property *f* at least one thing which possesses the property *h* possesses the property *g*."
= "For some *X* which is not *f*, *X* is both an *h* and *g*."

III *rūpa*:
"There is no occasion in which the property *g* is present in things which possess the property of *non-h*."
= "Nothing which possesses the property *non-h* possesses the property *g*."
= "For no *X*, *X* is both *non-h* and a *g*."

On the basis of this interpretation Chi proposes to resolve Dharmakīrti's dilemma on the interpretation of "*eva*" (only) in the second *rūpa* as follows:

"Only presence."

= "Only presence of the property of the *hetu* in similar instances but not otherwise."

= "Only presence of the property of the *hetu* in similar instances but not utter absence of its property in all similar instances."

= "The presence of the property of the *hetu* in at least one similar instance."

Understood in this way, the second *rūpa* doesn't overlap with the third *rūpa*, and the problem of redundancy is overcome.

After discussing the Buddhist theory of *hetu-trairūpya* in detail, let us attempt a comparative account of the different theories of *hetu-rūpa* attempted in the three systems of logic, namely, Buddhist, Nyāya, and Jaina. All three systems have differences with regard to the required *rūpas* of *hetu*. Buddhists insist on three *rūpas* only, but Naiyāyikas accept five *rūpas* of *hetu*, and Jainas emphasize that only one *rūpa* is necessary.

Nyāya Theory of *Pañcarūpya*

Nyāya logicians emphasize the fact that *hetu* or *liṅga* is the central element in the inferential process. It is related to *pakṣa* as well as *sādhya*, and it occurs in all significant premises, namely, *hetu, udāharaṇa,* and *upanaya*. The validity of inference depends, to a great extent, on *hetu;* and that is why a fallacious inference is known as having *hetvābhāsa*. Nyāya logicians therefore have taken great pains to expound the characteristics of a good *hetu*, because if the *hetu* is *sadhetu,* then the inference will be valid, and if it is *asadhetu,* the inference will be invalid. Naiyāyikas enumerate the following conditions of a *sadhetu*:

1. ***Pakṣadharmatvam.*** *Hetu* must be a *dharma* or characteristic of *pakṣa*. This means that the *hetu* should have its locus (*adhikaraṇa*) in *pakṣa*, that is, it should reside in, or be related to, *pakṣa*. Thus, the *pakṣa* should never be without *hetu*, and nothing can be *pakṣa* if there is no *hetu* related to it.

2. ***Sapakṣesattvam.*** *Hetu* must be distributively related to *sādhya*. This means that whenever *hetu* exists, in all such cases *sādhya* must be present. This means that the necessary condition for the occurrence of *hetu* is the occurrence of *sādhya*.

3. ***Vipakṣādvyāvṛttiḥ.*** *Hetu* must be absent in all such cases where *sādhya* is absent. This means that the absence of *sādhya* necessarily implies the absence of *hetu*. So, in all *asapakṣas*, that is, where *sādhya* is absent, *hetu* must also be absent.

4. ***Abādhitaviṣayatvam.*** *Hetu* should not be such as to be contradictory to, or incompatible with, the nature of *sādhya*. This is so because the function of *hetu* is to establish *sādhya*, but if it is incompatible with *sādhya*, it will disprove *sādhya*.

5. ***Asatpratipakṣatvam* or *Aviruddhatvam.*** *Hetu* should not be such as to have a rival *hetu* that is competent to invalidate it.

Of course, Naiyāyikas make it clear that all these five *rūpas* are not simultaneously present in all *hetu*. For example, in a *kevalānvayi anumāna* the third condition will not be applicable. Similarly, in the *kevalavyatireki anumāna* the second condition will not be applicable.[66] Hence, it has been said that a *sadhetu* satisfies the five or at least the four conditions.

If we compare the Nyāya theory of *pañcarūpya* with the Buddhist theory of *trairūpya*, we find that the first three *rūpas* of the Naiyāyikas correspond to the *trairūpya* of the Buddhists. Of course, the details in the formulation of these three *rūpas* are very much different in the two traditions, but we can still regard them as having some rough correspondence. But the last two *rūpas* of the Nyāya theory are not accepted and will not be acceptable to Buddhists. Now it can be asked why Buddhists do not accept the last two *rūpas*. The reason is that Buddhists believe in the theory of *pramāṇavyavasthā,* which is the opposite of the Nyāya theory of *pramāṇasaṁpalava*. So the verdict of one *anumāna,* if falsely drawn, can be contradicted by some other *pramāṇa* in the Nyāya position, but the verdict of one *anumāna* cannot be contradicted by another *pramāṇa* in the Buddhist position. Therefore, there is no possibility of *satpratipakṣa* here.[67] Second, the basis of *anumāna,* according to Buddhists, is *liṅga-liṅgī-bhāva*, between any two concepts. We shall never establish *liṅga-liṅgī-bhāva* if they are of opposite nature. Therefore, there will never be an occasion for *abādhitaviṣayatvam*.

Third, the introduction of the particle *eva* in (2) and (3) at proper places implies that a *hetu* has a necessary connection with the *sādhya*. Thus, as a *hetu's* necessary connection with the *sādhya* is covered by conditions (2) and (3)—they being a modification of the corresponding conditions of the Nyāya Vaiśeṣika scheme—there remains no possibility of its being either counterbalanced by another *hetu* or contradicted by a noninferential *pramāṇa*. So, for Buddhists conditions (4) and (5) formulated by the Nyāya-Vaiśeṣika logicians become redundant or inapplicable.

Though there has been a lot of controversy between Buddhists and Naiyāyikas as to whether only three *rūpas* or five *rūpas* are to be accepted, the whole controversy appears to be futile because they are two different traditions having different types of requirements. The Nyāya tradition stands in need of five *rūpas*, whereas in the Buddhist tradition only three *rūpas* are possible, and therefore the theories of *pañcarūpya hetu* and *trairūpya hetu* are perfectly in order in their respective systems.

Jaina Criticism of *Trairūpya*

The Jaina tradition maintains that *hetu* has a unitary nature, and therefore it possesses only one *rūpa*. *Hetu* is defined as that which is inseparably connected with *sādhya.* This means *hetu* is that which is present only in the presence of *sādhya* and which is necessarily absent in the absence of *sādhya*. Akalaṅkadeva defines *hetu* as "*sādhyāvinābhāva vinibodhaikalakṣaṇa.*"[68] Some Jaina logicians have described this fact with the help of another concept, namely, "*anyathānupapatti.*" Vādidevasūri puts it as "*niścitānyathānupapattyeka lakṣaṇohetuḥ.*"[69] The term "*anyathānupapatti*" means that in the absence of *sādhya* (*anyathā*), there should be absence of *hetu* (*anupapatti*). By implication it means that *hetu* should be present only in the presence of *sādhya*. So to be *sādhyāvinābhāvi* is the sole characteristic of *hetu*.

The Jainas have not only insisted on one and only one characteristic of *hetu* but they have also put forth a refutation of the theories of *trairūpya* and *pañcarūpya*.

Pātrasvāmin seems to be the first Jaina scholar, as quoted by Akalaṅka and Vinītadeva, who attempted refutation of the doctrine of *trairūpya* as follows:

Anyathānupapannatvam yatra tatra trayeṇa kim
Nānyathānupapannatvam yatra tatra trayeṇa kim,[70]

In the preceding verse Pātrasvamin emphatically maintains that "*anyathānupapannatvam*" is the only *rūpa* of *hetu*. If it is present, then what is the need of three *rūpas*, and if it is absent, then what is the purpose of having three *rūpas*? Following Pātrasvāmin, all subsequent Jaina logicians like Akalaṅka, Vidyānanda, Prabhācandra, Vādidevasūri, Anantavīrya, and Hemacandra have also refuted the doctrine of *trairūpya*. The preceding verse of Pātrasvāmin has been quoted by Śāntarakṣita in the *Tattva Saṁgraha* in the form of *pūrva-pakṣa* presenting the Jaina position, and there he has refuted the Jaina objections against *trairūpya*. The basic objection put forth by the Jainas is that even an invalid *hetu* may have the three *rūpas*, "*tasya hetvābhāsasyāpi sambhavāt.*" For example, the argument "There is smoke on the hill because there is fire" has all the three *rūpas*, namely, *pakṣadharmatvam, sapakṣesattvam,* and *vipakṣeasattvam,* but still it is logically invalid because there is no necessary connection (*avinābhāva*) between fire and smoke. In other words, there may be fire and smoke on the hill, and so the condition of *pakṣadharmatvam* is fulfilled. Similarly, there can be fire and smoke in the kitchen, and the condition of *sapkṣesattvam* is fulfilled. Likewise, there will be no fire and smoke in the lake, and the condition of *vipakṣeasattvam* is also fulfilled. Even then fire is an invalid *hetu* for smoke. Of course, Buddhists may point out that the *trairūpya* should be understood as qualified by *avinābhāva,* and there is no *avinābhāva* between fire and smoke because there may be fire without smoke, for example, in an electric hearth. So the relation of fire and smoke is conditional (*sopādhika*) and not unconditional (*nirupādhika*). To this Jainas have replied that if *avinābhāva* is to be emphasized, then this amounts to their position, which means *hetu* has only one *rūpa* and not three *rūpas*. Jaina's point of emphasis is that the *hetu* in an argument is valid and competent to prove the *sādhya* not because the two exist in the same *pakṣa,* as the Naiyāyikas say, but because the two are inseparably related. In the words of Jaina logicians the *hetu* is not cognized otherwise than in connection with the *sādhya*. Accordingly, so far as the essential characteristic of valid *hetu* is concerned, it is this and this one only.

Śāntarakṣita has stated and examined Pātrasvāmin's arguments in great detail. The basic point made by Pātrasvāmin is that *hetu* is valid if and only if it has "*anyathānupapatti*" with respect to *sādhya*. This is the only feature of *hetu* that is required, and it takes care of *pakṣadharmatvam, sapakṣesattvam,* and *vipakṣeasattvam*. To this Śāntarakṣita replies that this concept is nothing but an abbreviated form of *trairūpya*. *Anaythānupapatti* includes positive and negative concomitance, and by its presence in the object that is *pakṣa, pakṣadharmatva* is also admitted. Śāntarakṣita not only has defended *trairūpyavāda* against Pātrasvāmin's criticism but has himself raised some objections against Pātrasvāmin's theory of *ekarūpya*.[71]

Hetu Cakra Ḍamaru of Diṅnāga

The doctrine of *trairūpya* has been explicated by Diṅnāga in his work *Hetu Cakra Ḍamaru*,[72] a primer of Buddhist formal logic. In this work nine different conceivable relations of *hetu* with *pakṣa, sapakṣa,* and *asapakṣa* are presented. This presentation of the doctrine of *trairūpya* in a wider context was named by him as the doctrine of *hetucakra*.[73] Both these doctrines refer to the extension of *hetu*. This doctrine of *trairūpya* represents only three valid relations of *hetu* with *pakṣa, sapakṣa,* and *asapakṣa*, whereas the doctrine of *hetu cakra* takes for granted the presence of *hetu* in *pakṣa*, and its relations with *sapakṣa* and *asapakṣa* are alone taken into consideration. Here three possible ways of the relation between *hetu* and *sapakṣa* and *hetu* and *asapakṣa* are conceived and analyzed, namely, *vyāpaka* (pervasive presence), *avṛtti* (pervasive absence), and *ekadeśavṛtti* (partial presence).[74] He gives a formal schema of nine valid and invalid types of *anumāna* based on three possible relations of *hetu* with *sapakṣa* and *asapakṣa*. Since the text is very short we can have the advantage of giving it here in full.[75]

Hetu Cakra Ḍamaru (The Wheel of Reasons)

Homage to Mañjuśrīkumārabhūta.

Homage to the Omniscient One, who is
The destroyer of the snare of ignorance.
I am expounding the determination of
The *reason* with three-fold characteristics

Among the three possible cases of "presence," "absence" and "both"
Of the *reason* in the *probandum*,
Only the case of its "presence" is valid,
While its "absence" is not.
The case of "both presence and absence" is inconclusive,
It is therefore not valid either.
The "presence," "absence" and "both."

Of the *reason* in similar instances,
Combined with those, in dissimilar instances,
There are three combinations in each of three,

The top and the bottom are valid,
The two sides are contradictory.
The four corners are inconclusive because they are "too broad,"
The Centre is inconclusive because it is "too narrow."

Knowable, produced, non eternal,
Produced, audible, effort-made,
Eternal, effort-made and incorporeal,
Are used to prove the properties of being:
Eternal, non eternal, effort made,
Eternal, eternal, eternal,
Non effort-made, non eternal and eternal.

When two tops or two bottoms meet,
The *reason* is valid.
When two corresponding sides meet,
It is contradictory.

When corresponding corners meet,
It is inconclusive because it is "too broad."
When the centers of two crosses meet,
It is inconclusive because it is "too narrow."

Since there are nine classes of *reason*,
Accordingly we have nine sets of example:

Space-pot, pot-space,
Pot-lightning-space,
Space-pot-lightning,
Lightning-space-pot,
Pot-lightning-space,
Space-action-pot.
The above concerns the "determined *reason*" only;
As regards the "doubtful" ones,
There are also nine combinations of
"Presence," "absence" and "both."

Here the presence of *hetu* in *pakṣa* is combined with different types of relations that a *hetu* may possess with *sapakṣa* and *asapakṣa*. The combination of these two sets of possibilities gives rise to nine types. Among these nine possible relations between *hetu* and *sādhya*, only two are valid, and these constitute the II and III *rūpas* of the doctrine of *trairūpya*, and the remaining seven are graded as invalid as they are at variance with the doctrine of *trairūpya*. The nine possible relations are as follows:

I: *Sapakṣāsapakṣavyāpaka*: Pervasive presence in similar and dissimilar instances.

II: *Sapakṣavyāpaka asapakṣāvṛtti*: Pervasive presence in similar instances and necessary absence in dissimilar instances.

III: *Sapakṣavyāpaka asapakṣaikadeśavṛtti*: Pervasive presence in similar instances and partial presence in dissimilar instances.

IV: *Sapakṣāvṛtti asapakṣavyāpaka*: Necessary absence in similar instances and pervasive presence in dissimilar instances.

V: *Sapakṣāsapakṣāvṛtti*: Necessary absence in similar and dissimilar instances.

VI: *Sapakṣāvṛtti asapakṣaikadeśavṛtti*: Necessary absence in similar and partial presence in dissimilar instances.

VII: *Sapakṣaikadeśavṛtti asapakṣavyāpaka*: Partial presence in similar instances and pervasive presence in dissimilar instances.

VIII: *Sapakṣaikadeśavṛtti asapakṣāvṛtti*: Partial presence in similar instances and necessary absence in dissimilar instances.

IX: *Sapakṣāsapakṣaikadeśavṛtti*: Partial presence in similar and dissimilar instances.

These nine *rūpas* of the *hetu cakra* have been represented by Diṅnāga in the form of this diagram:

I	II	III
IV	V	VI
VII	VIII	IX

Referring to this diagram, he writes:

The top and the bottom are valid,
The two sides are contradictory,
The four corners are inconclusive because they are "*too broad.*"
The center is inconclusive because it is "*too narrow.*"

Keeping this in view, we can explicate the diagram as follows:

I (corner)	II (top)	III (corner)
IV (side)	V (center)	VI (side)
VII (corner)	VIII (bottom)	IX (corner)

After stating the *hetu cakra,* Diṅnāga proceeds to illustrate the different *rūpas* with the help of the following examples:

Knowable	Produced	Noneternal
Produced	Audible	Effort-made
Eternal	Effort-made	Incorporeal
Eternal	Noneternal	Effort-made
Eternal	Eternal	Eternal
Non effort-made	Non eternal	Eternal

With the help of these examples we can explain the earlier mentioned verse like this:

Two tops meet:

Whatever is produced is noneternal: VALID.

Two Bottoms meet:

Whatever is effort-made is noneternal: VALID.

Two corresponding sides meet:

Whatever is produced is eternal: Contradictory.
Whatever is effort-made is eternal: Contradictory.

Corresponding corners meet:

Whatever is knowable is eternal: Inconclusive, "too broad."
Whatever is eternal is noneffort-made: Inconclusive, "too broad."
Whatever is noneternal is effort-made: Inconclusive, "too broad."
Whatever is incorporeal is eternal: Inconclusive, "too broad."

Two Centers meet:

Whatever is audible is eternal: Inconclusive, "too narrow."

The statement of the *hetu cakra*, because of its cryptic wording, is unintelligible by itself, but with the help of examples given by Diṅnāga it can be better understood. Here we take an example of *anumāna* consisting of three steps because Buddhists accept only three steps. The three steps are *pratijñā*, *hetu*, and *udāharaṇa* of *sapakṣa* and *asapakṣa*. The three terms of *anumāna* are *pakṣa*, *hetu*, and *sādhya*. It is presumed that *hetu* is present in *pakṣa* (i.e., *pakṣadharmatva*). The relation of *hetu* with *sapakṣa* is conceived to be of three possible types, namely, *vyāpaka*, *avṛtti*, and *ekadeśavṛtti*. Similarly, the relation of *hetu* with *asapakṣa* can also be conceived of in the preceding manner. On the basis of the preceding stipulations the *hetu cakra* can be exemplified in the following way:

Statement of the example of first form:

Pratijñā : Sound is eternal.
Hetu : because it is knowable.
Udāharaṇa (of *sapakṣa* and *asapakṣa*): like space and unlike pot.
The three terms are:
Pakṣa : sound.
Hetu : knowable.
Sādhya : eternal.

In this example the *hetu*, apart from being present in *pakṣa*, is also present in both *sapakṣa* and *asapakṣa*. It renders this argument invalid. Here there is a fallacy of *sādhāraṇa anekāntika* (inconclusive, too broad), because the *hetu* is present in all three, whereas as per rule it should be present only in the first two.

Statement of the example of second form:

Pratijñā : Sound is noneternal.
Hetu : because it is produced.
Udāharaṇa (of *sapakṣa* and *asapakṣa*): like a pot and unlike space.
The three terms are:
Pakṣa : sound.
Hetu : produced.
Sādhya : noneternal.

In this example the *hetu* is present in *pakṣa*, is also present in *sapakṣa*, and is absent in *asapakṣa*. Thus, it satisfies all the three requirements of *trairūpya*. So it is valid.

Statement of the example of third form:

Pratijñā : Sound is effort-made.
Hetu : because it is noneternal.
Udāharaṇa (of *sapakṣa* and *asapakṣa*): like pot and unlike lightning and space.
The three terms are:
Pakṣa : sound.
Hetu : noneternal.
Sādhya : effort-made.

In this example, the *hetu* is no doubt present in *pakṣa* and *sapakṣa* but is absent in some instances of *asapakṣa* and is present in others. The *hetu* has *asapakṣaikadeśavṛtti* because (1) some noneffort-made things are noneternal like lightning whereas (2) some noneffort-made things are eternal like ether. Thus, the presence of *hetu* in some *asapakṣas* renders this argument invalid. Here there is a fallacy of *sādhāraṇa anekāntika* (inconclusive, too broad).

Statement of the example of fourth form:

Pratijñā : Sound is eternal.
Hetu : because it is produced.
Udāharaṇa (of *sapakṣa* and *asapakṣa*): like ether and unlike pot.
The three terms are:
Pakṣa : sound.
Hetu : produced.
Sādhya : eternal.

In this example, the *hetu* is present in *pakṣa*, is absent in *sapakṣa* and present in *asapakṣa*. Thus, *hetu* is contradictory of *sādhya*. This renders it invalid. Here there is a fallacy of *viruddha* (contradictory).

Statement of the example of fifth form:

Pratijñā : Sound is eternal.
Hetu : because it is audible.

Udāharaṇa (of *sapakṣa* and *asapakṣa*): Like space and unlike pot.

The three terms are:

Pakṣa : sound.
Hetu : audible.
Sādhya : eternal.

Here the *hetu* is present only in *pakṣa* and is absent not only in *asapakṣa* but also in *sapakṣa*. Here there is a fallacy of *asādhāraṇa anekāntika* (inconclusive, too narrow).

Statement of the example of sixth form:

Pratijñā : Sound is eternal.
Hetu : because it is effort made.

Udāharaṇa (of *sapakṣa* and *asapakṣa*) : Like space and unlike pot and lightning.

The three terms are:

Pakṣa : sound.
Hetu : effort made.
Sādhya : eternal.

Here the *hetu* is present only in *pakṣa*, absent in *sapakṣa*, but present in some instances of *asapakṣa* and absent in others. Here there is a fallacy of *viruddha* (contradictory).

Statement of the example of seventh form:

Pratijñā : Sound is noneffort made.
Hetu : because it is noneternal.

Udāharaṇa (of *sapakṣa* and *asapakṣa*) : Like lightning and space and unlike pot.

The three terms are:

Pakṣa : sound.
Hetu : noneternal.
Sādhya : noneffort made.

Here the *hetu* apart from its presence in *pakṣa* is present in some instances of *sapakṣa* and absent in others, whereas it is present in *asapakṣa*. Here there is a fallacy of *sādhāraṇa anekāntika* (inconclusive, too broad).

Statement of the example of eighth form:

Pratijñā : Sound is noneternal.
Hetu : because it is effort made.

Udāharaṇa (of *sapakṣa* and *asapakṣa*) : Like pot and lightning and unlike space.

The three terms are:

Pakṣa : sound.
Hetu : effort made.

Sādhya noneternal.

Here the *hetu* is present in *pakṣa*, present in some instances of *sapakṣa* and absent in others, whereas it is absent in all the cases of *asapakṣa*. Thus, the argument satisfies all the three requirements of the *trairūpya*. So, it is valid.

Statement of the example of ninth form:

Pratijñā : Sound is eternal.
Hetu : because it is incorporeal.
Udāharaṇa (of *sapakṣa* and *asapakṣa*) : like space and infinitesimal particles and unlike action and pot.

The three terms are:

Pakṣa : sound.
Hetu : incorporeal.
Sādhya : eternal.

Here, no doubt, *hetu* is present in *pakṣa* and in some instances of *sapakṣa* but is also present in some instances of *asapakṣa*. This renders it inconclusive (too broad). Here there is a fallacy of *sādhāraṇa anekāntika*.

THE *AVAYAVAS*

Anumāna is a complex cognition arrived at as an outcome of a thought process consisting of several stages known as *avayavas*. The entire inferential thought process, when expressed in language, is said to constitute one single unit named as *vākya*, having several constituent elements (*avayavas*).[76] In case of *pratyakṣa* being a simple cognition (in the Buddhist tradition) there are no parts, but that is not the case with *anumāna*, which is a complex cognition having several parts closely connected together by mutual requirement (*paraspara apekṣita sambandha*).

Daśāvayavī Tradition

As regards the complex character of *anumāna*, there is no difference of opinion among the different schools of Indian logic. But how many parts, this complex consists of, has been a matter of dispute. Several positions are available in Indian logical tradition about the number of *avayavas* ranging from ten to one. Vatsyāyana[77] refers to a view that held that *avayavas* of *anumāna* were ten, namely, *jijñāsā, saṃśaya, śakya prāpti, prayojana, saṃśayavyūdāsa, pratijñā, hetu, udāharaṇa, upanaya,* and *nigamana*. It seems to be a reference to some Jaina logicians of early time. Bhadrabāhu, for example, refers to the *daśāvayavī vākya*. He is of the view that the number of *avayavas* is really two only, namely, *pratijñā* and *hetu*, but it may be increased up to ten, depending on the grasping power of the other party. However, it is to be noted that Vādideva even grants that in dealing with a particular type of person, even one single *avayava*, namely, *hetu*, may constitute *anumāna*. Those who insist on ten *avayavas* were of the opinion that the five *avayavas* have to be added, taking psychological factors in consideration. But Vātsyāyana and other Naiyāyikas criticize this view on the ground that the first five members represent not so much the logical grounds needed for drawing the conclusion as the psychological or epistemological conditions involved in *anumāna*. *Jijñāsā*, though psychologically an antecedent condition of discussion of *hetu*, has no bearing on the *hetu* and so is outside the limit of *hetu*, which aims at proving *pratijñā*. *Saṃśaya*, too, is a purely psychical fact, and though it inspires the inquiry and as such initiates the argument, it has no probative value. *Śakyaprāpti* likewise is a question of psychological attitude and by itself has no logical consequence. Similarly, *prayojana* is only a by-product of the syllogistic argument insofar as it stands for practical application of the truth ascertained. The fifth factor, namely, *saṃśayavyūdāsa*, which is arrived at by the method of *tarka*, has a remote logical bearing on doubt, but it cannot, for that matter, be regarded as a part of the process of *anumāna* because its function is only to approve and confirm the truth of the conclusion logically deduced from the premises. Thus, the Naiyāyikas point out that the first five *avayavas* are of no logical use and therefore do not constitute a part of the process of *anumāna*. But the remaining five *avayavas* from *pratijñā* onward are the real *avayavas*, as each of them is essential to the deduction of the conclusion and to the conviction of the disputant. None of them can be omitted, as each has a distinct contribution that is not made by the other.[78]

Naiyāyikas consider the last five to be the real *avayavas*, and therefore their model is known as *pañcāvayavīvākya*.[79] In this context one may refer to a very interesting remark, though not very plausible, made by Vātsyāyana that in the Nyāya school only five *avayavas* have been accepted owing to a desire to equate "four premises" with the four *pramāṇas: pratijñā* = *śabda, hetu* = *anumāna, dṛṣṭānta (udāharaṇa)* = *pratyakṣa*, and *upanaya* = *upamāna*.[80] It is noteworthy that *anumāna* is here identified with *hetu* only. The Vedāntins admitted only the first or the last three members of the *pañcāvayavī vākya*.[81] A similar view is expressed by the Mīmāmsakas.

Pañcāvayavī Tradition

According to Naiyāyikas, *pratijñā* is the first *avayava* because it is the statement of the thesis to be proved in the process of *anumāna*. It is the first *avayava* insofar as it is the starting point of the process of *anumāna*. The second *avayava* is *hetu*, which consists in adducing a fact capable of proving the *sādhya*. The third *avayava* is *udāharaṇa*, which stands for a familiar instance known to possess the *hetu*, which is invariably concomitant with its *sādhya*. The fourth *avayava* is *upanaya*. It is an application of *hetu* to the disputed case after its probative value has been attested by the *udāharaṇa*. In the terminology of later Naiyāyikas, it is a statement of *parāmarśa*.[82] The last *avayava*, according to Naiyāyikas, is *nigamana*, which is a restatement of the thesis that is well established through *hetu* and *udāharaṇa*. The Nyāya *pañcāvayavī vākya* can be illustrated with the help of the classical example:

Pratijñā Word is noneternal.

Hetu	:	because it has a definite origin.
Udāharaṇa	:	A thing having a definite origin is seen to be nonetemal, as, for instance, a pot.
Upanaya	:	Word has a definite origin.
Nigamana	:	Therefore, word is noneternal.

Rejection of *Pañcāvavyavī* Tradition

In the Buddhist tradition there is a general acceptance of three *avayavas*, which may be either the first three or the last three.[83] The Buddhist formulation of *anumāna* can thus be:

Word is noneternal,
because it has a definite origin.
A thing having a definite origin is seen to be noneternal, as, for instance, a pot.

Dharmakīrti is perhaps the first Buddhist philosopher who questions the Nyāya theory of *pañcāvayavī vākya*. He argues that *pratijñā* has no probative value and, therefore, is not a part of the process of *anumāna*. *Nigamana* is proved by the virtue of the second and the third or the third and the fourth members, the fourth and the second members being identical in import. These two members alone are relevant, and since the *nigamana* follows irresistibly from these two, it need not be taken to be a part of the process of the *anumāna*. Moreover, *nigamana* is only a useless repetition of *pratijñā* and so should not be taken to be an *avayava*.

Vācaspati and Jayanta have, on the other hand, put forth a strong defense of *pañcāvayava*. Vācaspati argues that the arguer (*vādin*) has to state what is wanted by the opponent; otherwise, his or her statement will fail to receive attentive consideration at the hands of the opponent. The *pratijñā*, that is, "Word is noneternal," is what is wanted to be proved by both the opponent and the arguer, and unless this is stated, the *hetu*, "because it is a product," will be completely irrelevant. He, of course, concedes that the statement of *pratijñā* has psychological value as it directly enlists the attention of the opponent to the subject matter of dispute and thus renders the whole argument effective. The Buddhist model, of course, lacks this initial advantage and may fail to rouse the attention of the opponent.

The defense of Vācaspati does not seem to be convincing enough. The arguer advances an argument only when there is an occasion for it, and the opponent, too, cannot but give attention to the argument if he or she is serious of the purpose; otherwise, the Naiyāyika's *pratijñā*, too, would not receive attention from the opponent.[84]

Jayanta defends *pañcāvayavī* on a different line. He contends that the arguer should try to bring home an argument exactly in the order in which he or she has himself or herself reasoned out the conclusion. The arguer first observes the *pakṣa* being associated with *hetu* and then remembers the universal concomitance between *hetu* and *sādhya*. Although the *pakṣa* is observed without the *sādhya*, the association of *sādhya* with the *pakṣa* is stated in the *pratijñā* on the ground of the observation of *hetu*, but nonobservation of such an association leads to a feeling of uncertainty for which a proof has to be requisitioned. Jayanta's position also seems to be quite weak even from the psychological point of view because only in a complex and complicated situation do we need all three *avayavas;* otherwise, in normal situations *hetu* (reason) is enough.

Buddhists therefore contend that in an *anumāna* the *avayavas* should be chosen keeping in view their logical cogency, and the psychological order should have no bearing on it. If the psychological factors have a determining value, then even such factors as statement of approval should be incorporated as an *avayava*. If logical cogency is regarded as a criterion, then *pratijñā* should be excluded in the same way in which *jijñāsā, saṁśaya,* and so on, advocated by the exponent of *daśāvayava,* have been discarded by Naiyāyikas.

According to Buddhists, *upanaya*, which is an application of *hetu* and *udāharaṇa*, too, is superfluous and has no independent probative force, as it only reiterates the *hetu* and *udāharaṇa*.[85]

To this objection of Diṅnāga and Dharmakīrti, Uddyotakara has given the following reply.[86] The statement of *hetu* serves only to assign a reason and doesn't testify that the *hetu* exists in the *pakṣa*. The *upanaya* emphasizes the presence of *hetu* in the *pakṣa* and as such has a different function and value from the mere statement of *hetu*. Further, the *upanaya* doesn't reiterate the *hetu* as such; it applies the *hetu* along with *vyāpti* and *udāharaṇa* to the case in question and thus leads to the conclusion. The statement of *hetu* unbacked by *vyāpti* is ineffective and hence needs *upanaya*.

Śāntarakṣita, a later exponent of the Diṅnāga-Dharmakīrti tradition reacting to the Nyāya contention, argues that if *upanaya* is deemed necessary for pointing out the presence of *hetu* in *pakṣa,* then this amounts to usurping the task of *hetu*. In that case what shall be the function of *hetu*? Mere statement of *hetu* without reference to its presence in *pakṣa* is absolutely out of place. Therefore, any meaningful statement of *hetu* should always be in relation to *pakṣa* and *sādhya,* and if these two functions are served by the second and the third *avayavas*, then what is the need of having *upanaya*? In fact, the statement of *pakṣadharmatā* is the basis of *anumāna,* and if this is done by both the second and the fourth *avayavas,* then either of them should be jettisoned, and *upanaya,* is not necessary for bringing into relation the *vyāpti* with *hetu*, because this relation is understood eo ipso from the two premises, namely, *hetu* and *udāharaṇa,* and these two premises constitute a perfect *anumāna,* and nothing further is necessary.

In Śrīdhara we find a reply to Śāntarakṣita regarding the functions of *hetu* and *upanaya*. According to him, the two don't serve the same function. The second *avayava,* that is, *hetu,* also known as *apadeśa* in the Vaiśeṣika tradition, is the bare statement of the *liṅga* and not the assertion of the relation of *liṅga* with the *pakṣa*. This relation, known as *pakṣadharmatā,* is conveyed only by *upanaya,* and thus *upanaya* is not a duplication of *hetu*. This reply of Śrīdhara doesn't seem to be pertinent because it is commonly recognized that *hetu* is the statement of *pakṣadharmatā*.

Vācasapti and Jayanta fully realize the cogency of the argument as put forward by Śāntarakṣita and the weakness of Uddyotakara's defense. But they once again appeal to psychological evidence. Their contention is that our argument should be advanced in the same order in which we arrive at truth in our own experience. Now, we first observe the *pakṣa*, say, "the hill" and then the *hetu* "the smoke." Next we remember the invariable concomitance of smoke and fire as exemplified in the kitchen, and immediately this invariable concomitance is understood in relation to smoke on the hill, and the direct result of this is the deduction of the conclusion. Thus, the five *avayavas* embody only the order of our own subjective ratiocination and as such constitute the most satisfying process of *anumāna*.

It must, however, be stated in favor of Buddhist contention that the psychological account of the process of *anumāna,* should not be confused with the logical requirement of the truth and validity of *anuṁana* upon which alone its evidential value depends. Psychological evidence as to the subjective process of reasoning should not be allowed to dictate terms to the constituents of a logically sound *anumāna*. Logic, as has been pointed out, is concerned with validity and cogency, whereas psychology is interested in the natural history of mental phenomena. So, though psychologically *pratijñā* and *upanaya* may have a raison d'etre, they cannot on that account be taken to be *avayavas*.

As regards the *nigamana*, Buddhists insist that this also doesn't require to be stated, as it follows by a sheer logical necessity from the universal proposition as stated in the *udāharaṇa* and from the statement of *hetu*. Moreover, on the Naiyāyika's, own showing, it is perfectly redundant, being only a repetition of *pratijñā*.[87]

Uddyotakara, however, argues that *nigamana* is not a useless repetition of *pratijñā*, as the latter states only what is yet to be proved, and the former is the statement of the proven fact; nor is the statement of *nigamana* unnecessary because it serves to dispel a likely error or doubt. Unless the *nigamana* is stated, the opponent may still waver as to whether the *pratijñā* is acceptable or not. The clear statement of *pratijñā* dispels all such doubt and satisfies the opponent completely. Śāntarakṣita points out that this defense of the Naiyāyikas is not forceful. In fact, there can be no possibility of doubt if the *hetu* satisfies all the three logical requirements, that is, if it is *trairūpya liṅga*. The conclusion irresistibly follows from this and from none else. If, on the other hand, the three *rūpas* are lacking, the statement of *nigamana* by itself cannot remove doubt about its validity. Śāntarakṣita refers to Aviddhakarṇa, who contends that the premises, being scattered and piecemeal, cannot establish a unitary judgment unless they are shown to be mutually related, and this relationship is shown by the conclusion. To this he replies that though the premises are scattered and piecemeal, they are knit together by a logical bond of mutual compatibility and relevancy, and therefore the *nigamana* is unnecessary even for the purpose of showing the mutual relation of the premises.[88]

Because of the foregoing considerations Buddhist logicians reduce the *avayavas* to two, namely, *hetu* and *udāharaṇa,* and ultimately these two to one, namely, *hetu*, depending on the grasping power of the opponent.

It is proper to conclude this account concerning the number of *avayavas* with the words of S. Mookherjee. "From the doctrine of ten membered syllogism reduced to five in the *Nyāyasūtra* and still further reduced to two (or one) in Buddhist Logic, we can trace the history of the evolution of syllogism. Naturally the psychological and logical factors were mixed together in the doctrine of ten-membered syllogism. In the Nayiyāyika's syllogism there has been a bold attempt to shake off the psychological incumbus, but still the psychological influence did not cease to be at work. In the Buddhist syllogism as propounded by Diṅnāga and Dharmakīrti, the psychological factors were carefully eliminated and the syllogism received a perfectly logical shape. But the survival of the example was a relic of the ancient sway of psychology and this was destined to be unceremoniously brushed aside by the onslaughts of Jaina logicians."[89]

Avayavadvaya Tradition

Though the Buddhist account of the number of *avayavas* can be traced back to pre-Diṅnāga thinkers,[90] for want of some definite information we have to begin with the *Nyāya Bindu* of Dharmakīrti. In the *Nyāya Bindu* three *avayavas* of *anumāna* are jointly referred to as *sādhana*. The three *avayavas* are named *pakṣa, hetu,* and *dṛṣtānta*. The acceptance of *pakṣa*, that is, *pratijñā*, indicates that Dharmakīrti is not aversed to the *avayavatraya* tradition.

Here, though we find the statement of *pratijñā* it is not, in fact, a part of the process of *anumāna*.[91] Both in the *Pramāṇa Vārtika* and *Nyāya Bindu* we find elaborate arguments advanced by Dharmakīrti to point out the nonacceptance of *pratijñā* as an *avayava* of *anumāna*.[92] The main argument put forth by him is that the statement of *pratijñā* may be made, but it can be done away with also. In those cases where *pratijñā* is not stated, it is understood as implicit. In fact, from the context itself the reference to *pratijñā* is to be understood, even though it is not explicitly stated. Thus, only *hetu* and *udāharaṇa* are parts of the process of *anumāna*. In fact, Dharmakīrti goes a step further and states that *udāharaṇa* is needed for ordinary minds, but for an intelligent person only *hetu* suffices.[93]

In the statement of *parārthānumāna* Dharmakīrti advocates the model of *avayavatraya,* consisting of *pratijñā, udāharaṇa,* and *upanaya,* but maintains that only *udāharaṇa* and *upanaya* are real *avayavas* because they alone have probative value. The examples of the three types of *anumāna* are:

1. *Svabhāvānumāna* :
   Udāharaṇa : Everything that exists is momentary, like a jar.
   Upanaya : The sound exists.
   Nigamana : Therefore sound is momentary.

2. *Kāryānumāna*

Udāharaṇa	:	Wherever there is smoke, there is fire, like in kitchen.
Upanaya	:	Here there is smoke.
Nigamana	:	Therefore here there is fire.

3. *Anupalabdhyanumāna*

Udāharaṇa	:	Whatsoever is present and is perceptible is necessarily perceived, like a jar.
Upanaya	:	But there is no such jar being perceived.
Nigamana	:	Therefore a jar is not present here.[94]

For Diṅnāga and Dharmakīrti the *nigamana* is the *sādhya* for which *hetu* and *udāharaṇa* or *udāharaṇa* and *upanaya* are the *sādhana*. Therefore they are referred to as *sādhanāṅga* (constituents of proof), whereas *pratijñā* and *nigamana* are known as *asādhanāṅga*. In the case of *svārthānumāna, hetu* and *udāharaṇa* are *sādhanāṅga* and *pratijñā, upanaya* and *nigamana* are *asādhananga,* whereas in case of *parārthānumāna, pratijñā, hetu,* and *nigamana* are *sādhanāṅgas,* and *udāharaṇa* and *upanaya* are *asādhanāṅgas*. Thus, the Buddhist position is to be regarded as *avayavadvayi*.

In conclusion, for Buddhists a statement of *anumāna* is ordinarily expressed either as *pratijñā-hetu-udāhraṇa* or as *udāharaṇa-upanaya-nigamana*. But from a strict logical point of view neither *pratijñā* nor *nigamana* is a genuine part of the process of *anumāna*, and therefore the real process of *anumāna* consists of only two *avayavas,* namely, *hetu* and *udāharaṇa* or *udāharaṇa* and *upanaya*. This is a view advocated by Dharmakīrti and accepted by all of his followers, like Śāntarakṣita and Mokṣākaragupta.

Appendix 1

Nyāyapraveśakasūtram

Sādhanaṁ dūṣaṇaṁ caiva sābhāsaṁ parasaṁvide
pratyakṣamanumānaṁ ca sābhāsaṁ tvātmasaṁvide.
Iti śāstrārthasaṁgrahaḥ.

Tatra pakṣādivacanāni sādhanam. Pakṣahetudṛṣṭāntavacanairhi prāśnikānāmapratīto'rthaḥ pratipādyata iti. Tatra pakṣaḥ prasiddho dharmī prasiddhaviśeṣaṇa viśiṣṭatayā svayaṁ sādhyatvenepsitaḥ. Pratyakṣādyaviruddha iti vākyaśeṣaḥ. Tadyathā. Nityaḥ śabdo'nityo veti.

Hetustrirūpaḥ. Kiṁ punastrairūpyam. Pakṣadharmatvaṁ sapakṣe sattvam vipakṣe cāsattvamiti. Kaḥ punaḥ sapakṣaḥ. Ko vā vipakṣa iti. Sādhyadharmasāmānyena samāno'rthaḥ sapakṣaḥ. Tadyathā. Anitye śabde sādhhye ghaṭādiranityaḥ sapakṣaḥ. Vipakṣo yatra sādhyaṁ nāsti. Yannityaṁ tadakṛtakaṁ dṛṣṭaṁ yathākāśamiti. Tatra kṛtakatvaṁ prayatnānantarīyakatvaṁ vā sapakṣa evāsti vipakṣe nāstyeva. Ityanityādau hetuḥ. Dṛṣṭānto dvividhaḥ. Sādharmyeṇa vaidharmyeṇa ca. Tatra sādharmyeṇa tāvat. Yatra hetoḥ sapakṣa evāstitvaṁ khyāpyate. Tadyathā. Yatkṛtakaṁ tadanityaṁ dṛṣṭaṁ yathā ghaṭādiriti. Vaidharmyeṇāpi. Yatra sādhyābhāve hetorabhāva eva kathyate. Tadyathā. Yannityaṁ tadakṛtakaṁ dṛṣṭ aṁ yathākāśamiti. Nityaśabdenātrānityatvasyābhāva ucyate. Akṛtakaśabdenāpi kṛtakatvasyābhāvaḥ. Yathā bhavābhāvo'bhāva iti. Uktāḥ pakṣādayaḥ.

Eṣām vacanāni parapratyāyanakāle sādhanam. Tadyathā. Anityaḥ śabda iti pakṣavacanam. Kṛtakatvāditi pakṣadharmavacanam. Yatkṛtakaṁ tadanityaṁ dṛṣṭaṁ yathā ghaṭādiriti sapakṣānugamavacanam. Yannityaṁ tadakṛtakaṁ dṛṣṭaṁ yathākāśamiti vyatirekavacanam. Etānyeva trayo'vayavā ityucyante.

Sādhayitumiṣṭo'pi pratyakṣādiviruddhaḥ pakṣābhāsaḥ. Tadyathā. (1) Pratyakṣ aviruddhaḥ, (2) Anumānaviruddhaḥ, (3) Āgamaviruddhaḥ, (4) Lokaviruddhaḥ, (5) Svavacanaviruddhaḥ, (6) Apraṣiddhaviśeṣaṇaḥ, (7) Aprasiddhaviśeṣyaḥ, (8) Aprasiddhobhayaḥ, (9) Prasiddhasambandhaśceti. Tatra Pratyakṣaviruddho yathā. Aśrāvaṇaḥ śabda iti. Anumānaviruddho yathā. Nityo ghaṭa iti. Āgamaviruddho yathā. Vaiśeṣikasya nityaḥ śabda iti sādhayataḥ. Lokaviruddho yathā. Śuci naraśiraḥkapālaṁ prāṇyaṅgatvācchaṅkhaśuktivaditi. Svavacanaviruddho yathā. Mātā me vandhyeti. Aprasiddhaviśeṣano yathā Bauddhasya Sāṁkhyaṁ prati vināśī śabda iti. Aprasiddhaviśeṣyo yathā. Sāṁkhyasya Bauddhaṁ prati cetana ātmeti. Aprasiddhobhayo yathā. Vaiśeṣikasya Bauddham prati sukhādisamavāyikāraṇamātmeti. Prasiddhasambandho yathā. Śrāvaṇaḥ śabda iti. Eṣām vacanāni dharmasvarūpanirākaraṇamukhena pratipādanāsambhavataḥ sādhanavaiphalyataśceti pratijñādoṣāḥ. Uktāḥ pakṣābhāsāḥ.

Asiddhānaikāntikaviruddhā hetvābhāsāḥ. Tatrāsiddhaścatuḥprakāraḥ. Tadyathā. (1) Ubhayāsiddhaḥ, (2) Anyatarāsiddhaḥ, (3) Saṁdigdhāsiddhaḥ, (4) Āśrayāsiddhaśceti. Tatra śabdānityatve sādhye cākṣuṣatvādityubhayāsiddhaḥ. Kṛtakatvāditiśabdābhivya- ktivādinaṁ pratyanyatarāsiddhaḥ. Bāṣpādibhāvena sandihyamāno bhūtasaṁghāto" gnisiddhāvupadiśyamānaḥ saṁdigdhāsiddhaḥ. Dravyamākāśaṁ guṇāśrayatvādityā- kāśāsattvavādinaṁ pratyāśrayāsiddhaḥ.

Anaikāntikaḥ ṣaṭprakāraḥ. (1) Sādhāraṇaḥ, (2) Asādhāraṇaḥ, (3) Sapakṣ-aikadeśavṛttirvipakṣavyāpī, (4) Vipakṣaikadeśavṛttiḥ sapakṣavyāpī, (5) Ubhayapakṣ -aikadeśavṛttiḥ, (6) Viruddhāvyabhicārī ceti.

Tatra sādhāraṇaḥ śabdaḥ prameyatvānnitya iti. Taddhi nityānityapakṣayoḥ sādhāraṇatvādanaikāntikam. Kiṁ ghaṭavatprameyatvādanityaḥ śabda āhosvidākāśavatprameyatvānnitya iti. Asādhāraṇaḥ śrāvaṇatvānnitya iti. Taddhi nityānityapakṣābhyāṁ vyāvṛttatvānnityānityavinirmuktasya cānyasyāsaṁbhavātsaṁśayahetuḥ. Kiṁbhūtasyāsya śrāvaṇatvamiti. Sapakṣ aikadeśavṛttirvipakṣavyāpī yathā. Aprayatnānantarīyakaḥ śabdo'nityatvāt. Aprayatnānantarīyakaḥ pakṣaḥ. Asya vidyudākāśādiḥ sapakṣaḥ. Tatraikadeśe vidyudādau vidyate'nityatvam nākāśādau. Aprayatnānantarīyakaḥ pakṣaḥ. Asya ghaṭādirvipakṣaḥ. Tatra sarvatra ghaṭādau vidyate'nityatvam. Tasmādetadapi vidyudghaṭasādharmyeṇānaikāntikam. Kiṁ ghaṭavadanityatvātprayatnānantarīyakaḥ śabdaḥ āhosvidvidyudādivadanityatvādaprayatnānantarīyaka iti. Vipakṣ aikadeśavṛttiḥ sapakṣavyāpī yathā. Prayatnānantarīyakaḥ śabdo'nityatvāt. Prayatnānantarīyakaḥ pakṣaḥ. Asya ghaṭādiḥ sapakṣaḥ. Tatra sarvatra ghaṭādau vidyate" nityatvam. Prayatnānantarīyakaḥ pakṣaḥ. Asya vidyudākāśādīrvipakṣ aḥ. Tatraikadeśe vidyudādau vidyate'nityatvaṁ nākāśādau. Tasmādetadapi vidyudghaṭasādharmyeṇa pūrvavadanaikāntikam. Ubhayapakṣaikadeśavṛttir yathā. Nityaḥ śabdo'mūrtatvāditi. Nityaḥ pakṣaḥ. Asyākāśa paramāṇvādiḥ sapakṣ aḥ. Tatraikadeśa ākāśādau vidyate'mūrtatvaṁ na paramāṇau. Nityaḥ pakṣaḥ. Asya ghaṭa sukhādirvipakṣaḥ. Tatraikadeśe sukhādau vidyate" murtatvam na ghaṭādau. Tasmādetadapi sukhākāśasādharmyeṇānaikāntikam. Viruddhāvyabhicārī yathā. Anityaḥ śabdaḥ kṛtakatvād ghaṭavat. Nityaḥ śabdaḥ śrāvaṇatvāt śabdatvavaditi. Ubhayoḥ saṁśayahetutvād dvāvapyetāveko'naikāntikaḥ samuditāveva.

Viruddhaścatuḥprakāraḥ. Tadyathā. (1) Dharmasvarūpaviparītasādhanaḥ, (2) Dharmaviśeṣaviparītasādhanaḥ, (3) Dharmisvarūpaviparītasādhanaḥ, (4) Dharmiviśeṣ-aviparītasādhanaśceti. Tatra dharmasvarūpaviparītasādhano yathā. Nityaḥ śabdaḥ kṛtakatvāt prayatnānantarīyakatvādveti. Ayaṁ heturvipakṣa eva bhāvādviruddhaḥ. Dharmaviśeṣaviparītasādhano yathā. Parārthāścakṣurādayaḥ saṁghātatvācchayanāsanād- yangviśeṣavaditi. Ayaṁ heturyathā pārārthyaṁ cakṣ urādīnāṁ sādhayati tathā saṁhatatvampi parasyātmanaḥ sādhayati. Ubhayatrāvyabhicārāt. Dharmisvarūpaviparītasādhano yathā. Na dravyaṁ na karma na guṇo bhāvaḥ ekadravyavattvāt guṇakarmasu ca bhāvāt sāmānyaviśeṣ avaditi. Ayaṁ hi heturyathā dravyādipratiṣedhaṁ bhāvasya sādhayati tathā bhāvasyābhāvatvamapi sādhayati. Ubhayatrāvyabhicārāt. Dharmiviśeṣ aviparītasādhano yathā. Ayameva heturasminneva pūrva-pakṣe'syaiva dharmiṇo yo viśeṣaḥ satpratyayakartṛtvaṁ nāma tadviparītamasatpratyaya- kartṛtvamapi sādhayati. Ubhayatrāvyabhicārāt.

Dṛṣṭāntābhāso dvividhaḥ. Sādharmyeṇa vāidharyeṇa ca. Tatra sādharmyeṇa tāvad dṛṣṭāntābhāsaḥ pañcaprakāraḥ. Tadyathā. (1) Sādhanadharmāsiddhaḥ, (2) Sādhyadharmāsiddhaḥ, (3) Ubhayadharmāsiddhaḥ, (4) Ananvayaḥ, (5) Viparītānvayaśceti. Tatra sādhanadharmāsiddho yathā. Nityaḥ śabdo'mūrtatvāt paramāṇuvat. Yadamūrtaṁ tannityaṁ dṛṣṭaṁ yathā paramāṇuḥ. Paramāṇau hi sādhyaṁ nityatvamasti sādhanadharmo'mūrtatvaṁ nāsti mūrtatvātparamāṇūnāmiti. Sādhyadharmāsiddho yathā. Nityaḥ śabdo'mūrtatvād buddhivat. Yadamūrtaṁ tannityaṁ dṛṣṭaṁ yathā buddhiḥ. Buddhau hi sādhanadharmo'mūrtatvamasti sādhyadharmo nityatvaṁ nāsti. Anityatvād buddheriti. Ubhayāsiddho dvividhaḥ. Sannasanśceti. Tatra ghaṭavaditi vidyamānobhayāsiddhaḥ. Anityatvānmūrtatvācca ghaṭasya. Ākāśavadityavidyamānobhayāsiddhaḥ. Tadasattvavādinaṁ prati. Ananvayo yatra vinānvayena sādhyasādhanayoḥ sahabhāvaḥ pradarśyate. Yathā ghaṭe kṛtakatvamanityatvaṁ ca dṛṣṭamiti. Viparītānvayo yathā. Yat kṛtakaṁ tadanityaṁ dṛṣṭamiti vaktavye yadanityaṁ tatkṛtakaṁ dṛṣṭamiti bravīti. Vaidharmyeṇāpi dṛṣ ṭantābhāsaḥ pañcaprakāraḥ Tadyathā. (1) Sādhyāvyāvṛttaḥ, (2) Sādhanāvyāvṛttaḥ, (3) Ubhayāvyāvṛttaḥ, (4) Avyatirekaḥ, (5) Viparītavyatirekaśceti. Tatra sādhyāvyāvṛtto yathā. Nityaḥ śabdo" mūrtatvāt paramāṇuvat. Yadanityaṁ tanmūrtaṁ dṛṣṭaṁ yathā paramāṇuḥ. Paramāṇorhi sādhanadharmo" mūrtatvaṁ vyāvṛttaṁ mūrtatvātparamāṇūnāmiti. Sādhyadharmo nityatvaṁ na vyāvṛttaṁ nityatvātparamāṇūnāmiti. Sādhanāvyāvṛtto yathā. Karmavaditi. Karmaṇaḥ sādhyaṁ nityatvaṁ vyāvṛttam. Anityatvātkarmaṇaḥ. Sādhanadharmo'mūrtatvam na vyāvṛttam. Amūrtatvātkarmaṇaḥ. Ubhayāvyāvṛttaḥ. Ākāśavaditi. Tatsattvavādinaṁ prati. Tato nityatvamamūrtatvaṁ ca na vyāvṛttam. Nityatvādamūrtatvāccākāśasyeti. Avyatireko yatra vinā sādhyasādhananivṛttyā tadvipakṣabhāvo nidarśyate. Yathā ghaṭe mūrtatvamanityatvaṁ ca dṛṣṭamiti. Viparītavyatireko yathā. Yadanityaṁ tanmūrtaṁ dṛṣṭamiti vaktavye yanmūrtaṁ tadanityaṁ dṛṣṭamiti bravīti.

Eṣām pakṣahetudṛṣṭāntābhāsānām vacanāni sādhanābhāsam.

Ātmapratyāyanārthaṁ tu pratyakṣamanumānaṁ ca dve eva pramāṇe. Tatra pratyakṣ am kalpanāpodhaṁ yajjñānamarthe rūpādau nāmajātyādikalpanārahitam. Tadakṣ amakṣaṁ prati vartata iti pratyakṣam. Anumānaṁ liṅgādarthadarśanam. Liṅgaṁ punastrirūpamuktam. Tasmādyadanumeye'rthe jñānamutpadyate'gniratra anityaḥ śabda iti vā tadanumānam. Ubhayatra tadeva jñānaṁ phalamadhigamarūpatvāt. Savyāpāravatkhyāteḥ pramāṇatvamiti. Kalpanājñānamarthāntare pratyakṣ ābhāsam. Yajjñānaṁ ghaṭaḥ paṭa iti vā vikalpayataḥ samutpadyate tadarthasvalakṣ aṇaviṣ-ayatvātpratyakṣābhāsam. Hetvābhāsapūrvakaṁ jñānaṁ-anumānābhāsam. Hetvābhāso hi bahuprakāra uktaḥ. Tasmādyadanumeye'rthe jñānamavyutpannasya bhavati tadanumānābhāsam.

Sādhanadoṣodbhāvanāni duṣaṇāni. Sādhanadoṣo nyūnatvam. Pakṣadoṣaḥ pratyakṣ - ādiviruddhatvam. Hetudoṣo'siddhānaikāntikaviruddhatvam. Dṛṣṭāntadoṣaḥ sādhana-dharmādyasiddhatvam. Tasyodbhāvanam prāśnikapratyāyanaṁ dūṣ aṇam. Abhūtasādhanadoṣodbhāvanāni dūṣaṇābhāsāni. Sampūrṇe sādhane nyūnatvavacanam. Aduṣṭapakṣe pakṣadoṣavacanam. Siddhahetuke' siddhahetukaṁ vacanam. Ekāntahetuke'nekāntahetukaṁ vacanam. Aviruddhahetuke viruddhahetukaṁ vacanam. Aduṣṭadṛṣṭānte duṣṭadṛṣṭ āntadoṣavacanam. Etāni dūṣaṇābhāsāni. Na hyebhiḥ parapakṣo duṣyate. Niravadyatvāttasya. Ityuparamyate.

Padārthamātramākhyātamādau Diṅmātrasiddhaye;
Yātra yuktirayuktirvā sānyatra suvicāritā.
*** Iti NYĀYAPRAVEŚAKASŪTRAM samāptam***

Appendix 2

Nyāyapraveśakasūtram (Translation)

Giving arguments in support of one's own position and pointing out defects in the rival's position along with their respective fallacies are essential for communicating knowledge to others, whereas for acquiring knowledge for one's own sake, perception and inference and their respective fallacies are essential.

This is the sum and substance of the science of debate.[1]

Here, the statement regarding subject (*pakṣa*) and so on is means (*sādhana*).[2] The statements of subject, reason (*hetu*), and example (*dṛṣṭānta*) establish the hitherto not known object to the inquirer. Subject is a known substratum having the known qualifying property through which another property is desired to be proved by someone.[3] The subject must not be contrary to perception and so on. In the example of whether sound is eternal or noneternal, the subject is sound, and the property that is desired to be proved is whether it is eternal or noneternal. This is the point of debate.

Reason has three features.[4] Now the question is, Which are these three features? The necessary presence of reason in the subject, the presence of reason only in homologue (*sapakṣa*), and the necessary absence of reason always in heterologue (*vipakṣa*) are the three features of reason. Again, what is homologue?[5] What is heterologue? Homologue is what is similar (to subject) by virtue of having probandum (*sādhya*) as its common property. For example, in order to prove that "Sound is noneternal," pot and so on, which are noneternal, become homologue. Heterologue is that where probandum is absent for example, in the inference "Whatever is eternal is experienced to be nonproduced as space and so on." Being produced or being necessarily associated with effort is present only in homologue and is never present in heterologue. Here, reason is noneternal and so on.

Example is twofold.[6] One is based on similarity (*sādharmyeṇa*) and, the other is based on dissimilarity (*vaidharmyeṇa*). That which is based on similarity is where the existence of reason is known only in homologue. Its example is "Whatever is produced, is experienced as noneternal, for example pot and so on." That which is based on dissimilarity is where absence of reason is said to be in the absence of probandum, for example: "Whatever is eternal is experienced to be nonproduced as space and so on." "Eternal" means absence of noneternal. The word "nonproduced" means absence of being produced, as for example, "nonbeing" is absence of being. Thus, we have stated subject and so on.

Statements about all these are means of communicating knowledge to others. That can be explained as follows: "Sound is noneternal" is a statement of subject, and "because it is produced" is a statement of subject having reason as its property (*pakṣadharmatā*). "Whatever is produced is experienced to be noneternal like pot and so on" is the statement of homologue, which is based on similarity. The statement of dissimilarity (*vyatireka*) is "Whatever is eternal is experienced to be nonproduced like space and so on." These are said to be the three elements (*avayavas*) of the process of argumentation in support of one's own position.

Even though it is desired to be proved, a fallacious thesis (*pakṣābhāsa*) is (fallacious because it is) contrary to perception and so on.[7] It is of the following nine types: (1) contrary to perception (*pratyakṣa viruddha*), (2) contrary to inference (*anumāna viruddha*), (3) contrary to one's own scripture (*āgama viruddha*), (4) contrary to public opinion (*loka viruddha*), (5) contrary to one's own statement (*svavacana viruddha*), (6) a thesis whose subject is unacceptable (*aprasiddha viśeṣaṇa*), (7) a thesis whose predicate is unacceptable (*aprasiddha viśeṣya*), (8) unacceptable to both parties (*aprasiddhobhaya*), and (9) a thesis too well known or accepted universally (*prasiddha saṁbandha*).[(i)] A thesis contrary to perception is like "Sound is audible."[(ii)] A thesis contrary to inference is like "Pot is eternal."[(iii)] A thesis contrary to one's own scripture is like a Vaiśeṣika adherent trying to prove that "Sound is eternal."[(iv)] A thesis contrary to popular belief is like "A dead man's skull is pure because it is a limb of an animate being, as, for example, a conch or a shell."[(v)] A thesis contrary to one's own statement is like "My mother is barren."[(vi)] A thesis whose predicate is unacceptable is like while arguing with a Sāṁkhya adherent, a Buddhist taking his stand on such a proposition as "Sound is perishable."[(vii)] A thesis whose subject is unacceptable is like, while arguing with a Buddhist, a Sāṁkhya adherent taking his stand on such a proposition as "Self or ego is animate."[(viii)] A thesis whose both the terms — the subject and the predicate — are unacceptable is like a Vaiśeṣika adherent arguing with a Buddhist and taking his stand on such a proposition as "Soul is the inherent cause of pleasure and so on."[(ix)] A thesis universally accepted is like "Sound is audible."

These statements have a fallacious thesis (*pratijñādoṣa* = *pakṣābhāsa*) because they cannot be logically established and, second, they cannot serve as a means of proof. They negate the very property that is to be proved. Thus, fallacies of thesis are stated.

Unproved (*asiddha*), inconclusive (*anekāntika*), and contradictory (*viruddha*) are the fallacies of reason (*hetvābhāsas*).[8]

Unproved is divided into four types: (1) unacceptable to both (*ubhayāsiddha*), (2) unacceptable to either (*anyatarāsiddha*), (3) unproved because of doubt (*saṁdigdhāsiddha*), and (4) unproved locus (*āśrayāsiddha*).

In the argument "Sound is noneternal on account of being visible," sound is subject, noneternal is probandum, and visible is reason. Here visibility (of sound) is unacceptable to both parties, and, therefore, it is a fallacy of being unacceptable to both. Again, the inference "Sound is noneternal because it is effort-made," will not be acceptable to a person upholding the position that sound is eternal and that only its manifestations, which are effort-made, are noneternal. On the basis of doubtful existence (of reason), if one undertakes the inference like, inferring fire on the basis of doubting cluster of mist as smoke, then it is a fallacy of doubtful existence. "Space is a substance because it is a locus of quality (sound)": (this argument is valid) for believers in the reality of space; but (for Buddhists) it is not valid because (Buddhists) don't believe in the reality of space.

Inconclusive is sixfold: (1) too wide (*sādhāraṇa*), (2) too narrow (*asādhāraṇa*), (3) pervading one part of the homologue and pervading the entire heterologue (*sapakṣaikadeśavṛttiḥ vipakṣavyāpī*),[9] (4) pervading one part of the heterologue and pervading the entire homologue (*vipakṣaikadeśavṛttiḥ sapakṣavyāpī*),[10] (5) pervading one part of both (ubhayapakṣaikadeśavṛttiḥ)[11] and (6) contrary and nondivergent, (*viruddhāvyabhicārī*).[12] The example of "too wide" is that "Sound is eternal on account of its knowability." Here, the reason (knowability) is common to both eternal and noneternal things; therefore it is a fallacy of inconclusiveness of the variety of being "too wide." Is sound noneternal like a pot on account of its knowability or is it eternal like space on account of its knowability? The example of "too narrow" is "Sound is eternal on account of its audibility." Here, audibility is peculiar to sound and is not found in any other thing eternal or noneternal, and there is no other thing different from eternal or noneternal, and this gives rise to doubt as to what help audibility (as a reason) can render. "Pervading one part of the homologue and pervading the entire heterologue" is as follows: "Sound is naturally existing" (which can exist without any volitional effort on our part). Here, the term "natural" (*aprayatnānatarīyaka*) is subject. Its homologues are lightning, space, and so on. Here in one part of the homologue like lightning, noneternality resides, but it doesn't reside in some other parts like space and so on. Let us again take the term "natural" as subject. Pot and so on are its heterologues. Now this noneternality resides in all heterologues like pot and so on. Therefore, being common to both lightning (which is nonproduced) and pot (which is produced), it is inconclusive. Here a doubt arises whether sound is effort-made because of noneternality like pot or noneffort-made because of noneternality like lightning. "Residing in some part of heterologue and residing in whole of homologue" is as follows: "Sound is effort-made because it is noneternal." Here subject is effort-made. Pot and so on are its homologues. Everywhere in pot and so on noneternality resides. Again subject is effort-made; its heterologues are lightning, space, and so on. Here, in one part of the heterologue like lightning, noneternality resides but does not reside in other part like space and so on. Therefore, this also being common to both lightning and pot it is inconclusive as before. "Pervading one part of both (i.e., homologue and heterologue)" is like "Sound is eternal because it is incorporeal." Here subject is eternality. Space, infinitesimal particle, and so on are its homologues. In one part of the homologue, that is in space, incorporeality resides but not in the other part, that is, an infinitesimal particle. Again, subject is eternality. Pot, pleasure and so on are its heterologue. Here, in one part of the heterologue, that is, pleasure incorporeality resides but not in the other part of the heterologue like pot and so on. Since it is common to both pleasure (which is heterologue) and space (which is homologue), it is inconclusive. An example of "Contrary and nondivergent" is as follows: "Sound is noneternal on account of being produced like a pot" and "Sound is eternal on account of audibility like soundness," in both these arguments, the two reasons taken together cause doubt and are therefore inconclusive (here, about the same thesis two different reasons lead to two contradictory conclusions).

Contradictory is of four types. They are as follows: (1) reason contradictory to probandum (*dharmasvarūpaviparītasādhana*),[13] (2) reason contradictory to a particular probandum (*dharmaviśeṣaviparītasādhana*),[14] (3) reason contradictory to thesis (*dharmisvarūpavīparitasādhana*),[15] (4) reason contradictory to a particular thesis (*dharmiviśeṣaviparītasādhana*).[16] "Reason contradictory to probandum" is as follows: "Sound is eternal on account of being produced or effort made." This reason belongs to the side of heterologues. Therefore, it is known as contradictory. "Reason contradictory to a particular probandum" is as follows: eyes and so on exist for the sake of others on account of their composite character like bed, seat etc. which are composite in nature. This reason not only proves that eyes and so on exist for the sake of others but also proves that self (as conceived by the Sāṁkhyas) is of a composite nature because reason is invariably applicable to both. "Reason contradictory to the thesis" is as follows: "*Summum genus* (*bhāva*) is not a substance or action or quality, because of its possessing one substance and because of its presence in qualities and actions like the universal and the particular." This reason not only proves that *summum genus* is the opposite of substance and so on but also proves the absence of *summum genus* itself because it is invariably common to both. "Reason contradictory to a particular thesis": this very reason in this very argument of the opponent proves the presence as well as the absence of "being based on being" and "being based on nonbeing" and is common to both.[17]

The fallacy of examples is twofold, on the basis of similarity and on the basis of dissimilarity.

The fallacy of example based on similarity is fivefold. It is as follows: (1) incompatibility of the example with the reason (*Sādhanadharmāsiddha*),[18] (2) incompatibility of the example with the probandum (*Sādhyadharmāsiddha*),[19] (3) incompatibility of the example with both (reason and probandum) (*Ubhayadharmāsiddha*),[20] (4) absence of statement of positive invariable concomitance (*Ananvaya*),[21] and (5) contrary to the statement of positive invariable concomitance (*Viparītanvayaḥ*).[22] "Incompatibility of example with the reason" is as follows: "Sound is eternal on account of its being incorporeal like infinitesimal particle." In infinitesimal particle the probandum, that is, eternality, exists, but the reason, namely, incorporeality, doesn't exist because infinitesimal particles are corporeal. "Incompatibility of the example with the probandum" is as follows: "Sound is eternal on account of its being incorporeal like intelligence." In intelligence, the reason, that is incorporeality, exists, and the probandum, that is eternality, doesn't exist because intelligence is noneternal. Incompatibility of the example with both (reason and probandum) is twofold, positive and negative. The positive is as follows: "Sound is eternal on account of being incorporeal like a pot." Here, the example is contrary to both reason and probandum because pot is noneternal (contrary to probandum) and corporeal (contrary to reason). The example of negative is as follows: "Sound is eternal on account of being incorporeal like space." This argument contains an example that is not acceptable to a person who doesn't believe in the reality of space. "Absence of statement of positive invariable concomitance" is as follows: the coexistence of probandum and reason is stated without stating their invariable concomitance, for example in the statement "In the pot there is the property of being produced and noneternality." "Contrary to the statement of positive invariable concomitance" is as follows: instead of saying, "Whatever is produced is experienced to be noneternal," we say, "Whatever is noneternal is experienced to be produced." (Here concomitance is stated in a reverse order.)

Fallacy of example based on dissimilarity[23] is fivefold, which is as follows: (1) nonabsent probandum (*Sādhyavyāvṛtta*),[24] (2) nonabsent reason (*Sādhanavyāvṛtta*),[25] (3) both are nonabsent (*Ubhayavyāvṛtta*),[26] (4) absence of statement of negative concomitance (*Avyatireka*),[27] and (5) contrary to the statement of negative invariable concomitance (*Viparītavyatireka*).[28] "Nonabsent probandum" is as follows: "Sound is eternal on account of incorporeality like infinitesimal particle. Whatever is noneternal is experienced to be corporeal like infinitesimal particle." Of infinitesimal particle, reason is incorporeality, but incorporeality, in fact, is absent from infinitesimal particles because they are corporeal, whereas the probandum, namely, eternality, is not excluded because infinitesimal particles are eternal. "Nonabsent reason" is as follows: "Sound is eternal on account of incorporeality like action." Here, the probandum, that is, eternality, is excluded in respect of action because all actions are noneternal, but the reason, that is incorporeality is not excluded because an action is incorporeal. "Both are nonabsent" is as follows: "Sound is eternal on account of incorporeality like space." This is fallacious for one who believes in the existence of space. Here, both eternality (probandum) and incorporeality (reason) are not excluded because space is both eternal and noncorporeal. "Absence of statement of negative concomitance" is that where without negating probandum and reason, their presence in the heterologue is stated, as, for example, in pot there are incorporeality and noneternality. "Contrary to the statement of negative invariable concomitance" is as follows: instead of saying "Whatever is noneternal is experienced to be corporeal," we say, "Whatever is corporeal is experienced to be noneternal."

These are the statements of the fallacies of thesis, reason, and example, and they are known as fallacies of demonstration or means of proof.

In order to acquire knowledge for one's own sake perception and inference are the only two means of knowledge. Perception is bereft of conceptualization. It is that knowledge that is devoid of all determinations in terms of words and concepts like class and so on. That which depends on each individual cognitive sense is perception. Inference is knowledge of objects on the basis of a necessary mark. Necessary mark is said to have three features. Therefore, it is that knowledge that arises concerning the inferential object, for example, "Here is fire (because of smoke)" or "Sound is noneternal (because it is produced)." In both (perception and inference) the same knowledge is both the cause and its result, which is in the form of cognition of an object. Knowledge is always of functional character, and, therefore, it is true cognition. (The truth of knowledge consists in its ability to be functional.) A determinate knowledge is a fallacious perception if it is taken in the context of objective reality.

The object of determinate knowledge is a universal, but if a unique particular is taken to be its object, then it is fallacious. So, (determinate) knowledge like "This is a pot" or "This is cloth," which arises through a judgment, is fallacious perception because it takes the objective reality (unique particular) as its object. Fallacious inference is that which is due to fallacious reason. Fallacious reason is said to be of many kinds. Thus, concerning the inferential object, that knowledge that arises in one who doesn't take cognizance of (fallacies like unproved and so on) is fallacious inference.

To point out defects in means of proof is known as fallacies in means of proof or refutation *(dūṣaṇa)*. Deficiency in means of proofs is (known as) its defect. Defect in thesis consists in incompatibility with perception and so on. Defect in reason is unproved, inconclusive, and contradictory. Defect in example is where reason and so on as property are not proved. To point out the defects to the inquirer is for his or her knowledge.

To point out that the defects are not, in fact, defects is known as fallacious refutation. To point out deficiency in a perfect reason, to point out defects in nondefective thesis, to point out unprovenness of a proved reason, to point out inconclusiveness in a conclusive reason, to point out contradiction in a noncontradictory reason, to point out defects in a nondefective example—these are fallacious refutations. By these the rival position is not vitiated because they are not refutable. This is the end.

The entire discourse on (logical) categories is stated to prove the philosophical position of Diṅnāga. Whatever is argued or not argued here is well discussed (in *Pramāṇa Samuccaya*) (by us).

Notes

CHAPTER 1

1. In Buddhist epistemology the Sanskrit word for knowledge is *pramāṇa*, and the words *pramā, samyag-jñāna*, and so on are also used as its synonym.
2. Dharmakīrti, *Nyāya Bindu*, p. 1.
3. Dharmakīrti, *Pramāṇa Vārtika*, p. 3.
4. Ibid., p. 8.
5. Dharmottara, *Nyāya Bindu Ṭīkā*, p. 10.
6. Diṅnāga, *Pramāṇa Samuccaya*, Tr. by Hattori, *Diṅnāga on Perception*, p. 28.
7. Ibid, p. 29.
8. Dharmottara, *Nyāya Bindu Ṭīkā*, pp. 82-85.
9. Aniruddha, *Abhidhammamatasaṁgaho*, IV.8.
10. Edited by Kashyap, Jagdish, *Kathāvatthu*, p. 374.
11. Th. Stcherbatsky, *Buddhist Logic*, vol. 2, p. 311.
12. Ibid., Appendix—IV.
13. Ibid., vol. 1, p. 552.
14. (a) Diṅnāga, *Pramāṇa Samuccaya*, Tr. by Hattori, *Diṅnāga on Perception*, p. 28.
    (b) Dharmakīrti, *Pramāṇa Vārtika*, pp. 479, 480, 491.
15. Dharmakīrti, *Pramāṇa Vārtika*, p. 337.
16. Diṅnāga, *Pramāṇa Samuccaya*, Tr. by Hattori, *Diṅnāga on Perception*, p. 28.
17. Ibid., p. 29.
18. Ibid., p. 108.
19. Ibid., p. 28.
20. Ibid., p. 29.
21. Ibid., p. 28.
22. Dharmottara, *Nyāya Bindu Ṭīkā*, pp. 69ff.
23. Diṅnāga, *Pramāṇa Samuccaya*, Tr. by Hattori, *Diṅnāga on Perception*, p. 30.

CHAPTER 2

1. Diṅnāga, *Pramāṇa Samuccaya*, Tr. by Hattori, *Diṅnāga on Perception*, p. 32.
2. See Bhatt, *Basic Ways of Knowing*, p. 31.
3. Diṅnāga, *Pramāṇa Samuccaya*, Tr. by Hattori, *Diṅnāga on Perception*, p. 24.
4. Ibid, p. 25.

5. *Tatra sandhāne na pramāṇāntaram aniṣṭāsakteḥ*, ibid., p. 24.
6. Ibid., p. 28.
7. Ibid., p. 29.
8. Ibid., pp. 25-26.
9. Vasubandhu, *Abhidharmakośa*, p.145.
10. Dharmakīrti, *Nyāya Bindu*, p. 32.
11. Dharmottara, *Nyāya Bindu Ṭīkā*, pp. 12ff.
12. Dharmakīrti, *Nyāya Bindu*, p. 42.
13. Ibid., pp. 42ff.
14. Cf. *avyapadeśyam* of the Nyāya school.
15. Dharmottara, *Nyāya Bindu Ṭīkā*, p. 44.
16. *Vikalpa yonayaḥ śabdāśca śabdā vikalpa yonayaḥ*.
17. *Dharmottara, Nyāya Bindu Ṭīkā*, pp. 32ff.
18. Ibid., pp. 51ff.
19. Ibid., pp. 54.
20. Śāntarakṣita, *Tattva Saṁgraha*, verses 1220-23.
21. Ibid., verse 1223
22. Ibid., verse 1224.
23. Ibid., verse 1236.
24. Ibid., verse 1312.
25. Th. Stcherbatsky, *Buddhist Logic*, vol. 1, pp. 153-45.
26. Dharmottara, *Nyāya Bindu Ṭīkā*, p. 36.
27. Śāntarakṣita, *Tattva Saṁgraha*, verse. 1313.
28. Dharmottara, *Nyāya Bindu Ṭīkā*, pp. 36-40.
29. Śāntarakṣita, *Tattva Saṁgraha*, verse. 1323.
30. Kamalaśila, *Tattva Saṁgraha Pañjikā*, p. 482.
31. Dharmarāja Adhvarindra, *Vedānta Paribhāṣā*, p. 32.
32. Bhartṛhari, *Vākyapadīya*, I, verses 123-24.
33. Iśvara Kṛṣṇa, *Sāṅkhya Kārikā*, pp. 27-28.
34. Bhatta, Kumarila, *Śloka Vārtika, pratyakṣa khaṅda*, p. 133.
35. Ibid., p. 73.
36. Bhatta, Jayanta, *Nyāya Mañjarī*, p. 92.
37. Viśvanātha, *Bhāṣā Pariccheda*, p. 58.
38. Diṅnāga, *Pramāṇa Samuccaya*, Tr. by Hattori, *Diṅnāga on Perception*, p. 88.
39. Bhaṛtrhari, *Vākyapadīya* Ch. II, verse 48. Kamalaśila in *Pañjikā* quotes this verse in order to substantiate the Buddhist position, which Śāntarakṣita presents in *Tattva Saṁgraha* in another verse with similar import.
40. Śāntarakṣita, *Tattva Saṁgraha*, verses 1292ff.
41. Śāntarakṣita, *Tattva Saṁgraha*, verses 1268-90.
42. Diṅnāga, *Pramāṇa Samuccaya*, Tr. by Hattori, *Diṅnāga on Perception*, Appendix 1.5. *Atra viśeṣaṇam paramatāpekṣam sarvetvavikalpakā eva*.
43. The Buddhist theory of *mānasa pratyakṣa* is different from that of the Nyāya. In Nyāya *mānasa pratyakṣa* is internal perception of the self and mental states through the mind, which is an inner cognitive sense organ.
44. Diṅnāga, *Pramāṇa Samuccaya*, Tr. by Hattori, *Diṅnāga on Perception*, Appendix, I.6.
45. Ibid.
46. Dharmottara, *Nyāya Bindu Ṭīkā*, pp. 46-48.

47. Kamalaśīla, *Tattva Saṁgraha Pañjikā*, pp. 1260-61.
48. Dharmottara, *Nyāya Bindu Ṭikā*. pp. 419-50.
49. Ibid., pp. 56ff.
50. Dharmakirtī, *Pramāṇa Vārtika*, p. 243.
51. Ibid., p. 239.
52. Dharmottara, *Nyāya Bindu Ṭikā*, pp. 56ff.
53. Ibid., p. 60.
54. Th. Stcherbatsky, *Buddhist Logic*, vol. 1, p. 162.
55. Dharmottara, *Nyāya Bindu Ṭikā*; See *Buddhist Logic*, vol. 2, Appendix 3.
56. Dharmottara, *Nyāya Bindu Ṭikā*, p. 59.
57. Ibid.
58. Miśra, Durveka, *Dharmottara Pradipa*, p. 62.
59. Dharmottara, *Nyāya Bindu Ṭikā*, pp. 62-63.
60. Ibid.
61. Dharmakīrti, *Pramāṇa Vārtika*, pp. 268-69.
62. Ibid., pp. 281-86.

CHAPTER 3

1. *Encyclopaedia of Religion and Ethics*, vol. 8, p. 133, fn. 4.
2. Edited by Swami Dwarikadas Shastri, *Sutta Nikāya*, vol. II, p. 58, *Digga Nikāya*, vol. III, p. 226.
3. *Samyutta Nikāya*, vol. 2, p. 57.
4. Ibid., p. 58.
5. Asaṇga, *Mahāyānasūtrālaṅkāra*, I.12.,
6. Sugiura, Sadajvio, *On Some Aspects of the Doctrines of Maitreyanātha and Asaṅga*, pp. 52-53.
7. Ibid., p. 74.
8. Ibid., p. 81.
9. Vidyabhushan, *History of Indian Logic*, p. 267.
10. Ibid., p. 269.
11. Th. Stcherbatsky, *Soul Theory of the Buddhists*, quoted from *Buddhist Logic*, vol. 1, p. 31.
12. Uddyotakara, *Nyāya Vārtika*, p. 300.
13. Diṅnāga, *Pramāṇa Samuccaya*, Tr. by Hattori, *Diṅnāga on Perception*, II.1.
14. Keith, *Indian Logic and Atomism*, p. 43.
15. Chatterjee, *Nyāya Theory of Knowledge*, pp. 244-45.
16. Diṅnāga, *Pramāṇa Samuccaya*, Tr. by Hattori, *Diṅnāga on Perception*, I. 7-8.
17. Vācaspati, *Nyāya Vārtika Tātparya Tīkā*, p. 9.
18. *Pariśuddhi*, Asiatic Society edition, p. 113.
19. Diṅnāga, *Pramāṇa Samuccaya* Tr. by Hattori, *Diṅnāga on Perception*, I.9.
20. Ibid., I.10.
21. Dharmakīrti, *Nyāya Bindu*, I.1.
22. Dharmottara, *Nyāya Bindu Ṭīkā*, p. 131.
23. From the epistemic angle the relation can be named as *gamaka-gamya-bhāva*, but from the ontological angle it can be put as *gamya-gamaka-bhāva*. In the text it is put in the latter form.
24. Dharmottara, *Nyāya Bindu Ṭīkā*, pp. 111ff.
25. Ibid., p. 97.

26. Diṅnāga, *Pramāṇa Samuccaya* Tr. by Hattori, *Diṅnāga on Perception*, II.1.
27. Dharmakīrti, *Nyāya Bindu*, p. 98.
28. Dharmottara, *Nyāya Bindu Ṭīkā*, pp. 98-99.
29. Th. Stcherbatsky, *Buddhist Logic*, vol. 1, p. 236.
30. Dharmottara, *Nyāya Bindu Ṭīkā*, p. 97. *Parārthānumānam śabdātmakam, śvārthānumānam tu jñānātmakam.*
31. Ibid., p. 30.
32. Quoted from Randle, *Fragments from Diṅnāga*, section 14.
33. Dharmakīrti, *Nyāya Bindu*, p. 186.
34. Ibid.
35. Dharmottara, *Nyāya Bindu Ṭīkā*, p. 97.
36. Dharmakīrti, *Nyāya Bindu*, p. 98.
37. The word "individual" should not be understood as referring to *svalakṣaṇa*. Here it means every individual object belonging to the category of *vikalpa* or *sāmānya lakṣaṇa*.
38. Dharmakīrti, *Nyāya Bindu*, p. 111.
39. Vācaspati, *Nyāya Vārtika Tātparya Ṭīkā*, p. 199.
40. Dharmakīrti, *Nyāya Bindu*, Ch. 2. pp. 122ff.
41. Ibid., p. 126.
42. Ibid., pp. 117, 140.
43. *Pramāṇa Vārtika*, p. 260 (Vṛtti by Manorathanandi).
44. Dharmakīrti, *Nyāya Bindu*, pp. 152ff.
45. *Bauddha Tarka Bhāṣā*, Mokṣākaragupta p. 62.
46. Randle, *Fragments from Diṅnāga*, p. 46.
47. Dharmakīrti, *Nyāya Bindu*, p. 129. *Svabhāva pratibandhe hi satyartho'rtham gamayet.*
48. Ibid., p. 131. *Tadapratibaddhasya tada vyabhicāraniyamābhāvāt.*
49. Dharmakīrti, *Nyāya Bindu Ṭīkā*, p. 129.
50. *Hetu Bindu*, Dharmakīrti, p. 53. *Tasya vyāptirhi vyāpakasya tatra bhāva eva. vyāpya vā tattraiva bhāva. Etena anvayo vyatireko vā.*
51. Arcaṭa, *Hetu Bindu Ṭīkā*, pp. 17-18.
52. Dharmakīrti, *Nyāya Bindu*, p. 134.
53. Dharmakīrti, *Nyāya Bindu*, pp. 134ff.
54. Shah, *Akalaṅka's Criticism of Dharmakīrti's Philosophy*, p. 264, fn. 49.
55. Dharmakīrti *Nyāya Bindu*, p. 112.
56. Dharmottara, *Nyāya Bindu Ṭīkā*, *Samānasya ca sa śabdādeśaḥ*, p. 112.
57. Ibid., p. 113. *Na ca viśeṣaḥ sādhyaḥ apitu sāmānyam.*
58. Dharmakīrti, *Nyāya Bindu*, p. 114.
59. Ibid.
60. Ibid.
61. Th. Stcherbatsky, *Buddhist Logic*, vol. 1, p. 243.
62. Uddyotakara, *Nyāya Vārtika*, I.1.5, p. 301.
63. Th. Stcherbatsky, *Buddhist Logic*, vol. 1, p. 244.
64. Dharmottara, *Nyāya Bindu Ṭīkā*, p. 103. *Yadyapi cātra niścitagrahaṇam na kṛtam tathāpi ante kṛtam prakrāntayordvayorapi rūpayorapekṣaṇiyam.*
65. Dharmottara, *Nyāya Bindu Ṭīkā*, pp. 109-10.
66. Buddhist logicians do not admit the possibility of *kevalānvayi* and *kevalavyatireki vyāptis*; the metaphysics of Naiyāyikas, however, permit them to do so. In a situation

where there is only the possibility of co-occurrence of *hetu* and *sādhya* in their presence, and there is no possibility of their co-occurrence in absence, it is known as *kevalānvayi vyāpti*. Likewise, if in a situation there is a possibility of co-occurrence of *sādhya* and *hetu* only in their absence, and there is no possibility of their co-occurrence in their presence, it is known as *kevalavyatireki*. The *kevalānvayi* is purely affirmative concomitance, whereas the *kevalavyatireki* is purely negative concomitance. The example of former is, "Whatever is knowable is nameable." The example of latter is, "In any pure substance different from earth, there is absence of earth because there is absence of smell."

67. Establishing a contradictory thesis based on a rival reason.

68. Cf. Hemchandra, *Pramāṇa Mīmāmsā*, p. 72, and Akalaṅka, *Laghīyastraya* III.12, published in Sindhi Grantha Mala.

69. Vādi Deva Sūri, *Pramāṇanayatattvālokālaṁkāra*, Ch. 3, p. 142.

70. Quoted by Śāntarakrita in *Tattva Saṁgraha*, verse 1368.

71. For details see Śāntarakrita, *Tattva Saṁgraha*, verses 1363-1428.

72. *Hetu cakra* is also called *pakṣadharma cakra*; see Vidyabhushana, *A History of Indian Logic*, p. 299, fn. 2.

73. The doctrine of *Hetu cakra* is also mentioned in *Nyāya Praveśa*.

74. In the *Nyāya Vārtika* of Uddyotakara in the context of examination of the doctrine of *trairūpya* there is a statement of another doctrine of seven possible types of relations *hetu* may have with *pakṣa*, *sapakṣa*, and *asapakṣa*. The seven possibilities are:

1. present in *pakṣa*, absent in *sapakṣa*, and present in *asapakṣa*.
2. present in *sapakṣa*, absent in *pakṣa*, and present in *asapakṣa*.
3. absent in *asapakṣa*, absent in *pakṣa*, and absent in *sapakṣa*.
4. present in *pakṣa*, present in *sapakṣa*, but not absent in *asapakṣa*.
5. present in *pakṣa*, absent in *asapakṣa*, but not present in *sapakṣa*.
6. present in *sapakṣa*, absent in *asapakṣa*, but not present in *pakṣa*.
7. present in *pakṣa*, present in *sapakṣa*, and absent in *asapakṣa*.

Of these the first three fail to satisfy two requirements, the next three fail to satisfy one requirement, but the last one satisfies all three requirements. Thus, the first six are rejected, and the seventh alone is regarded as valid. The *hetu* in the seventh placement is *trairūpya hetu*. This septenary is different from the *Hetu cakra* insofar as it takes into consideration the relation of *hetu* with *pakṣa* apart from its relation with *sapakṣa* and *asapakṣa*. Here the possibility of *asiddha hetu* is also taken into consideration. But the doctrine *hetu cakra* presumes that *hetu* must necessarily be present in *pakṣa*. With this presumption it considers nine possible ways of the relation of the *hetu* with *sapakṣa* and *asapakṣa*.

75. Borrowed from Chi, *Buddhist Formal Logic*.

76. Vācaspati, *Nyāya Vārtika Tātparya Ṭikā*, p. 266. *Avayavatvenaikavākyatā darśitā, sa ca padānām parasparāpekṣita sambandha yogyārthapratyayena bhavanti*.

77. Vātsyāyana, *Nyāya Bhāṣya* I. 1.32.

78. Ibid., I.1.1. *Āgamaḥ pratijñā heturanumānam udāharaṇam pratyakṣam upamāna upanayaḥ. Sarveṣāmekārtha samavāye sāmarthya pradarśanam nigamanamiti. So'yam param nyāya iti*.

79. Ibid., I.1.32.

80. Pārthasārathi Miśra, *Nyāya Ratna Mālā on Śloka Vārtika, anumāna khaṇḍa*, p. 54.

81. Vācaspati, *Nyāya Vārtika Tātparya Ṭīkā*, p. 267.
82. *Vyāpti viśiṣṭa pakṣadharmatā jñānam parāmarśam.*
83. In the Buddhist literature prior to Diṅnāga there is an acceptance of eight *avayavas*, which have only been stated and not analyzed (cf. *Tucci*, *Buddhist Logic before Diṅnāga*, pp. 461-65). In the *Nyāya Praveśa*, however, only three *avayavas*, namely, *pratijñā*, *hetu*, and *dṛṣṭānta*, are put forth (pp. 1-2).
84. Śāntarakṣita, *Tattva Saṁgraha*, verse 1435.
85. According to them, in *parārthānumāna* we have five *avayavas*, but in *svārthānumāna* three are enough.
86. Quoted in Śāntarakṣita, *Tattva Saṁgraha*, pp. 514ff.
87. Ibid.
88. Ibid., p. 516.
89. Satkari Mookerjee, *Buddhist Philosophy of Universal Flux*, p. 364.
90. Diṅnāga, *Nyāya Praveśa*, Tr. by Dhruva.
91. Kamalaśila, *Tattva Saṁgraha Pañjikā*, p. 516.
92. Dharmakīrti, *Pramāṇa Vārtika*; Ch. 4, *verses* 16, 17, 20, and 26.
93. Dharmakīrti, *Pramāṇa Vārtika*, Ch. 3, verse 27. *Tadbhāvahetubhāva hi dṛṣṭānte* tadvedinaḥ.
94. Dharmakīrti, *Nyāya Bindu*, Ch. 2, p. 117.

APPENDIX 2

1. According to Buddhist tradition, the purpose of acquiring knowledge is either for one's own awareness or for communicating it to others. Buddha acquired knowledge for his own enlightenment and also communicated knowledge for the enlightenment of others. So, Buddhist epistemological thinkers draw a distinction between knowledge for one's own sake (*ātmasaṁvit*) and knowledge for the sake of others (*parasaṁvit*). Perception (*pratyakṣa*) and inference (*anumāna*) are the two means to acquire knowledge for one's own sake. *Anumāna* in this context is *svārthānumāna* only. For communicating knowledge to others there is only one mode, which is *sādhana*, also known as *parārthānumāna*. In this text first there is exposition of *sādhana*, and then *pratyakṣa* and *anumāna* are discussed with their respective fallacies. So, in total, there are eight topics discussed in this text. They are as follows: (1) *Sādhana*, (2) *Sādhanābhāsa*, (3) *Duṣaṇa* (4) *Dūṣaṇābhāsa*, (5) *Pratyakṣa* (6) *Pratyakṣābhāsa* (7) *Anumāna* (8) *Anumānābhāsa*.

In a proper epistemological order first there should have been discussion on perception and inference and then on *sādhana* and *dūṣaṇa*. But the order is reversed here. The tradition explains it by saying that this book is intended for the sake of others (*parasaṁvit*) and therefore *ātmasaṁvit* is made subservient to *parasaṁvit*. Buddha also acquired enlightenment not for his own sake primarily but for suffering beings (*Bahujana hitāya bahujana sukhāya*).

The word "*sādhana*" is used in two different senses. One is the mode of demonstration or giving arguments in support of one's own position, and the other is for one of the constituents of the process of inference, that is, *hetu* (reason). Here, it is used in the former sense. The entire process of argumentation consisting of different elements and stages is collectively known as *sādhana*. The elements are thesis (*pakṣa*), reason (*hetu*), homologue (*sapakṣa*), and heterologue (*vipakṣa*). The stages are thesis, reason, and example (*dṛṣṭānta*). Pointing out fallacies in *sādhana* is known as *dūṣaṇa*. *Dūṣaṇa* means pointing a fallacious *sādhana, that is sādhanābhāsa*. It means pointing out such defects in *sādhana* that are existent here. *Dūṣaṇa* is directed against *sādhanābhāsa* and can never be directed against *sādhana*. For a genuine *sādhana* there cannot be any *dūṣaṇa*. Only when the *sādhana* is fallacious is there a possibility of *dūṣaṇa*. In fact, *sādhana* and *dūṣaṇa* are the two positions adopted by the two parties in a debate. The proponent puts forth one's position through *sādhana*, and the opponent tries to refute it through *dūṣaṇa*. A fallacious *sādhana* is known as *sādhanābhāsa*. A fallacy may be because of defect in thesis or reason or example. To catch the fallacious *sādhana*, that is, to point out *sādhanābhāsa*, is known as *dūṣaṇa*.

Dūṣaṇabhāsa means pointing out defects in a *sādhana* that are nonexistent. It is allegating defects in a *sādhana* that are not there. *Sādhana* and *dūṣaṇa*, along with their respective fallacies, are meant for communicating knowledge to others. All these four are involved in a debate where one party tries to refute the other. These are, therefore, different aspects of *vāda-vidhi* (art of debate).

Perception and inference are the two modes of acquiring knowledge. Buddhists belonging to the Diṅnāga-Dharmakīrti tradition accept only two *pramāṇas*, namely, perception and inference. A knowledge is acquired by a knower for one's own sake. According to Buddhists, perceptual knowledge concerns the objective real known as *svalakṣ aṇa*. A *svalakṣaṇa* is devoid of all determinations and characterizations; therefore, a perceptual knowledge is also indeterminate. In this respect Buddhists fundamentally differ from Naiyāyikas, according to whom a perceptual knowledge can be determinate as well. Buddhists accept five types of determinations (*kalpanā*), namely, in terms of substance, qualities, action, class-character, and language. Buddhists insist that perception is devoid of all determinations, and, therefore, they define perception as *kalpanāpoḍha*. Knowledge of an object by means of a necessary mark is known as *anumāna*. A distinction is drawn between *svārthānumāna* and *parāthānumāna*. *Svārthānumāna* is just cognitive (*jñānātmaka*), whereas *parārthānumāna* is expressed in verbal propositions (*śabdātmaka*). *Parāthānumāna* is covered up under *sādhana*, and under *anumāna* as a mode of knowing *svārthānumāna* is accepted. There is a possibility of defects in both these modes of knowing. The defective perception is known as *pratyakṣābhāsa*, and defective *anumāna* is known as *anumānābhāsa*. Perceptual knowledge is necessarily indeterminate. But if it is misunderstood as determinate knowledge, then it is a fallacious perception. Perceptual knowledge concerns objective reality (*svalakṣaṇa*). A *svalakṣaṇa* can only be grasped (*grāhya*) and not conceptualized (*adhyavasita*). But if in a perceptual knowledge the objective reality is conceptualized, then it becomes *pratyakṣābhāsa*.

Anumānābhāsa is fallacious inference on account of fallacious reason (*hetvābhāsa*). Since *anumāna* is taken here as *svārthānumāna*, only *hetvābhāsa* is mentioned, not *pratyakṣ ābhāsa* and *dṛṣṭāntābhāsa*, which come under *sādhanābhāsa*.

This is the synoptic account of the *vāda-vidhi* (theory of debate) and *pramāṇa-vidhi* (theory of knowledge), which are the two aspects of *nyāya* concerning knowledge. There are works dealing exclusively either with *pramaṇa* or with *vāda*, but here both are discussed together. The verse that occurs at the beginning of the text sums up the entire discussion on *vāda* and *pramāṇa* presented in this text, and therefore it prefaces the text.

2. *Sādhana* consists of three elements. They are *pakṣa*, *hetu*, and *dṛṣṭānta*. A *sādhana* is always employed to establish something that is not known to the other party. Therefore, it is necessarily communicative (*vacana*). In fact, it is employment of *parāthānumāna* in debate. When *svārthānumāna* is verbalized, it becomes *parāthānumāna*, and when *parāthānumāna* is used in debate, it is known as *sādhana*.

3. *Pakṣa* is that which is brought to consciousness or manifested (*pacyate iti pakṣaḥ*). *Pakṣa* is always a subject taken with its predicate. It has two predicates. One is known or

wellknown, whereas the other is yet to be known. The latter is to be known on the basis of the former. According to Buddhists, the *pakṣa* is the object of inferential inquiry and subject of proof. The definition of *pakṣa* in the Buddhist tradition as *svayam sādhyatvenepsitaḥ* means that it is something that one desires to prove; that is, it is something that is upheld by the proponent (*vādi*) and directed to the opponent (*prativādi*) for proving.

Reason is the means through which the hitherto not proved is proved. Etymologically, *hetu* means *hi, hinoti,* to know, which means that by which something is proved. The *pakṣa* and the *hetu* should be accepted by both the parties; only then can they make the hitherto unproved, proved.

4. These three features of reason constitute the formal conditions of the validity of *anumāna* and therefore of *sādhana*. Violation of any of these three results in a fallacy. Since there are three features of reason, therefore, there are three types of fallacy pertaining to reason.

5. Homologue and heterologue are the supporting factors for proving a thesis. Homologue is affirmative, and heterologue is negative in nature. Both are grounded in experience, and their veracity is wellestablished. Homologues are known substrata of the presence of probandum, and heterologues are the known substrata of the absence of probandum. The homologue provides positive support, and the heterologue provides negative support to reason in proving the probandum. Since the relation of probandum with the substrata involved in homologues and heterologues is that of logical necessity, both of them provide the logical ground for the relation of invariable concomitance between reason and probandum. The homologue points out that there is at least one such case that is similar to subject and that can serve as a corroborative instance for the existence of probandum in the particular subject where reason is also present. The heterologue also provides a negative support insofar as it points out that there cannot be any presence of reason in the absence of the presence of probandum, and, therefore, the presence of reason in the particular subject provides the necessary ground for the presence of probandum in that particular subject.

6. Enumeration of example provides further support to the reason in proving its probandum. Since the relation between the reason and the probandum can be either positive or negative, accordingly, there can be two types of example. The positive example instantiates the homologue, and the negative example instantiates the heterologue. The difference between heterologue and homologue and their corresponding examples can be understood in terms of a formal statement of a relation and its concrete instantiation. Historically, before the idea of generalization or universalization came to be formulated, examples alone served as the basis for proof. But when the need and necessity of generalization were met in terms of *vyāpti* or the "relation of invariable concomitance," the role of example became subservient to that of *vyāpti*. Nevertheless, the probative role of the latter was not discarded or belittled. The *sādharmya dṛṣṭānta* is of the same nature as that of the *sapakṣa*. Likewise, *vaidharmya dṛṣṭānta* is of the same nature as that of the *vipakṣa*.

In the Buddhist tradition *sādhana*, which stands for a means to communicate knowledge to others, always consists of three elements, the thesis, the reason, and the example. All three have to play their respective role in the *sādhana*. In other words, the thesis must be wellformulated, the probative reason must be welladduced, and the corroborative examples must be suitably enumerated.

7. In the formulation of a *sādhana* if any of the three constituents are vitiated by some defects, then it is known as *sādhanābhāsa*. The *sādhanābhāsa* can be of three types: *pakṣ ābhāsa, hetvābhāsa,* and *dṛṣṭāntābhāsa*. In the Nyāya system the roles of *pakṣa* and *dṛṣṭ*

ānta are made subservient to the role of *hetu*, and therefore it concentrates on *hetvābhāsas* alone, but Buddhist logicians take into account the other two types of fallacy also. Let us clarify some points regarding these nine *pakṣābhāsas* one by one.

(i) Since we know by perception that words are audible (or there is audibility in words), the statement "Words are inaudible" is contradicted by perception,

(ii) It is contradicted by the inference "A pot is noneternal because it is a product".

(iii) In Vaiśeṣika metaphysics sound is regarded to be produced, and, therefore, it is noneternal.

(iv) According to popular belief, the former is regarded as untouchable, though not the latter.

(v) It is not clear here whether a statement that contradicts one's former statement will also come under this head.

(vi) According to Buddhists, everything is momentary and therefore noneternal; but according to *satkāryavāda* of Sāṁkhya, all entities preexist in their cause, and, therefore, they cannot agree to *śabda* being perishable.

(vii) Here, the existence of self is denied by Buddhists. They deny both the subject and the predicate.

(viii) They don't believe in the existence of soul or hold that pleasure and so on are qualities inhering in soul.

(ix) 'Sound is audible" is a fallacious thesis because something is desired to be proved (*sādhyatvenepsitaḥ*) only when its truth is at issue between the two parties, but this is not the case with "Sound is audible", and so it is a fallacious thesis. This is a fallacy of triviality because it is absurd and fallacious to offer as a thesis a statement that everyone would accept as a plain statement of fact.

8. According to the doctrine of *trairūpya* there are three conditions which regulate the validity of a reason (*hetu*). Violation of any of the three conditions results in making the reason invalid. Thus, there are three types of fallacies of reason.

9. *Sapakṣaikdeśavṛttiḥ vipakṣavyāpi*: Inconclusive (*anekāntika*) is sixfold. The first two, being easy to understand, do not require explaination. Here we are giving the detailed explanation for the remaining four.

Thesis: Sound is naturally existing (non effort-made)
Reason: Noneternality
Homologoue: Lightning, space, and so on

In one part of homologue, that is, lightning, reason (noneternality) resides but not in the other part, that is space.

Thesis: Sound is naturally existing (non effort-made)
Reason: Noneternality
Heterologue: Pot

Reason (noneternality) resides in the entire class of heterologues; therefore, the reason is inconclusive here.

10. *Vipakṣaikadeśavṛtti sapakṣavyāpi:*

Thesis: Sound is effort-made
Reason: Noneternality
Homologue: Pot, and so on

Here, reason resides in the entire class of homologues.

Thesis: Sound is effort-made
Reason: Noneternality
Heterologue: Lightening, space, and so on

Here, reason resides in one part of the class of heterologues, that is, lightning and so on, and doesn't reside in another part, that is space and so on. Therefore, the reason is inconclusive here.

11. *Ubhayapakṣaikadeśa vṛtti:*

Thesis:	Sound is eternal
Reason:	Incorporeality
Homologue:	Space, infinitesimal particles, and so on

Here, reason resides in one part of the homologue, that is space and so on and does not reside in another part, that is infinitesimal particles and so on.

Thesis:	Sound is eternal
Reason:	Incorporeality
Heterologue:	Pot, pleasure and so on

Here, reason (incorporeality) resides in one part of the heterologue, that is, pleasure and so on, and does not reside in another part, that is, pot and so on. Therefore the reason is inconclusive here.

12. *Viruddhāvyabhicārī*:

Here, two different theses are given, one put forth by Vaiśeṣikas and another by Mīmāmsakas. According to Vaiśeṣikas "Sound is noneternal because it is produced, like a pot and so on", and, on the contrary, according to Mīmāmsakas, "Sound is eternal because of its audibility, like "soundness."

(a) Thesis: Sound is noneternal
Reason: Produced

(b) Thesis: Sound is eternal
Reason: Audibility

Here, we have two contradictory theses supported by two different valid reasons about the same subject, sound. As Vidyabhushana puts it, "This fallacy arises when a thesis and its contradictory are both supported by what appear to be valid reasons." This fallacy is known as *viruddhāvyabhicārī* because the theses are mutually contradictory, but they are validly established by their respective reasons. If taken separately, each appears to be valid, but doubt arises only when they are taken together. Here it can be asked how this fallacy is not different from the fallacy of "too narrow" discussed earlier. The reply is that it arises only when one argument alone is taken independently of the other. But when both are taken together, it would be the fallacy of "*viruddhāvyabhicārī*".

In the *Nyāya Bindu Tikā* Dharmottara gives two possible meanings of the term "*viruddhāvyabhicāri*":

1. *avyabhicāri of viruddha,* that is, that which invariably proves the opposite of what is proved by another *hetu.*

2. *viruddha,* which is at the same time *avyabhicāri*, that is, that which is opposed to another *hetu* inasmuch as it proves its contradictory and is at the same time invariably accompanied by its own *sādhya*, that is, which is good in itself, so far as its own *vyāpti* is concerned.

In the example "Sound is noneternal on account of being produced like a pot," "being produced" is opposed to, or contradicted by, "Sound is eternal on account of audibility like soundness." The two reasons taken together cause doubt and are inconclusive.

The function of a reason is to prove the existence of the probandum in a particular locus or *pakṣa*. A reason can perform this function if and only if it stands in the relation of necessary concomitance with its probandum. This implies that the reason should not be such as to prove the opposite of either the probandum or the thesis concerning the probandum. Likewise, it should not disprove the very existence of the probandum or the thesis, nor should it disprove any essential property of the probandum or the thesis. Accordingly, four varieties can be conceived of the contradictory reason, namely, pertaining to reason or to a particular reason and pertaining to a thesis or to a particular thesis. One type of fallacy is general, and the other one is specific or particular; one covers up the entire existence, whereas the other covers up only a particular property.

13. *Dharmasvarūpaviparīta sādhana:*

Thesis:	Sound is eternal
Probandum:	Eternal
Reason:	Produced / effort made

If anything is produced, it can't be eternal. Likewise, if anything is effort made, it must be naturally existing, and, therefore, must have a beginning. These two reasons don't reside in eternal entities (homologues) like sound; rather, they reside only in noneternal entities (heterologues). Thus, instead of proving eternality of sound, they would prove the opposite of eternality.

14. *Dharmaviśeṣa viparītasādhana:*

In the argument "Eye and so on exist for the sake of others (i.e., self) on account of their being of the nature of aggregates like bed, seat, and so on, which have parts", here, we have,

Thesis:	Eyes and so on exist for the sake of others
Reason:	Aggregateness
Probandum:	To exist for the sake of others

This argument not only proves the existence of eyes and so on for the sake of others on the ground of being aggregates, but also proves the aggregateness of the "self". This is because if eyes and so on are aggregate, then one whose purpose they serve should also be aggregate. This is because of transference of property. However, this is not acceptable to the Sāṁkhya school, which is the opponent here because, according to the Sāṁkhya school, self is not an aggregate. In this argument the reason is fallacious because it proves the opposite of the particular *dharma* or property that it is intended to prove. The reason, that is, aggregateness, while proving that there is something beyond eyes, proves also that something, namely, *ātman*, which Sāṁkhya desires to prove, for the same reason is proved to be having aggregation, a position that Sāṁkhya is not prepared to hold. Sāṁkhya thinkers on the basis of the previously stated reason want to prove not only the existence of the individual self but also its being noncomposite. But, this argument not only proves the existence of self but also proves its composite character.

15. *Dharmisvarūpaviparītasādhana:*

The example given here is "Existence (*bhāva*) is not a substance or action or quality, because of its possessing one substance and because of its presence in qualities and actions like the universal and particular.''

Thesis	:	Existence (*mahāsāmānya*) is *summum-genus*
Probandum	:	Existence is different from substance or action or quality

But this argument is vitiated by a fallacy of *hetu* contradicting a thesis, say Buddhists. Because the same bipartite *hetu*, namely,

Reason:	(a) Because it possesses a single substance
	(b) Because of its presence in qualities or actions,

would prove the absence of the thesis, that is, *bhāva* as well as absence, that is, *abhāva*. Thus, this bipartite *hetu* may prove that *bhāva* is *abhāva*, which is the very opposite of the thesis. Buddhists here are refuting the Vaiśeṣika concept of *bhāva,* which is the *summum genus,* on the ground that the reason put forth to establish the existence of *bhāva,* in fact, disproves its very existence. It no doubt proves that existence is different from substance, qualities, and actions, but it also proves the absence of existence.

16. *Dharmiviśeṣa viparītasādhana:*

Here, the example given is the same as before with the addition that the thesis is taken along with its particular property, namely, the causal capability of giving rise to the notion "It is existent". In this argument both the reasons not only prove the property of causing the notion "it is existent" but also prove the absence of this property. The Vaiśeṣikas are realists in their epistemology, and therefore they argue that existence alone is the cause of the notion that "it is existent."

17. In the theory of inference, example plays a significant probative role. It acts as a support to the reason in terms of a concrete exemplification. It enumerates a case similar to the *vyāpti* situation, that is, a locus in which reason necessarily coexists with the probandum. Such cases are known as *sapakṣa* or homologue. A *sapakṣa* is always similar to *pakṣa* insofar as it possesses the coexistence of reason and probandum. But in terms of assuredness of the coexistence of reason and probandum, it is on a strong footing compared to that of *pakṣa*. An example based on similarity reinforces the positive concomitance, and an example based on dissimilarity reinforces negative concomitance. So, the former consists of enumeration of homologue, and the latter consists of enumeration of heterologue. If the example is not in conformity with homologue or heterologue, it is fallacious. Thus, there are two types of fallacy of example: one in which *sapakṣa* is not valid, and the other in which *vipakṣa* is not valid.

18. *Sādhana dharmāsiddha:*

The example given is "Sound is eternal on account of its being incorporeal like infinitesimal particle." Here,

Thesis:	Sound
Reason:	Incorporeality
Probandum:	Eternality
Homologue:	Infinitesimal particle

Here the homologue (i.e., infinitesimal particle) no doubt possesses the probandum (i.e., eternality) but doesn't possess the reason (i.e., incorporeality). Therefore, the homologue is not similar to the thesis. The reason does not exist in the homologue, and therefore the homologue does not have any probative value. Only that homologue has probative value that has the presence of both the reason and the probandum.

19. *Sādhyadharmāsiddha:*

In the example "Sound is eternal on account of its being incorporeal like intelligence",

Thesis:	Sound
Probandum:	Eternality
Reason:	Incorporeality
Homologue:	Intellect

Here the homologue (i.e., intellect) no doubt possesses the reason (i.e., incorporeality) but does not possess the probandum (i.e., eternality). Therefore, the homologue is not similar to the thesis. As before, the homologue does not have the probative value because it lacks the probandum.

20. *Ubhayadharmāsiddha:*

This is twofold: affirmative and negative. An example of the former is "Sound is eternal on account of being incorporeal like a pot". Here,

Thesis:	Sound
Reason:	Incorporeality
Probandum:	Eternality
Homologue:	Pot

The homologue (i.e., pot) has absence of both reason and probandum; therefore, the homologue is not similar to the thesis and therefore has no probative worth.

An example of the latter is "Sound is eternal on account of being incorporeal like space". (This argument is valid only for those who believe in the reality of space, but it will not be valid for Buddhists, who do not believe in the reality of space.) Here,

Thesis:	Sound
Reason:	Incorporeality
Probandum:	Eternality
Homologue:	Space

The existence of homologue (i.e., space) is not acceptable to one party (i.e., Buddhists).

21. *Ananvaya:*

The statement of invariable concomitance is the very backbone and logical foundation of inference. No inference can be valid in the absence of such a statement. An example is attached to such a statement. If an example is given without a statement of invariable concomitance, then it cannot have firm probative worth. Such an example will be fallacious. In such a situation the mere coexistence of probandum and reason is stated without pointing out their relationship of invariable concomitance.

22. *Viparītānvaya:*

In the argument in the pot there are the properties of "producedness" and "non eternality", the example lacks positive invariable concomitance. It would be a valid example if it is restated as "Whatever is produced is noneternal like a pot." This fallacy occurs when a positive invariable concomitance is stated inversely and therefore wrongly. Thus, instead of saying, "Whatever is produced is noneternal," if it is said that "Whatever is noneternal is produced," then the order of reason and the probandum are reversed, but thereby the pervader becomes the pervaded, and the pervaded becomes the pervader.

23. In dissimilarity we have a statement of heterologue that should have the absence of both reason and probandum. Like the fallacies based on similarity these are also of five types. In the classification of the fallacies based on similarity, the starting point is reason because the presence of reason implies the presence of probandum, whereas in the classification based on dissimilarity, the absence of probandum implies the absence of reason.

24. *Sādhyavyāvṛtta:*

The example "Sound is eternal on account of incorporeality like infinitesimal particle", if converted to a statement of negative invariable concomitance containing dissimilar example of heterologue, would then run as: "Whatever is noneternal is corporeal like infinitesimal particle." As per the rule, the same example cannot be adduced both as heterologue and homologue. But in this case, the same example, that is, infinitesimal particle, is put forth in both situations. Just as in the invariable concomitance between smoke and fire, where kitchen can serve as a homologue, but it cannot serve as a heterologue, whereas lake can serve as a heterologue, likewise, in this case also infinitesimal particle can serve only as a homologue and cannot serve as a heterologue. In infinitesimal particle incorporeality, which is reason, is absent, but noneternality, which is probandum, is not absent, whereas as per the rule both should be absent. Thus, it contains the fallacy of nonabsent probandum.

25. *Sādhanavyāvṛtta:*

Here, the thesis is same as before, but the example is different. Instead of infinitesimal particle here we have action. In this argument, the statement of positive invariable concomitance, "Whatever is incorporeal is eternal", if converted to a statement of negative invariable concomitance containing dissimilar example of heterologue, would then run as, "Whatever is noneternal is corporeal like action". As explained before, the same example cannot serve as both homologue and heterologue. In "action" the probandum, that is, eternality, is excluded, but the reason, that is, incorporeality, is not excluded.

26. *Ubhayavyāvṛtta:*

Again, the thesis is the same as before but the example is different. Instead of an infinitesimal particle or action, we have space here. In this argument the statement of positive invariable concomitance, "Whatever is corporeal is eternal," if converted to a statement of negative invariable concomitance containing dissimilar example or heterologue, would then run as, "Whatever is noneternal is corporeal like space". Here, both reason and probandum are not absent because space is both eternal and incorporeal.

27. *Avyatireka:*

Only the absence of probandum and reason is said to belong to the example without stating their negative invariable concomitance. Thus, instead of saying, "Whatever is noneternal is not incorporeal like a pot," if we simply say, "In pot reside corporeality and noneternality", then it is a case of nonstatement of negative invariable concomitance.

28. *Viparīta vyatireka:*

While stating negative invariable concomitance, first the absence of probandum is stated, and thereafter the absence of reason is stated. But here, first the absence of reason is stated, and thereafter absence of probandum is stated. This is the fallacy of reversed absences because here the logical order of absences is not followed. Only absence of probandum implies absence of reason, not vice versa (*sādhyābhāve sādhanābhāvaḥ*).

The treatment of the fallacious means of proof comes to an end with the exposition of its three varieties. The author discusses the means of knowledge that are helpful in acquiring knowledge for oneself. Thus, *svasaṁvit* and *ātmapratyāyana* are synonyms, as *parasaṁvit* and *parapratyāyana* are synonyms.

According to Buddhists, the theory of knowledge is dependent on the theory of reality. Since there are two and only two types of objects, there are two and only two modes of knowing. One and the same mode of knowing cannot cognize both types of objects. Thus, for Buddhists perception and inference are the only two ways of knowing. It is not that Buddhists deny other ways of knowing accepted in other schools. They only deny their independent status and reduce them to inference.

Glossary

1.	*Ābhāsa*:	Fallacy
2.	*Abhūta sādhanadoṣa*:	Nonexistent defect in means of proof
3.	*Āgamaviruddha*:	Contrary to one's own scripture
4.	*Ananvaya*:	Absence of statement of invariable concomitance
5.	*Anekāntika*:	Inconclusive
6.	*Anumāna*:	Inference
7.	*Anumānābhāsa*:	Fallacious inference
8.	*Anumānaviruddha*:	Contrary to inference
9.	*Anyatarāsiddhaḥ*:	Unacceptable to either
10.	*Aprasiddhaviśeṣaṇa*:	A thesis whose subject is unacceptable
11.	*Aprasiddhaviśeṣya*:	A thesis whose predicate is unacceptable
12.	*Aprasiddhobhaya*:	Unacceptable to both parties
13.	*Aprayatnānantarīyaka*:	Natural, noneffort-made
14.	*Asādhāraṇa*:	Too narrow
15.	*Asiddha*:	Unproved
16.	*Avidyamāna*:	Absent
17.	*Avyatireka*:	Absence of negative concomitance
18.	*Āśrayāsiddha*:	Fallacy of unproved locus
19.	*Dharmasvarūpaviparītasādhana*:	Reason contrary to probandum
20.	*Dharmaviśeṣaviparītasādhana*:	Reason contrary to a particular probandum
21.	*Dharmisvarūpaviparītasādhana*:	Reason contrary to thesis
22.	*Dharmiviśeṣaviparītasādhana*:	Reason contrary to a particular thesis
23.	*Doṣa*:	Defect
24.	*Dṛṣṭānta*:	Example

25. *Dṛṣṭānta-doṣa*: Fallacy in example, fallacious example
26. *Dūṣaṇa*: Fallacy in means of proof or refutation
27. *Dūṣaṇābhāsa*: Fallacious refutation
28. *Hetu*: Reason
29. *Hetvābhāsa*: Fallacy in reason, fallacious reason
30. *Kalpanā*: Conceptualization
31. *Liṅga*: Necessary mark
32. *Lokaviruddha*: Contrary to public opinion
33. *Pakṣa*: Subject, thesis, locus
34. *Pakṣābhāsa = pratijñādoṣa*: Fallacious thesis
35. *Pakṣadharmatā*: Necessary presence of reason in the thesis
36. *Pakṣadharmatva*: Thesis having reason as its property
37. *Paramāṇu*: Infinitesimal particle
38. *Prasiddha Sambandha*: A thesis too well known or accepted universally
39. *Prāśnika*: Inquirer
40. *Pratyakṣa*: Perception
41. *Pratyakṣābhāsa*: Fallacious perception
42. *Pratyakṣaviruddha*: Contrary to perception
43. *Prayatnānantarīyaka*: Effort made
44. *Sādhana*: Means of proof
45. *Sādhānābhāsa*: Fallacy in the means of proof
46. *Sādhanadharmāsiddha*: Incompatibility of the example with the reason
47. *Sādhanadoṣa*: Defective means of proof
48. *Sādhanāvyāvṛtti*: Nonabsent reason
49. *Sādhāraṇa*: Too wide
50. *Sādharmya*: Similarity
51. *Sādharmya dṛṣṭāntābhāsa*: Fallacy of example on the basis of similarity
52. *Sādhya*: Probandum
53. *Sādhyadharmāsiddha*: Incompatibility of the example with the probandum
54. *Sādhyāvyāvṛtti*: Nonabsent probandum
55. *Sāmānyalakṣaṇa*: Generalised image
56. *Sapakṣa*: Homologue
57. *Sapakṣaikadeśavṛtti*: Pervading one part of homologue
58. *Sapakṣavyāpi*: Pervading entire homologue
59. *Svalakṣaṇa*: Unique particular
60. *Svavacanaviruddha*: Contrary to one's own statement
61. *Ubhayadharmāsiddha*: Incompatibility of the example with both (reason and probandum)

62. *Ubhayapakṣaikadeśavṛtti*: Pervading one part of both
63. *Ubhayāsiddha*: Unacceptable to both
64. *Ubhayāvyāvṛtta*: Both are nonabsent
65. *Ubhayāvṛtta*: Both are absent
66. *Vaidharmya (vyatireka)*: Dissimilarity
67. *Vaidharmya dṛṣṭāntābhāsa*: Fallacy of example based on dissimilarity
68. *Vidyamāna*: Present
69. *Vikalpa*: Concept
70. *Vipakṣa* (*Asapakaṣa*): Heterologue
71. *Vipakṣaikadeśavṛtti*: Pervading one part of the heterologue
72. *Vipakṣavyāpī*: Pervading entire heterologue
73. *Viparītānvaya*: Contrary to the statement of positive concomitance
74. *Viparītavyatireka*: Contrary to the statement of negative concomitance
75. *Viruddha*: Contradictory
76. *Viruddhavyabhicāri*: Contradictory and divergent
77. *Viṣayākāra (arthākāra)*: Form of the object

Bibliography

Aniruddha, *Abhidhammatasaṁgaho*. Translated by Shwe Zan Aung and C.A.F. Rhys Davids, London, Pali Text Soceity, 1910.

Asaṇga, *Mahāyānasūtrālaṅkāra*. Edited by Vaidya P.L., Darbhanga, Mithila Institute, 1960-64.

Akalaṅka, *Laghīyastraya*. Edited by Mahendra Kumar, Ahmedabad, Sindhi Jain granth Mala, 1939.

Arcaṭa, *Hetu Bindu Ṭīkā*. Baroda, Gaekwad Oriental Institute, 1949.

Bhartṛhari, *Vākyapadīya*. Edited by Pillai K.R., Delhi, Motial Banarsidass, 1971.

Bhatt, G. P., *Basic Ways of Knowing*, Delhi, Motilal Banarsidass, 1989.

Bhatta, Jayanta, *Nyāya Mañjari*. Edited by Surya Narayana Shukla, Varanasi, 1971.

Bhatta, Kumarila, *Śloka Vārtika*. Darbhanga, K.S. Darbhanga Sanskrit University, 1979.

Chatterji, Durgacharana, "*Hetucakranirṇaya,*" *Indian Historical Quarterly* 9, 1933, pp. 266-272,

———. "Sources of Buddhist Logic" (From the Traditional Point of View). *Indian Historical Quarterly* 9, 1933, pp. 499-02.

———. "The Doctrine of Trirūpa Hetu." *Indian Historical Quarterly* 9, 1933, pp. 503-10.

———. "Sources of Knowledge in Buddhist Logic." *Indian Culture*, Calcutta, no. 2- Oct. 1934 pp. 263-74.

———. "*Hetucakrahamaru*" (also known as *Hetucakranirṇaya* or *Hetucakraḍamaru*) (Translation into English), *Indian Historical Quarterly*, 9, 1933, pp. 511-14.

Chatterji, S.C., *Nyāya Theory of Knowledge*. Calcutta, Calcutta University, 1939.

Chi, Richard S. Y., *Buddhist Formal Logic* (A Study of Diṅnāga's *Hetucakra* and K'Uei-Chi's Great Commentary on the *Nyāya Praveśa*). Delhi, Motilal Banarsidass, 1984.

Chinchore, Mangala R, *Vādanyāya; A Glimpse of Nyāya-Buddhist Controversy*, Delhi, Sri Sadguru Publications, 1988.

———."Some Thoughts on Significant Contribution of Buddhist Logicians." *Journal of Indian Philosophy*, 15, no. 2 June 1987, pp. 155-71.

Croce, Bendetto, "On Indian Logic." *East and West* (Roma), 4, 1953, pp.1-30.

Das, Rasvihary, "Relations in Modern Indian Logic." *The Calcutta Review*, 45, no. 2, 1932, pp. 143-60.

Dasgupta, S. N., *A History of Indian Philosophy*, 5 vols. Cambridge, Cambridge University Press, 1951.

Dharmakīrti. *Hetu Bindu* (with *Ṭīkā* by Arcaṭa and *Āloka* by Durveka Miśra). Edited by

Sanghavi, Sukhalalji, and Muni Jinavinayaji, Baroda, Baroda Oriental Institute, 1949.

——. *Nyāya Bindu*. Edited by Shastri, Chandrasekhara, Banaras, 1954.

——. *Pramāṇa Vārtika*. Edited by Pandeya R.C., Delhi, Motilal Banarsidass, 1989.

——. *Santānāntarasiddhi*. Edited by Kitagawa and Hidenoir. *Journal of Greater India Society*, 14, no. 1,2, 1955, pp. 407-29.

——. *Svārthānumāna-pariccheda*. Edited by Dalasukha Bhai Malvaniya, Varanasi, 1959.

——. *Vāda Nyāya* (with *Vipañcitārtha* by Śāntarakṣita). Edited by Sankrityayana, Rahula. Appendix to *Journal of Bihar and Orissa Research Society*, 1949, pp. 21-22.

——. *Vāda Nyāya* (with by *Vipañcitārtha* and *Saṁbandhaparīkṣā*). Edited by Swami Dwarikadas Shastri, Varanasi, 1972.

——. *Pramāṇa Viniścaya*. Edited by Steinkellner, Wien, Verlag Der Ostereichischen Akademe Der Vissenschaften, 1973.

Dharmottara, *Nyāya Bindu Ṭīkā*. Edited by Shastri Chandrasekhar, Banaras, Chaukhamba, 1954.

Dharmarāja Adhvarīndra, *Vedānta Paribhāṣā*. Translated by Swami Madhvananda, Belur Math, Rama Krishna Mission, 4th edition, 1972.

Diṅnāga. *Ālambana Parīkṣā Vṛtti*. Edited by N. Shastri Aiyaswami, Madras, Adyar Library, 1942.

——. *Nyāya Mukha*, Edited by Tucci Guiseppe, vol. 1. Heidelberg, *Jabuch des Institutes fur Buddhismus Kunde*, 1930.

——. *Nyāya Praveśa*. Edited by B. J. Sandesara, Baroda, Baroda Oriental Institute, 1968.

——. *Pramāṇa Samuccaya* (*Pratyakṣa Khaṇḍa*) (*Svavṛttisahita*). Edited by H. R. Iyengar Rangaswamy, Mysore, Mysore Press, 1930.

Durveka, Miśra, *Dharmottara Pradīpa*. Edited by Dalsukhabhai Malvania, Patna, Kashi Prasad Jayaswal Research Institute, 1971.

Gokhale, P. P., *Inference and Fallacies Discussed in Ancient Indian Logic*. Delhi, Sri Satguru Publications, 1973.

Gupta, Prajñākara, *Pramāṇavārtikālaṅkāra* (also known as *Pramāṇavārtika Bhāṣya*). Edited by Sankrityayana, Rahul, Patna, Kashi Prasad Jayaswal Research Institute,1953.

Gupta, Rita, "The Buddhist Doctrine of Momentariness and Its Presuppositions." *Journal of Indian Philosophy* 8, no. 1, March 1980.

Hastings, James, *Encyclopaedia of Religion and Ethics*. Edinburah: T. & T. Clark, New York.

Hattori, Masaki. *Diṅnāga on Perception* (*Pratyakṣa Pariccheda* of Diṅnāga's *Pramāṇa Samuccaya*). Cambridge, 1968.

——. "Fragments from *Pramāṇa Samuccaya*." *Journal of Indian Buddhist Studies*, no. 1, 1958, pp. 330-35.

——. "*Pratyakṣābhāsa*" (Diṅnāga's View and Dharmakīrti's Interpretation), *Miscellanea Indologica Kiotiensa*, 6-7, March 1965, pp. 122-28.

Hayes, Richard P., "Diṅnāga's Views on Reasoning" (First half of *Svārthānumāna Pariccheda* of *Pramāṇa Samuccaya*), translated into English in *Journal of Indian Philosophy*, 3, 1980, pp. 219-77.

Hemchandra, *Pramāṇa Mīmāmsā*. Varanasi, Tara Publications, 1970.

Herzberger, H. G., "Double Negation in Buddhist Logic." *Journal of Indian Philosophy*, 3, March/April 1975, pp. 3-16.

Īśvara Kṛṣṇa, *Sāmkhya Kārikā*. Edited by Chaturvedi Brij Mohan, Delhi, National Publishing House, 1970.

Iyengar, Rangaswami

———. "Some Theories of Buddhist Logic in the Kāvyālaṅkāra of Bhāmaha." Proceedings of All India Oriental Conference, No. 8, 1935, Mysore, pp. 419-25.

———. "The *Vāda Vidhi* and the *Vāda Vidhāna* of Vasubandhu." *Brahmavidyā. The Adyar Library Bulletin* 17, part I, 1953, pp. 9-19.

Jayatilake, K. N., *Early Buddhist Theory of Knowledge*. London, George Allen and Unwin, 1963.

Jitāri, *Hetutattvopadeśa*. Edited by Chattopadhyaya, Durgacarana, Calcutta, University of Calcutta, 1939.

Joshi, Rasik Vihari, *Treatment of Fallacy in Indian Logic*. Nagpur, Vidarbha Samshodhan Mandal, 1965, pp. 270-301.

Kajiyama, Yuichi, "On the Theory of Intrinsic Determination of Universal Concomitance in Buddhist Logic." *Journal of Indian Buddhist Studies*, 7, pp. 354-60.

———. "The *Avayavi Nirākaraṇa* of Paṇḍita Aśoka." *Journal of Indian Buddhist Studies*, 9, no. 1 1961, pp. 371-76.

Kamalaśila, Tattva Saṁgraha Pañjikā, 2 Vols., Edited by Shastri Dwarikadass, Varanasi, Bauddha Bharati, 1981, reprint Delhi, Motilal Banarsidass, 1986.

Kashyap, Jagdish. (Edited). *Kathāvatthu*. Bihar Pali Publication Board, 1961.

Katsura, Shoryu, "New Sanskrit Fragments of the *Pramāṇa Samuccaya*," *Journal of Indian Philosophy* 3, March/April 1975, pp. 67-78.

Keith, A. B. "Vasubandhu and His *Vāda Vidhi*." *Indian Historical Quarterly* 4, 1928, pp. 221-27.

———. *Indian Logic and Atomism*. New Delhi, Oriental Reprint, 1977.

Kenneth, K. I., "Some Basic Misconceptions of Buddhism." *International Philosophical Quarterly* 10, no. 1, March 1969.

Kher, Chitrarekha, "The Concept of *Pramāṇa* according to Diṅnāga and Dharmakīrti." *Journal of the Oriental Institute* 22, no. 3, March 1973, pp. 256-64.

Kitagawa, Hidenoir, (Edited). "*A Refutation of Solipsism* (An Annotated Translation of the *Santānāntarasiddhi*)." *Journal of Greater India Society*; 14, no.1,2, 1955, pp. 407-29.

———. "A Note on the Methodology in the Study of Indian Logic." *Journal of Indian Buddhist Studies* 8, no.1, 1960, pp. 380-90.

Matilal, B. K., and Robert D. Evans, Editors, *Buddhist Logic and Epistemology; Studies in the Buddhist Analysis of Inference and Language*. Dordrecht, D. Reidel, 1986.

Miśra, Durveka, *Dharmottara-Pradīpa*. Edited by Malvania Dalsukhabhai, Patna, K.P. Jayaswal Institute, 1971.

Miśra, Pārthasārathi, *Nyāya Ratna Mālā*. Baroda, Gaekwad Oriental Institute, 1937.

Miśra, Vācaspati, *Nyāyavārtikatātparyaṭīkā*. Edited by Dravid Shastri. R., vols. 1, 2, Varanasi, Chowkhamba Sanskrit Samsthana, 1926.

Mokṣākaragupta, *Bauddha Tarka Bhāṣā*. Edited by Giri, Raghunatha, Varanasi, Prāchya Prakāshana, 1969.

Mookerjee, Satkari, (Edited). Vols. 1, 2, Patna, Nav-Nalanda Mahavihara Research, 1937.

———. *Buddhist Philosophy of Universal Flux*. Delhi, Motilal Banarsidass, 1975.

———. *Mānasa pratyakṣa: A Conundrum in the Buddhist Pramāṇa System*. Dordrecht,

D. Reidel, 1980, pp. 243-60.
Oliver, J.W., "Formal Fallacies and Other Invalid Arguments." *Mind*, 76, 1967.
Randle, H. N. *Fragments from Diṅnāga*. Delhi, Motilal Banarsidass, 1981.
——. *Indian Logic in the Early Schools*. Delhi, Oriental Books Reprint, 1976.
——. *"A Note on the Indian Syllogism." Mind*, 33, 1924, pp. 398-414.
Saradchandra, E. R., "From Vasubandhu to Śāntarakṣita." *Journal of Indian Philosophy* 4, no. 1, 1976, pp. 67-77.
Shah, Nagin J., *Akalaṅka's Criticism of Dharmakīrti's Philosophy*. Ahmedabad. L. D. Institute of Indology, 1967.
Sharma, Brajanarayana, *Bhāratīya Darśana main Anumāna*. Bhopal, M. P. Hindi Granth Academy, 1973.
Shastri, D.N., *The Philosophy of Nyāya-Vaiśeṣika and Its Conflict with the Buddhist Diṅnāga School (Critique of Indian Realism)*. New Delhi, Bharatiya Vidya Prakashana, 1976.
Shastri Dwarikadas, (Edited). *Sutta Nikāya*. Varanasi, Bauddha Bharati.
——. *Uddyotakara kā Nyāya Vārtika eka Adhyayana*. Kanpur, Bharatiya Prakashana, 1974.
Stall, J. F., "Correlations between Language and Logic in Indian Thought." *Bulletin of the School of Oriental and African Studies*, 23, no. 1, 1960, pp. 109-22.
Śāntarakṣita, *Tattva Saṁgraha*, Edited by Shastri Dwarikadass, Varanasi, Bauddha Bharati, 1981, reprint Delhi, Motilal Banarsidass, 1986.
——. "The Concept of *Pakṣa* in Indian Logic" *Journal of Indian Philosophy*, 2, no. 2, 1973.
Sugiura, Sadajvio. *Hindu Logic as Preserved in China and Japan*. University of Pennsylvania Press, 1900.
——. "Is the *Nyāya Pravesa* by Diṅnāga." *Journal of the Royal Asiatic Society* 82, 1928, pp. 7-13.
——. "Buddhist Logic before Diṅnāga." *Journal of the Royal Asiatic Society* 81, 1929, pp. 451-88.
——. *On Some Aspects of the Doctrines of Maitreyanātha and Asaṅga*. Calcutta, Calcutta University, Press, 1930.
——. *Pre-Diṅnāga Buddhist Texts on Logic from Chinese Sources*. Madras, Vesta, 1981.
——. "The Problem of *Svalakṣaṇa* in Sautrāntika Epistemology." *Journal of the Oriental Institute* 20, 1970-1971, pp. 216-25.
Th. Stcherbatsky, *Buddhist Logic* Vols. 1 and 2. Delhi, Motilal Banarsidass, 1993.
Uddyotakara, *Nyāya Vārtika*. Edited by Thakur, Anant Lal, Vaishali, Prākrita Jain Institute.
Vācaspati, *Nyāya Vārtika Tātparya Ṭīkā*. Edited by Thakur, Anant Lal. Vaishali, Prakrita Jain Institute.
Vādi Deva Suri, *Pramāṇanayatattvālokālankāra*. Bombay, Jain Shitya Vikas Mandal, 1967.
Vasubandhu, *Abhidharmakośa*, 4 vols. Edited by Shastri Dwarikadass, Varanasi, Bauddha Bharati, 1970-74.
Vātsyāyana, *Nyāya Bhāṣya*. Edited by Thakur Anant Lal, Vaishali, Prakrita Jain Insititute.
Vidyabhushana, S. C., "Requisites of a Good *Hetu*." *Annals of the Bhandarkar Oriental Research Institute*, 46, 1965, pp. 43-48.

——. *A History of Indian Logic*. Delhi, Motilal Banarsidass, 1978.

Vinītadeva, *Nyāyabinduṭīkā*. Edited by Mrinalakanti Gangopadhyaya, Calcutta, Indian Studies Past and Present, 1971.

Viśvanātha, *Bhāṣā Pariccheda*. Varānasi, Chaukhamba Sanskrit Series, 1972.

Wayman, Alex. "The Rules of Debate according to Asaṅga." *Journal of the American Oriental Society* 78, no.1, 1958, pp. 29-40.

——. A Reconsideration of Dharmakīrti's Deviation from Diṅnāga on *Pratyakṣābhāsa*. Pune, *Annals of the Bhandarkar Oriental Research Institute*, Vol.8, 49. 1977-1978.

Index

AUTHORS, WORKS, AND SCHOOLS

About the Authors

S. R. BHATT is Senior Professor of Philosophy at Delhi University. His research interests include Indian philosophy, logic and epistemology, social and political thought, and philosophy of religion. He has published numerous scholarly articles and seven books, including *The Philosophy of Pancaratra* (1968) and *Knowledge, Values and Education* (1986).

ANU MEHROTRA is senior scholar of Philosophy at Delhi University. Her research interests include Indian Philosophy, logic and epistemology, philosophy of religion, and social and political thought. She has published scholarly articles on Nehru and Buddhist Philosophy.

BUDDHIST TRADITION SERIES

Gen. Ed. E. Steinkellner and Jt. Gen. Ed. A. V. Rospatt,
Founder Ed. Late *ALEX WAYMAN*

1 **Indian Buddhism**—*Hajime Nakamura*
2 **Nagarjuniana**—*Chr. Lindtner*
3 **Chinese Monks in India**—*Latika Lahiri*
4 **Buddhism in Central Asia**—*B.N. Puri*
5 **Dharmakīrti's Theory of Hetu-Centricity of Anumāna**—*Mangala R. Chinchore*
6 **The Legend of King Aśoka**—*John S. Strong*
7 **Buddhist Insight**—*George R. Elder*
8 **Buddhism Transformed**—*Richard Gombrich* and *Gananath Obeyesekere*
9 **The Buddhist Tantras**—*Alex Wayman*
10 **The Lion's Roar of Queen Śrīmālā**—*Alex Wayman* and *Hideko Wayman*
11 **The Buddha Nature**—*Brian E. Brown*
12 **Evolution of Stupas in Burma**—*Sujata Soni*
13 **Buddhist Parables**—*Eugene Watson Burlingame*
14 **The Debate of King Milinda**—*Bhikku Pesala*
15 **The Chinese Madhyama Āgama and the Pāli Majjhima Nikāya**—*Bhiksu Thich Minh Chau*
16 **Sudden and Gradual**—*Peter N. Gregory*
17 **Yoga of the Guhyasamājatantra**—*Alex Wayman*
18 **The Enlightenment of Vairocana**—*Alex Wayman* and *R. Tajima*
19 **A History of Indian Buddhism**—Tr. *Hirakawa Akira*, Ed. *Paul Groner*
20 **Introduction to the Buddhist Tantric Systems**—*F.D. Lessing* and *Alex Wayman*
21 **Anāgatavaṃsa Desanā**—Tr. *Udaya Meddegama*, Ed. *John C. Holt*
22 **Chinnamasta**—*Elisabeth Anne Benard*
23 **On Voidness**—*Fernando Tola* and *Carmen Dragonetti*
24 **Nāgārjuna's Refutation of Logic (Nyāya) Vaidalyaprakaraṇa**—*Fernando Tola* and *Carmen Dragonetti*
25 **The Buddhist Art of Nagarjunakonda**—*Elizabeth Rosen Stone*
26 **Discipline**—*J.C. Holt*
27 **Philosophy and its Development in the Nikāyas and Abhidhamma**—*Fumimaro Watanabe*
28 **Untying the Knots in Buddhism**—*Alex Wayman*
29 **Early Buddhist Theory of Knowledge**—*K.N. Jayatilleke*
30 **Calming the Mind and Discerning the Real**—Tr. *Alex Wayman*
31 **A Comparative Study of the Pratimoksha**—*W. Pachow*
32 **Rise of the Esoteric Buddhism in the Tibet**—*Eva M. Dargyay*
33-35 **Saṃyuktābhidharmahṛdaya (3 Parts)** *Bart Dessein*
36 **A Millennium of Buddhist Logic (Pt. I)**—*Alex Wayman*
37 **The Buddhist Pilgrimage**—*Duncan Forbes*
38 **Chanting the Name of Mañjuśrī**—*Alex Wayman*
39 **The Literature of the Personalists of Early Buddhism**—*Bhikshu Thich Thien Chau*
40 **The Laṅkāvatāra Sūtra** —*D.T. Suzuki*
41 **Studies in the Laṅkāvatāra Sūtra**—*D.T Suzuki*
42 **The Vimalakīrti Sūtra**—*Burton Watson*
43 **The Gāndhārī Dharmapada**—*John Brough*
44 **Imaging Wisdom**—*Jacob N. Kinnard*
45 **Pain and Its Ending**—*Carol S. Anderson*
46 **Apparitions of the Self**—*Janet Gyatso*
47-49 **Rules for Nuns according to the Dharmaguptakavinya (3 Parts)**—*Ann Heirmann*
50 **The Chinese Hevajraṭantra**—*Ch. Willemen*
51 **The Historical Buddha**—*H.W. Schumann,* Tr. from the German *M.O'c Walshe*
52 **Dana:** Giving and Getting in Pali Buddhism—*Ellison Banks Findly*
53 **Hermeneutics and Tradition in the Samadhinirmocana Sutra**—*John Powers*
54 **Skillful Means**—*John W. Wchroeder*
55 **The Two Truths in Chinese Buddhism**—*Chang-Qing Shih*
56 **The Bodhisattva Path**—*Jan Nattier*
57 **Becoming the Buddha**—*Donald K. Swearer*
58 **Approaching the Land of Bliss**— Eds. *Richard K.Payne* & *Kenneth K. Tanaka*
59 **Indian Monastic Buddhism**—*Gregory Schopen*
60 **Caste and Buddhist Philosophy**—*Vincent Eltschinger*